Praise for *Emotional Advantage*

"*Emotional Advantage* takes a fresh approach to making sense of our emotions. Randy Taran, in a clear and accessible way, reminds us that life isn't about avoiding pain; it's about removing the mental resistance to its inevitability. Even negative emotions are arrows pointing to our evolution. Every emotion has much to reveal when we know how to chart our inner landscape." —Dr. Shefali Tsabary, author of *The Awakened Family*

"Randy Taran's words are informative and transformative, interesting and enlightening. Reading *Emotional Advantage* felt like embarking on a journey, at the end of which I felt more deeply connected to myself and to others, better understood and more understanding, lighter as well as happier." —Tal Ben-Shahar, *New York Times* bestselling author of *Happier*

"Happiness is an evolving field and *Emotional Advantage* is the up-to-date dispenser of the latest in research and practices. Promoting the subtle intersection of enjoyment and purpose, *Emotional Advantage* engagingly shows how to handle one's negative emotions and sustain one's positive emotions. Written in a friendly yet carefully researched manner, this book offers clear guidance to a better and more skillful life."
—Dr. Fred Luskin, bestselling author of *Forgive for Good*

"I LOVE THIS BOOK! I'm going to get it for all four of my teenagers and every single one of my clients. Well-researched, soulful, and eminently practical, *Emotional Advantage* is eye-opening and inspiring. Randy Taran shows us how even the most difficult emotions have upsides: they can be used to guide us towards our best lives. An absolute must-read for anyone seeking inner peace, greater confidence, or unlimited joy."
—Christine Carter, Ph.D., author of *Raising Happiness* and *The Sweet Spot*

"*Emotional Advantage* illuminates a new path to working with all your emotions to reconnect with your authenticity and create a more fulfilling life. With its simple and accessible strategies, it provides actionable ways to positively impact your life and the lives of those you love."
—Emma Seppälä, Ph.D., author of *The Happiness Track*

ALSO BY RANDY TARAN
(and Maria Lineger)

Project Happiness Handbook

Emotional Advantage

Embracing *All* Your Feelings
to Create a Life You Love

Randy Taran

ST. MARTIN'S
ESSENTIALS
NEW YORK

For David, Alex, Ben, and Zoe—
you are my greatest gifts.

Published in the United States by St. Martin's Essentials,
an imprint of St. Martin's Publishing Group

EMOTIONAL ADVANTAGE. Copyright © 2019 by Randy Taran.
Foreword copyright © 2019 by His Holiness the Dalai Lama.
All rights reserved. Printed in the United States of America. For information,
address St. Martin's Publishing Group, 120 Broadway, New York, NY 10271.

www.stmartins.com

The Library of Congress has cataloged the hardcover edition as follows:

Names: Taran, Randy, author.
Title: Emotional advantage : embracing all your feelings to create a life you love /
Randy Taran.
Description: First edition. | New York : St. Martin's Essentials, [2019] | Includes
bibliographical references.
Identifiers: LCCN 2019001795| ISBN 9781250200051 (hardcover) |
ISBN 9781250200068 (ebook)
Subjects: LCSH: Emotions. | Well-being.
Classification: LCC BF561 .T37 2019 | DDC 152.4—dc23
LC record available at https://lccn.loc.gov/2019001795

ISBN 978-1-250-76577-2 (trade paperback)

Our books may be purchased in bulk for promotional, educational, or business use.
Please contact your local bookseller or the Macmillan Corporate and Premium
Sales Department at 1-800-221-7945, extension 5442, or by email at
MacmillanSpecialMarkets@macmillan.com.

First St. Martin's Essentials Trade Paperback Edition: 2020

10 9 8 7 6 5 4 3 2 1

Contents

THE DALAI LAMA

Foreword

THE MORE I SEE of the world, the clearer it becomes that no matter what our situation, whether we are rich or poor, educated or not, of one race, gender, religion, or another, we all desire to be happy and to avoid suffering. The purpose of life is happiness.

By happiness I do not only mean the temporary pleasure of comfort alone. I am thinking more of the enduring happiness that results from the thorough transformation and development of the mind. This can be achieved by cultivating such qualities as compassion, patience, and wisdom. If you are able to develop these on a personal level, you will immediately find that they are a true source of happiness.

We can all achieve peace and happiness, because we all possess some basic good human values. For example, if you can be friendly and trusting toward others, you become more calm and relaxed. You lose the sense of fear and suspicion that we often feel about other people, either because we don't know them well or because we feel they are threatening or competing with us in some way. When we are calm and relaxed, we can make proper use of our mind's ability to think clearly, so whatever we do, whether we are studying or working, we will be able to do it better.

Randy Taran, in this book, provides an opportunity for people to look beyond narrow self-interests, to find out and consider what is of interest and benefit to others. The idea of the basic sameness of human beings is as simple as it is true; we all want happiness. We can learn much from each other, for understanding each other's needs also means respecting people's natural desire to make their own choices.

It is tremendously important that we try to make something positive of our lives. We were not born in order to cause trouble and harm. But for our lives to be of value, we need to foster and nurture such basic good human qualities as warmth, kindness, and compassion. If we can do that, the happier and more meaningful life can be for everyone.

—His Holiness the Dalai Lama

Introduction

HAVE YOU EVER HAD an emotion that hijacked your mind, and you didn't know where it came from or what to do about it? Have you ever felt that diving into that emotion was something you would rather not do at that moment? Join the human race! We don't have a problem with the emotions we approve of: happiness, acceptance, desire, and love—bring 'em on. . . . It's the other side of the emotional spectrum that bothers us: the iceberg of fear, the flames of anger, the cave of despair. How fast can we run? It's hard enough to live through these challenging emotions, never mind make sense of them. And it's not like they wait patiently to be looked at, either—emotions change dramatically from one minute to the next. Sure, we are supposed to "be" with our emotions, but for most people, they would rather be anywhere but.

I know this feeling well. For so many years, I favored the "happy" side. I was the optimistic one, the one who found solutions to every problem, and the one who could find the good in every situation. But that all changed one day, sitting at the kitchen table with my teenager, who said to me, "Mom, I'm stressed out. I want to be happy, I just don't know how." Every cell in my body

ached to help, but every "solution" I tried to offer did not resonate even one bit. I sought out experts only to discover that, according to the World Health Organization, depression is now
the leading cause of suffering worldwide. That means in our
own backyard, and in every country globally, women, men, and
children are suffering. And the thing is, we're not talking about it
nearly enough; the stigma is still real.

The stigma and the accompanying silence are territories that
I do know well. My grandfather had been suicidal, my mom had
chronic depression, and on my dad's side of the family, my aunt
was schizophrenic. My sister faces these challenges, too. Every
family has its issues, and, of course, I was not immune. So . . . you
can imagine, after the conversation around the kitchen table, my
inner alarms were piercingly loud. While I was a child, I was in
no position to help my mother, but now that I was a mom myself,
I would do anything to help my child.

This ignited a spark in me to do something, not only to help
my own family, but kids all over the globe. With a background
in film, I produced *Project Happiness*, a documentary bringing
together young people from the United States, Nigeria, and
Tibet to find answers for one question—What is happiness? We
interviewed George Lucas, Richard Gere, and neuroscientist
Richard Davidson and met with the Dalai Lama at his home in
Dharamsala, India.

That led me to writing a book to teach kids positive psychology, mindfulness, and the neuroscience of happiness, and to found-
ing a nonprofit that provides curriculum for K–5, middle school,
and high school that has been utilized digitally in 120 countries.
As suicides infiltrate the news, along with school shootings and
massive anxiety at all levels, I feel more passionate than ever about

sharing these materials to inspire kids and adults everywhere to develop their *inner* resources. My own journey took me on a mission to learn the tools I would later share with others, like gratitude, mind-set, emotional resiliency, and the power of identifying your strengths, and I am grateful for every step along the way.

It's so important, even necessary, to know that happiness is not just a state, it's a skill that we can all develop. I have seen that to be true, and the science backs it up.

But something in my heart felt that there was more. What about those spiraling worries at three A.M.; what about the anger that flares at unexpected times; what about the sadness that drifts in like a dark cloud? Are there any skills that could be learned to navigate those emotions, the ones we do not consider "socially acceptable," especially in a culture that values appearance over authenticity?

As I delved into the subject, it was amazing to discover that each emotion had its own brand of wisdom. The word "emotion" comes from the Latin word "emovere," which means "energy in motion." Emotions, whether considered "positive" or "negative," are packed not only with energy, but a lot of information. Though I will use the words "emotions" and "feelings" interchangeably in the book, in the same way we do in real life, there is actually a distinction.

Neuroscientist Antonio Damasio explains that emotions are the signals that happen inside the *body* itself and have evolved to serve as an automated response to take care of a danger or opportunity. This often happens spontaneously and without our awareness. Feelings are sparked by emotions but occur in our *minds*, from the thoughts and images associated with the emotion. According to Damasio, feelings are "the process of perceiving what is going on in the organism (yourself) when you are in the throes of an emotion. Because we have feelings and because feelings can actually stay in memory, then we have a possibility of using feelings of certain emotions for future planning. It helps us construct a view of the world and take that into consideration when we plan future events."[1] This awareness opens up an important opportunity.

What if we could actually use our emotions and feelings as a pathway to guide us back like an inner compass? What if, like alchemists, we had the tools to transform every emotion to recalibrate us toward creating our very best life? If instead of hijacking us and taking us off course, they could be touchstones to help reconnect us with our true nature? What if we could comprehend how even the most troublesome emotions and feelings are sending messages to alert, protect, and fuel us forward?

The challenge of our times is not only what we can achieve on the outside, but how we can connect with our deepest core self on the inside. We are here to experience the vastness and breadth of life, including our inner landscapes. This can only come from engaging fully with all the emotions—and understanding how to work *with* them, rather than pretending they don't exist. Then we can use them skillfully, instead of having them take us on a wild ride.

One thing for sure is that each and every person is more powerful than they know, and the more we understand about how we think, act, and relate, the better we will do in life. This is not only helpful for ourselves but ripples out to the people we love and care about, to our communities, and into our world. All emotions are contagious.

In this time of escalating anxiety and confusion, we need more than ever to take charge of our lives. Understanding the tough emotions as well as the easier ones gives us the clarity, fuel, and energy to reveal who we really are, beyond the frustrations, the judgments, and the fears. Each emotion has the power to bring us back to our true essence. As Marcus Aurelius once said, "The impediment to action advances the action—what stands in the way becomes the way." This book was written to give you a new way of looking at your emotions' hidden gifts as well as your own.

How to Use This Book

As you read through the book, you'll see that it is organized by emotion. Each chapter delves into the science behind the emotion, the messages it offers, and practical time-tested strategies to make the most of each one. There are various systems of organizing emotions—ranging from five individual "families" of emotions (enjoyment, anger, fear, disgust, and sadness)[2] to seven to ten emotions, all the way to the latest research by Dr. Dacher Keltner and Dr. Alan Cohen pointing to smooth gradients of twenty-seven emotions.[3] Brené Brown's research has highlighted thirty emotions.[4] For the purpose of this book, in order to take a deep dive in on selected emotions, I have narrowed it down to ten. Each one is more fascinating than the last. Of course, you will have your favorites:

- **Desire** looks at the nature of desire, how it is different from hope or expectation, the two types of passion to watch out for, and what to do if it gets extreme.
- **Tolerance** explores two layers: tolerance for some aspects of ourselves and tolerance for others. We'll look

at the difference between tolerance and acceptance, and how to have more *self*-acceptance now. You'll discover how tolerance relates to empathy and how to use it to deepen every relationship.

- **Happiness** discusses how to change the brain to bring forward the best of ourselves.

  We'll also dive into the Seven Happiness Habits and how little shifts can change everything. The chapter concludes with a section on PTG—post-traumatic growth— and why some people are so resilient even after tragedy.

- **Sadness** is often confused with depression. In this chapter we explore the difference. You will also discover the hidden gifts of sadness and why it is an important part of life.

  Finally, we look at what it means to architect your life to be free of regrets.

- **Fear** looks at the different types of fear—there are many! You will take a fear quiz and find out what happens when fear is suppressed. You'll also learn some strategies to make fear your friend.

- **Anxiety** will explain the difference between fear and anxiety. When is anxiety a healthy reaction, and when is it called a disorder? We'll also look at ways to navigate this much misunderstood emotion.

- **Confidence** discusses two causes of confidence: it can be the result of inner alignment or externally learning something new. You will learn the different mind-sets that will support or sabotage your dreams and why self-esteem alone is not enough.

- **Anger** will look at the downsides of this emotion but also at its gifts. How can you harness its power for good? You'll learn the many faces of anger and proven strategies that help when anger arises.

- **Guilt** is one of the most potent guides to get you back to what you value most. You'll look at the difference between guilt and shame. You'll also explore three types of guilt that can keep you stuck and seven action steps to take you through even the muddiest of waters.
- **Love** introduces you to the six types of love, the three stages of love, and how the chemicals in your brain move you to love, lust, and connection. You'll also learn what helps love go the distance.

Each chapter will also give you opportunities to tie what you are reading to your personal life. Get yourself a new journal and be ready for reflection questions and challenges to help you discover more about yourself and the insights that are waiting to emerge.

Along this journey, you will receive prompts, such as "In your journal, jot down the following question . . ." This is your time to write from the heart—no judgment allowed! This is all about tapping into your inner wisdom, reconnecting with your intuition, and uncovering insights that may surprise you. You will learn a lot about yourself, your strengths, and your choices as you progress through the chapters.

Before you start, there is something you should know about. Though each emotion has its own characteristics and message, it is fascinating to recognize that there is a progression that helps us understand anger, fear, and other challenging feelings. Author Dr. Paul Ekman and contemplative social scientist Dr. Eve Ekman have researched emotions and their stages and point to a timeline[5] that helps us make sense of this sometimes disruptive energy. With emotional episodes (and who doesn't get them occasionally), it's good to know that there is a predictable pattern and a way to get to the other side.[6] I like the analogy of a sports game—sometimes it can be relatively smooth, and sometimes it can be unpredictably intense. But if you know the drill and can anticipate what can come up, you'll have a game plan. Here are some questions to ask yourself to help you make it through not only in one piece, but with a feeling of exhilaration and discovery. Game—on!

Pregame

This is the time for a precheck. When our feelings start to stir, before an emotion gains momentum, it helps to take a quick inventory: "How do I feel? Is my energy level low; am I sleep-deprived or worried about a few things in particular? What is on my mind (job, kids, health, finances, politics)? Am I hungry, hangry (low blood sugar levels), or did I just get up on the wrong side of the bed?" All these things, though seemingly inconsequential, really can influence how you feel physically, mentally, and emotionally, and how you react to what's to come.

WHAT ARE MY MENTAL TRIGGERS?

Next, looking at it from a mental perspective, ask yourself, "What is this feeling coming up now? What is the trigger? Is it an *event* (job interview, date, presentation) that is nerve-racking, or is this state of heightened emotion coming from my *perception* and how I'm seeing the world (life is easy; life is a struggle;

people are kind; can't trust anyone . . .)? Is there an old memory, a recurring belief, or a theme that inflames the emotion?" Check in with this statement: "When _____ happens (or when I think_____), I usually feel _____."

WHAT ARE MY PHYSICAL AND EMOTIONAL CLUES?

It also helps to look at the emotion itself. What are the clues our body is giving us (racing heart, clenched fist, tightness in the torso) that this emotion is taking over? What are the psychological changes we are experiencing? What makes anxiety feel like anxiety; how does anger feel like anger? If you were to explain how you felt to a friend, what words best describe these emotional and physical changes?

WHAT ARE MY CHOICES?

This information brings us to a new level of choice with several paths to select from. We can use this new awareness to take action in a **constructive** way. Check in with this statement: "I know by how my body feels and by my thoughts that I'm getting triggered (by this person or situation), so I will _____." By doing so, we are taking action in advance.

Then there's the other option: choosing behaviors that turn out to be **destructive**. We also have to remember that by simply not making any choice at all, we also end up defaulting to old (usually destructive) patterns. Some people react *internally*, preferring to suppress uncomfortable feelings deep inside. While that may sound like the path of least resistance, these intense emotions can build and then rudely crash in later like uninvited guests at a party. Others react to challenging feelings *externally*, either by exploding and lashing out at another, or by imploding and lashing inwardly. Constructive or destructive—if we plan potential plays in advance, we really do have a choice.

Postgame

After the emotional incident, there is a wind-down period, an opportunity to reflect, to become aware of what caused the incident, how it felt in the body, and how it played out . . . what the consequences were. If we take this opportunity of reflection, we are less likely to be retriggered when similar situations come about again. It may seem like, "It's over; why bother?" But this is a huge opportunity to hone our awareness. It's one of the most important stages of an emotion and can help predict the outcome of future plays, too.

Repeating the same patterns over and over again, especially if we keep getting hurt, can get old really fast. Through the vehicle of our emotions, our mind, body, and spirit are sending signals that something has to shift. By using the emotions and their stages as important messengers of greater awareness, we set ourselves up to enjoy the game, reduce injuries, and do really well. We open the doors to greater understanding, agency, and happiness, too. When we put this into practice, we gain new freedom and the power of knowing we are in charge of our own game.

These topics are transformational. Since I started taking this on fully in my own life, I have noticed a change in myself as well. I have become more accepting of all the shades of emotion and learned to understand them better. That causes such a huge shift, because when we understand, we can no longer react to whatever triggered us in the same way. It feels like I am now partners with my emotions, instead of being stuck in the old game of tug-of-war. It is so much easier to access my inner resources and feel released from the grip of ego-driven limitations. I feel a sense of freedom and a lightness that I never had, as well as an unshakable sense that I have so much more agency in my life, which is exactly what I want for you.

If we know how to work with any emotion that comes our way (and you know they all will), we can get through to the other side. In the words of Jon Kabat-Zinn, "You can't stop the waves, but you can learn to surf." This book is designed to offer you surfing lessons, but more than that, the opportunity to know yourself at an even deeper level and to connect with your true nature: peaceful, knowing, and confident to the core. These qualities are already there inside of you. This is about connecting to that part of you so you can see through the illusion of separation and lack and know to your very essence how strong, capable, and loved you really are. I am so excited to share this book, so you can, through all your emotions, reveal to yourself the power of you.

Happiness

*Don't ask what the world needs. Ask what makes you come
alive, and go do it. Because what the world needs is people who
have come alive.*

— HOWARD THURMAN

WHAT DOES THE WORD "happiness" mean to you? Though we
all want the same things—happiness, love, to live a meaningful
life, to rise to our potential—there is no set formula; the path is
different for each one of us. But one thing is sure: happiness is at
the core. Our natural state is one of joy; we are here to feel alive.
When we vibrate from a place of joy, we are attuned to who we
really are. This allows life to open up to us and allows us to meet
that energy in ways we might not have previously imagined.

I have come to see happiness as an umbrella that covers
so many aspects of living life fully: it embraces joy, gratitude,
compassion, connection, physical wellness, mental fitness, generosity, purpose, and even grace. It operates on every level: physical, emotional, mental, and spiritual. But what I love most about
it is that it strengthens the inner resources that allow us to handle

the full range of life . . . including the tough stuff. Happiness does not mean that our problems magically disappear—it means that we are more able to deal with them. I want more of that in my life, and I want it in yours—that is why I started Project Happiness, and really that is why I'm writing this book.

We are all on a journey. Think of your body as a ship, a vessel that allows you to go wherever you choose to, as far as the eye can see. On this journey, you will have untold adventures that allow you to learn more about not only the places you travel to, but also about yourself, the capacities you know about and those that are getting ready to emerge. Storms may come up, and if you are not taking care of your boat, it could spring a leak, take on too much water, and, if things get too critical, get so heavy it could even sink. In the same way, the body itself has to be taken care of. The sea of negativity, if it fills up your boat, could become a threat to your body and mind.

Ships don't sink because of the water around them; ships sink because of the water that gets in them. Don't let what's happening around you get inside you and weigh you down.

— UNKNOWN

Just like a captain has daily protocols to keep her/his vessel shipshape, you can develop habits that will keep you afloat no matter if the seas are stormy or calm. You can also use these habits to intentionally check in with your vessel and plug up any leaks before they get dangerously large. You can learn to navigate the waves.

In this chapter, we'll look at the different types of happiness. We'll see what positive psychology tells us about happiness and well-being and how to change our brains to bring forward the best within ourselves. We'll explore the Seven Happiness Habits and simple practices to expand happiness in day-to-day life. Then we'll see how it is possible to thrive, even after trauma. Happiness is a journey, one of the most important ones we can ever take—let's get started!

What Is Happiness, Anyway?

First of all, having all the toys in the store, all the shoes in your closet, all the friends at the party does not determine your happiness. For happiness to last it cannot, does not, and will not come from outside sources. Well, maybe temporarily, but soon enough the thrill is gone. Happiness is, as the saying goes, an inside job. External validation does not last. Only we can really make ourselves happy.

Does that put you off; does it all seem like too much work? Actually, it involves no work at all—just a shift in perspective. We are all born to be happy—it is our true nature just as it is our birthright. That's right. You, like everyone, deserves happiness, and you *can* have it.

What we don't always realize is that so much of happiness depends not on what happens to you, but on how you interpret life's events. How you hold them. The story you tell yourself. If you have been a victim in your story, you can find out how to reframe it to underline what you have learned in the last phases, what you are doing now, and what you plan to do in the chapters to come.

We have more influence than we may know. Our thoughts and the beliefs they produce are like boomerangs—what we send out comes back to us. Have you noticed that when we release thoughts out into the world, the results of those thoughts often show up in our lives? When you have a bad day and send out angry thoughts, you usually get some angry responses in return. If you send out thoughts that life is pretty good, chances are that you are seeing evidence of that, too. But let's be clear. This is not about lying to yourself—it's about what you are choosing to bring to the forefront of your mind.

The good news is that we can train ourselves to activate what we want, just by giving our attention to it. What we focus on grows, so imagine purposely focusing on feeling good—that we have everything we need inside of us, that we are supported, that we are already loved, and that there is so much to be grateful for. We can reframe the challenging stuff (for example: *I sprained my ankle*. Reframe: *If I hadn't sprained my ankle, I would not have paused long enough to see that I was ready to change jobs, friends, cities*—you get the idea). When you choose to focus on all the good things here and on all the unknown gifts to come, you position your mind and your vibration to welcome them in.

By intentionally focusing on what you want (not what you have settled for, not what you feel stuck in right now), you create a strong intention to bring that into your life. By practicing visualizing and even happily feeling it happen, similar to what athletes do when preparing for a game, you light the fire to move forward in that direction.

So, back to the emotion of happiness. Some experience it from personal pleasures—the little things in life. Others would say it is in the unforgettable moments that take your breath away. Some see happiness as personal while others insist it involves the greater good. . . . Happiness is best when it is shared. There are people who feel it's about igniting your emotions through passion;

others might think it's about managing your mind and choosing a better attitude.

Could it be that different aspects of happiness arise at different times and under different circumstances? Your definition may very well change according to your age, stage, and situation. Pull out your **journal** now. Here is your first question.

JOURNAL CHALLENGE

In the left margin, write down "age 1–10," then beside it describe the moments of happiness that come to mind. Next, repeat below that for ages fifteen, twenty, twenty-five, and so on. Take a moment to reflect on how your most memorable moments of happiness have changed over time. Is there a thread that unites some of them, like the warmth of human connection, the majesty of nature, or the excitement of creativity? What clues do these memories give you for today?

Though happiness appears in special moments, we all want it to linger. One thing that has become clear is that for happiness to have a lasting quality, rather than being a momentary high, it has to be tied to longer-term meaning. The rush of pleasure from having an ice cream on a hot day is over quickly, but the warm connected feeling of doing something special for a friend lasts much longer.

Yet pleasure is an important part of it, too. The question is how *much* pleasure works best? Think of it as a banquet, filled with a huge variety of flavors. By trying the dishes for ourselves, we discover which ones make us feel good and which don't agree with us at all. If we don't sample any, we'll likely be hungry and may sense that something is missing, but if we binge on every option, we just end up feeling sick.

What about meaning? On one extreme, devoting 100 percent of our life to a singular source of meaning while denying laughter, play, or the beauty of the senses can produce a dry, ascetic, maybe even obsessive life. Yet, at the other end, having no meaning at all can make us feel empty, like we're just going through the motions, and for what?

Author and happiness expert Tal Ben-Shahar says it well: "Happiness lies at the intersection of pleasure and meaning." We need both. Pleasure motivates the journey, and meaning makes it worthwhile.

Three Types of Happiness

1. **Hedonic happiness** is all about increasing pleasure and decreasing pain. It is a temporary good feeling from getting or enjoying something new (new phone, shoes, job . . .) that is outside of you and not necessarily in your control. If you get the new thing, you might be very happy, but you adapt quickly to having it (hedonic adaptation), and the pleasure doesn't last. If you don't get it, as it's outside of your control, you could be upset. If your happiness is tied to that "thing," where does it leave you?

2. **Eudaemonic happiness** involves being a mensch—that is, a good-spirited person. The literal translation for "eu" is good, and "daemon" means spirit. There is a sense of personal fulfillment, being your authentic self, and drawing from your strengths. It is also explained as living

well and doing well, and being loved by your family and friends. If you are living a meaningful life, you are feeling eudaemonia.

3. **Chaironic happiness** can occur even in difficult situations when you feel connected to something greater.[1] For some that's found in the grandeur of nature, when you feel a sense of awe witnessing the power of the universe. This type of happiness can feel like a blessing in the midst of suffering, or can be experienced in spiritual or religious practice, meditation, or whatever evokes a feeling of profound communion.

These categories of happiness originated in the time of Aristotle. More recently, though, the word "happiness" has come under fire. In this culture, it's very easy to bash happiness and see it through the narrowest of lenses. There are those who equate it with living life through rose-colored glasses, replacing reality with wishful thinking, and pretending everything is "fine."

But let's clarify that living a happy life does not mean we are supposed to be upbeat all the time. A: that is impossible, and B: it would deny a whole aspect of experiencing the richness and reality of life. Happiness is not about experiencing a set of thrills or an endless pursuit of pleasure. Rather than chasing constant euphoria (a setup for disaster any way you look at it), what if we could see how restrictive that definition is and accept that real life is complex and kinda disruptive—it is designed that way to help us grow. Psychologist and author of *Emotional Agility*[2] Susan David explains, "Research now shows that the radical acceptance of all of our emotions, even the difficult and messy ones, is the cornerstone to resilience, thriving, and true authentic happiness."

The more emotions we can work with, the better. In one study, 35,000 participants were measured on "emodiversity," the variety and abundance of their emotions.[3] This took into account not only pleasant ones, like happiness, awe, and gratitude, but others, like sadness, anger, and worry. Results showed that "people high in 'emodiversity' [meaning they could express a diverse range of emotions] were less likely to be depressed than people high in positive emotion alone."[4] Everyone at birth is given a spectrum of emotions. They are here for a reason, to help guide us through life.

Authentic happiness is about choosing intentional strategies to navigate the painful moments, as well as making the most of the pleasing ones. It is about looking for the good amid the challenges, such as appreciating the kindness of others while you are going through an unusually hard time (like a sudden loss, a transition, or a health crisis). While we can't necessarily change what life throws our way, we can influence how we view it. The Dalai Lama suggests that the feeling of being content or unhappy rarely depends on our absolute state, but on our perception of the situation.[5]

The unhappy emotional states are more challenging; that's certain. But the problem is not those emotions themselves; it is opening to their lessons and having the mind-set and strategies to move through them. Happiness helps us gain access.

Positive Psychology

PERMA is a framework developed by Dr. Martin Seligman, widely known as the founder of Positive Psychology, to describe what it takes to live a flourishing life.[6] See which aspects make you the happiest.

- **P:** There are proven ways to increase **positive emotions**, like gratitude, generosity, and mindfulness. What we intentionally focus our attention on will grow. But apart from putting our attention on appreciation and other good feelings, we can also choose to frame the events in our lives in a way that makes sense of where we have been and where we are going, a narrative that supports our goals. What actually happened to us is certainly important, but it is how we *interpret* those events that determines our happiness.

JOURNAL CHALLENGE

In your **journal**, give yourself some time to reflect on these questions: Are you the hero in your story, or the victim? What have you learned by facing the monsters along your journey? Rewrite the script to give yourself the strong lead.

- **E: Engagement** is another aspect of flourishing. How great is it to experience total immersion in an activity? Hours feel like minutes and you feel engaged for the love of what you're doing, not for any external reward.[7] This "flow" experience can happen in many ways, from rock climbing to reading, from gardening to going on a run, to losing yourself in a creative project (writing, painting, music). It's unique for everyone. What is your favorite way to be 100 percent fully engaged?
- **R: Relationships** are another key to thriving. How you relate to others, the friendships you nurture, the cama-

raderie, laughter, and sense of closeness all contribute to a
happy life. Even having one person (or furry friend) to be
with makes all the difference. With self-reported feelings of loneliness now up to 40 percent of adults in the
United States alone and loneliness increasing the odds
of an early death by 26 percent, so many feel disconnected. We need to know we are here for one another.

- **M**: Having a sense of **meaning** and purpose also makes
  people happier. If you've ever asked "Why am I here?" you
  know the depth of this question. Meaning can be found
  through connecting with something greater, through the
  work you do, the people you connect with, or the cause you
  support. Some good questions to ask yourself are: "What
  makes me feel most alive? What touches my heart so
  deeply that I want to help?"

- **A**: The best type of **accomplishment** is putting your
  energy into something that is aligned with your values,
  something that sits well with you and makes you feel that
  you are making a difference. That's your "why." Chunking
  goals down to smaller tasks is often "how" to see them
  through. Working backward to chart the steps you'll
  need to take can give you the road map. Finally, rewarding yourself, or at least taking the time to savor the accomplishment (even small steps count) allows you to take
  it in. Otherwise, even with all the accomplishments, you
  will never have any satisfaction. Your focus will always
  be on the next goal, the next mountain to climb, which
  can lead to burnout. Instead, celebrate the little wins.

Training Your Brain

What would it be like if you could actually train your brain to be more positive? The good news is that you can.

We used to think that the brain never changed, but according to the neuroscientist Richard Davidson, we now know that this is not true—specific brain circuits grow stronger through regular practice, which is called neuroplasticity. He explains, "Well-being is fundamentally no different than learning to play the cello. If one practices the skills of well-being, one will get better at it." What this means is that you can actually train your brain to become more grateful, relaxed, or confident, by repeating experiences that evoke gratitude, relaxation, or confidence. Your brain is shaped by the thoughts you repeat. The more neurons fire as they are triggered by repeated thoughts and activities, the faster they develop into neural pathways, which cause lasting changes in the brain. Or in the words of Donald Hebb, "Neurons that fire together wire together." This is such an encouraging premise: bottom line—we can intentionally create the habits for the brain to be happier.

One of the easiest ways to do this is called "taking in the good." Neuropsychologist and author Rick Hanson explains how to get this positive neuroplasticity in motion.[8] First of all, it is necessary to overcome the brain's built-in negativity bias. This evolved for a reason: the survival of the species. It was way more prudent for humans to focus on negative threats such as animals that could eat them for lunch than to be daydreaming about something frivolous. To stay alive, you had to be on guard. Today, we are not living under the same conditions, so always scanning the horizon for danger is like a being stuck in overdrive and burning out our engine.

As an antidote, Hanson points out a simple three-step practice to amplify your well-being while growing your inner resources:

1. **Look for positive facts and let them become positive experiences.** Instead of mindlessly jumping to the next thing on your to-do list, allow yourself to feel good right then and there. Turn that feeling on whenever you can. If you have a pleasant conversation, feel it! When you notice something good in yourself, or when you achieve a small goal, pause a moment and take it in.

2. **Savor the positive experience**—think about it for ten, twenty, or thirty seconds. Feel and intensify it in your body and emotions. (Picture an imaginary dial that controls the intensity of the experience. Now dial it up.)

3. **Intentionally feel that the positive experience is soaking into your brain** and body like water into a sponge, becoming part of your emotional memory. Imagine this is now embedded in your cells.

The more you practice this, the more you are using your mind to reshape the brain. And the more you can experience this feeling in your body as well, in the words of Rick Hanson, over time, "passing states become installed as lasting traits."[9] The exciting thing is that over time, instead of defaulting to the negativity bias and getting trapped in it, we can literally train our brains to be more positive and more resilient no matter what life presents.

The Seven Happiness Habits

While we're on the topic of training your brain, if there was an easy way to develop the habits that helped your inner resources get stronger, would you be interested? Research proves that while 50 percent of our happiness is based on genetics and 10 percent is due to external circumstances, a full 40 percent relates to the intentional daily activities and the choices that we make.[10]

So we now know that happiness is a skill set we can learn through practice, but with so much research on the science of happiness, the challenge we faced at Project Happiness was how to take all that information and offer it in a way that was brain-friendly and accessible. The Seven Daily Happiness Habits were designed in this exact way—using social media as a psycho-educational intervention through the days of the week: Mindful Monday, GratiTuesday, Wellness Wednesday, Thoughtful Thursday, Freedom Friday, Social Saturday, and Soul Sunday. The days are just a guideline. It is this daily practice that actually changes the brain. The power is in practicing these habits consistently.

Each of the seven habits offers practical ways to integrate it into your life. As you go through all of the habits, choose one that resonates with you the most right now, and practice it for several days. Then move to another habit until you have covered all seven. Even just a few moments of practice a day can shift your perspective and move you forward. If you miss a day, do not beat yourself up, just pick up where you left off. Consider this a smorgasbord of happiness—take a taste of each and see which offerings you like the best.

HABIT 1: MINDFULNESS (MINDFUL MONDAY)

Mindfulness, the ancient practice of focusing nonjudgmental awareness on the present moment, is now recognized as an effective way to help us navigate through everyday life. From athletes to CEOs, from students to those on the front lines under severe stress, mindfulness meditation is now mainstream. There is good reason.

In our busy and half-crazed modern lifestyle with all its digital distractions, sleep deprivation, comparison culture, and endless obligations, mindfulness or meditation in general is a proven way to re-center, collect your energy, and literally come back to yourself, to be present in your own life. It helps you regulate your attention and emotions so that even in challenging situations, you can be less reactive and not take things as personally.

INCREASES	DECREASES
Increases focus and concentration	Reduces loneliness
Improves relationships and social connection	Lowers blood pressure
Helps you sleep better	Decreases painful thoughts and feelings
Boosts immune system	Lowers cortisol, easing stress and anxiety
Enhances mental strength	Reduces depression
Improves empathy and compassion	Eases inflammation[11]
Physically changes the brain	Reduces heart risk[12]
Increases self-awareness	Lowers emotional reactivity
	Decreases emotional eating

In as little as a minute, you can reset your mind and come out refreshed. Mindfulness doesn't have to be rigid or regimented. It's as easy as remembering to be aware of your breath or even lying outside and gazing at the sky. Guided meditations are designed to reduce stress, increase positivity, and even get you to sleep. There are many apps you can use right on your phone.

Mindfulness will also help you take a step back so you can observe the situation from a place of greater awareness (like a deep ocean that is not disturbed by the temporary waves on the surface). From this more peaceful place you can make a choice of how you want to handle any given situation.

Viktor Frankl explains it beautifully: "Between stimulus and response there is a space. In that space is our power to choose our response. In our response lies our growth and our freedom."

Habit 2: Gratitude (GratiTuesday)

Gratitude is like a magic sword—it can cut away the feeling of not having enough, not doing enough, or not being enough. It connects us with what is already working in life and helps us see the small moments of pleasure or grace that are always around, if we take the time to notice them. A great cup of tea—gratitude; the sun that warms your back—gratitude; a smile on the way to work—gratitude, a meaningful conversation—well, you see how it works.

When you think of it, there is so much to be thankful for: from nature to family to friends to our bodies, our food, water, and places of shelter. We can be grateful for our passions and hobbies, our jobs, our community, and our ability to give back. We can appreciate the devices that make life more convenient, as well as our ability to put them away. We can be grateful for the people who fill our days with good feelings and the situations that challenge us—perhaps they are our greatest teachers.

If you want to be happier (and who doesn't), the simple practice of gratitude can set you up for a lifetime of expansiveness. It truly can open your world and ignite a renewed energy. This is such a powerful practice that I want you to take a moment and really take in the benefits. Gratitude improves sleep, immune function, and longevity. People become more emotionally resilient, relaxed, and optimistic. Robert Emmons, the leading scientific expert on gratitude and author of *Thanks!*, reports that the result of practicing gratitude is about a 25 percent increase in well-being.[13] Really think about that—this is a game changer.

It will lead you to be more optimistic, feel better about yourself and your life, and connect more with your inner values. Gratitude helps you be more social, more caring; it leads to more meaningful friendships and kinder relationships. More gratitude also leads to less jealousy, less feeling like a victim, and less bitterness. In the workplace, use it as your secret weapon to create deeper social connections, manage people better, and see your productivity go up. This practice alone can jump-start you and keep you going—it is that powerful.

Here are some easy ways to start:

- **A gratitude journal:** The landmark research study led by Robert Emmons instructed one group to write five things they were grateful for once a week for ten weeks. The second group was told to jot down five things they were not happy about each week, and the third was a neutral group. The results stated, "Participants who'd kept a gratitude journal felt better about their lives as a whole and were more optimistic about the future than participants in either of the other two groups. To put it into numbers, according to the scale we used to calculate well-being, they were a full 25 percent happier than other participants."[14] If you are ready to take charge of your happiness, would you be willing to write five things you are grateful for once a week?

JOURNAL CHALLENGE

Now create a page in your **journal** called "Gratitude." Track how you feel during the next few weeks and notice the changes.

Three Good Things: While the gratitude list focuses on what or who you are grateful for, the "Three Good Things" activity asks you to write down three good things that happened to you today and the reasons why. Include how it made you feel in that moment and also how it makes you feel now, as you remember it. You can vary this to write down three good qualities you saw *in yourself* today and why. This is a good one for building self-awareness. If you want to work on your confidence, this is also a good one to add to your journal.

- **A gratitude letter:** Think of one special person who you are deeply grateful for, someone who believed in you. Maybe they saw things in you that you did not even see in yourself. You knew they wanted the best for you and had your back. Write them a letter expressing how you feel and why. You can send the letter, but if it is possible to call them up and read it to them or deliver it in person, that is even better. If they are no longer here, writing the letter is still very powerful, as you will experience a renewed connection just by putting your thoughts on paper. This simple exercise will open your heart.

- **A gratitude email:** This is very useful for a wider range of people and great when you don't have much time. Simply send a few words of thanks to a friend or colleague. It will make you feel better, lighten their day, and chances are they will send you back a similar note, bringing your thoughtfulness full circle.

- **How would you feel without it?** Think of a positive event or a relationship that you value and imagine how you might feel if for whatever reason, it was no longer in your life. Think of the moment that started it all and ask yourself, "What if it had transpired differently?" What would your life be like now without that positive event or person? Now recognize that you did not have to face that loss—everything is still standing. Allow yourself to feel not only relief, but full-on gratitude.

Gratitude takes no time, it's easy to do, and you never have to pay money to be grateful for what you already have. In the words of Seneca, "True happiness is to enjoy the present, without anxious dependence upon the future, not to amuse ourselves with either hopes or fears but to rest satisfied with what we have, which is sufficient, for he that is so wants nothing. The greatest blessings of mankind are within us and within our reach." If your grandmother told you to count your blessings, she was right. Take on this potent practice and you will see how your life can change.

Habit 3: Well-being (Wellness Wednesday)

According to the Harvard School of Public Health, happiness and health are clearly linked as "scientific evidence suggests that positive emotions can help make life longer and healthier."[15] It makes sense that happiness supports health, and health allows for greater happiness. It is no surprise that we have more vitality when we exercise, eat a balanced diet, and get enough sleep. The more interesting question is why?

- Moving the body not only builds your muscles, it also builds your brain. Exercise releases a protein called BDNF (brain-derived neurotrophic factor) in the learning (prefrontal cortex) and memory (hippocampus) areas of the brain.[16]
- A lack of sleep leads to increased inflammation and decreased strength in the immune system. It also makes it harder to fight off colds and disease. Cortisol also stays at a high level, making you more susceptible to feeling stressed.
- Giving the body mostly fast foods, refined sugars, and saturated fats makes it sluggish and puffy (inflamed). Choosing foods that are high in omega-3 fatty acids and fiber from fruits and vegetables helps in fighting inflammation as well as in regulating your emotions.

The good news is that simple shifts can cause big changes. By tweaking your calendar to build in regular workouts, by choosing an earlier bedtime, and by replacing fast food with options that sustain you, your sense of well-being will go up. It's not a question—this will happen. And if you bring in a friend and do it together, you will keep each other on track!

Then, as you develop a better sense of well-being, it becomes easier to maintain wellness habits. You want to. So these habits not only make you feel happier and more hopeful and have a more optimistic mind-set, they also open you to healthy behaviors because they support how you want to feel and how you want to be. Feeling better motivates you to keep doing what keeps your energy up. As you vibrate with more energy and positivity, you recognize that this is who you really are.

Self-care Starter Kit
We cannot talk about well-being without mentioning self-care. (Self-love is different and will be covered in the love chapter.) Though life can be ridiculously fast-paced, with plenty of turbulence, you must take care of the vessel to keep yourself afloat. You might say, "I don't have the time," but think of what it could be like if you got really run-down. A little self-care now prevents any deterioration later on. One thing to remember: self-care is not selfish; it is the opposite. It will restore you so you can handle what's front and center. This is actually the most responsible thing you can do. It's a way of taking charge of your energy, instead of seeing it steadily slip away. It helps you return to your natural state of happiness. This practice looks different for everyone, but here are a few ideas to get you started.

- **The body** needs to rest and recharge. Take a spa evening, get a massage or pedicure, take a yoga class or a nap, dance to your favorite music, drop into a relaxing bath, drink more water. Be good to your body—it wants to take care of you.

- **The mind** also needs some TLC. Don't "should" on it! Examine with a discerning eye what you feel pressed to do, think, or say. Set boundaries—your mind needs time to relax and do nothing. Listen to some great music, watch a show, stare at a candle—your choice. Release the pressure; this is your time to let go of stress.
- **Tend to your spirit.** Make some time to take a look at your priorities. Get a gut feeling to know if they still hold true or if it's time to course correct. Connect with something bigger, through meditation, a spiritual or religious group, or time with yourself in nature. Slow down the breath so you can listen to the whispers of your heart. The best information is right there—inside of you. This is your time to listen and to take it in. Trust that you are being guided.

HABIT 4: TO FEEL GOOD, DO GOOD
(THOUGHTFUL THURSDAY)

Have you ever done an act of kindness for someone else? How did it make you feel? Doing good is a vital pillar of happiness. Neuroscientist Richard Davidson writes, "The best way to activate positive-emotion circuits in the brain is through generosity."[17] Generosity also triggers a bath of chemicals that makes us feel good: serotonin levels rise, making us happy; cortisol decreases, reducing stress; and oxytocin elevates, making us feel more connected. It's as if the body is rewarding us for being kind. In ancient times, members of a group had to look out for one another to survive. It's not that different today.

Generosity does not even have to be about money—a kind word or a sincere smile can touch a heart in profound ways. It doesn't stop there. Doing good makes you feel good, which in turn motivates kindness and generosity in the future. Some call it a virtuous cycle—you don't want to stop.

Who benefits most—the giver or the recipient? Sometimes it's a toss-up. But how we spend our time and money is just as important, and often more important than the amount of money we make. It also contributes to a sense of purpose in our lives. Those who help others know they matter; they know they are making a difference.

Maybe this is already part of your practice. If not, challenge yourself to find a cause that resonates with you and give a few hours of your time, meet some new people, and know you are helping out. There are volunteering websites that direct you to one-time opportunities or those you can do regularly. If you have ever volunteered or given of yourself with no expectation of return, you know how good it feels.

> Happiness is a perfume you cannot pour on others without getting a few drops on yourself.
>
> —RALPH WALDO EMERSON

As a species, we are wired to care for one another, and age is not a factor. Some experiments showed how toddlers were innately happier to give than to receive.[18] At the heart of it, people are good, and kind, and *feel* good when they lend a hand. You see the mass outpouring of support in every natural disaster. When you do good, you feel good—maybe it is really that simple. Altruism activates the best within us and models that for others, too. Some say you can measure a person not by what they have, but by what they give. I am convinced that the coolest and most interesting people on earth are givers. And this type of gift comes right back to you.

> When you give others a new chance, a new chance is really being given to you.
>
> BRYANT MCGILL

HABIT 5: AUTHENTICITY, VULNERABILITY, FORGIVENESS, LETTING GO (FREEDOM FRIDAY)

It is so easy to get caught up in comparison and the pressure to look or act in a certain way. Achieve the right goals, wear the right clothes, eat the right food, be in the right mood. (As you can see, I am a fan of Dr. Seuss.) But seriously, so many people are trapped in a narrow expression of perceived expectations—and it can be stifling.

Have you ever noticed that when people are guarded, it creates a wall? Unless you can see through to their tenderness inside, you may react by becoming guarded, too. On the other hand, when you have the courage to be vulnerable and to be seen, it gives others more courage to be themselves, too, and to shed the burden of appearing a certain way. Your ego, in its efforts to maintain the status quo, wants to keep you small and scared to step out, but that is not your true nature. You are much more expansive than that. There is a side of you that delights in being yourself: quirky, unique, and filled with possibility. When you take an authentic stance, people will meet you there in that openness, easing the way for you both to experience true connection.

Though sharing your real self makes you seem more vulnerable, showing vulnerability does not mean you are weak. It's

the opposite—when you allow yourself to be vulnerable, you reveal your inner strength. In personal relationships, if you care
about someone but never take the risk to let them know, they
may never find out how you really feel. By keeping your heart
"safe," it is also shielded. It may seem that nothing bad can get in,
but neither can the beautiful, magical, and poignant moments.
Vulnerability opens doors. In business, if things are not going
well, if you keep it inside and pretend, you'll never get another
perspective. But if you share your worries, you discover there is
no shame in being human. We all go through challenges.

Forgiveness plays an important role here, too. When we
forgive ourselves for holding on to old patterns because they
kept us feeling safe, we free ourselves from the chains of denial
and self-judgment and create the space to move on. When we can
forgive someone else, or at least recognize that they are dealing
with their own demons, and sometimes it is not personal, that can
be liberating, too. When you connect with your true nature, you
see that these old cords can no longer keep you imprisoned—
there is so much more waiting for you when you realize that
you have the choice to let go of any attachment to other people's
dramas.

One way to move this along is an intuitive visualization
called "Cutting the Cord." The purpose of this is to free yourself
from the mental attachments that keep that person front and center in your mind, and to no longer feel exhausted by them whenever you are in their presence. The visualization goes like this:
Slow down your breathing and close your eyes. Imagine there
is a cord connecting your heart or solar plexus to theirs. Visualize that cord draining you of your energy while filling you with
self-doubt and negativity. Then imagine yourself feeling all the

tension from that relationship in every part of your body—your hands clench, your shoulders tense, your face gets tight. That is when you reach for an imaginary pair of heavy-duty golden scissors. You take them in both hands and effortlessly cut the cord. Visualize the severed cord just falling away. Immediately exhale fully and feel all the tension leaving your body along with old attachments. Whether you can forgive the other person now or not isn't the issue. What's most important is taking a stand for yourself. By realizing how holding on to hurt and anger only ends up hurting you, you have already taken the first step to greater freedom. After you cut the cord, notice how you can breathe more easily and experience a greater sense of peace.

A more scientific approach, based on the work of Dr. Fred Luskin, author of *Forgive for Good*, involves nine steps[19]:

1. Be clear on what upset you, and tell a few trusted people.
2. Since forgiveness is for you, not anyone else, decide that you want to feel better for yourself.
3. The aim is not to reconcile with that person, but to take their offenses less personally.
4. Adjust your perspective to realize that the upset you are feeling is predominately from the hurt feelings and thoughts that are dominating your mind now—not from what hurt you in the past.
5. Take charge of how you feel now by managing your stress through taking a walk or doing exercise or deep breathing to soothe your body's fight-or-flight response.
6. Realize that you are not in control of other people's actions and adjust your expectations accordingly.
7. Find other ways to have your positive goals met rather

than hoping the experience you went through will some-how dramatically change. Manage your expectations.

8. Make a choice to focus on the goodness, kindness, beauty, and opportunities around you rather than your wounded feelings and your attachment to a dysfunctional situation. A life well lived is the best revenge.

9. Rewrite the story of your past to include your heroic choice to forgive as a means of moving your life forward. Recognize that you are the author of your future.

Both exercises will help you shift your perspective and reclaim both your energy and your life. It is time to honor your innate strength and rediscover the amazing parts of you that are poised to emerge.

HABIT 6: SOCIAL CONNECTION
(SOCIAL SATURDAY)

Since the earliest days, human beings have depended on their tribes for safety, food, and shelter. Through working together, traveling together, living cooperatively, and caring for one another, the tribe could thrive. Even today, we gather in workplaces, schools, sports arenas, book clubs, and spiritual groups to combine our resources and energies and to bond.

Even a baby will literally not survive without feeling connected. In 1995, two twins were born twelve weeks premature, weighing only two pounds. They were placed in separate incubators, according to the hospital's protocol. One was doing well, but her sister was struggling to breathe, and it looked like she might not make it. When a nurse had the idea to transfer the healthier sister into the weaker sister's incubator, something unexpected happened. The stronger sister, just three weeks old, put her arm around her twin, whose breathing and vital signs instantly stabilized. A photographer happened to be there at the time, and the photo of one tiny infant hugging another was featured in *Life* magazine. Worldwide this was called "The Rescue Hug."[20]

For human animals or animals of any age, we all need to connect in order to thrive, illustrated by the research conducted on rats. In one experiment, a rat in a solitary cage was given the choice between drinking water or drinking a solution of water and morphine. The result: the rat became addicted to the morphine drip and died. This became an often-cited example of the danger of drugs and was highlighted to support the war on drugs. But . . . if you look closer, that was just one part of the story.

What was not considered was the fact that these caged rats were in the equivalent of a prison, and not just prison—this was solitary confinement. What if the rats had turned to the morphine solution to numb themselves from the isolation and depression they felt, much in the same way that people do?

A fascinating study led by Bruce Alexander at Simon Fraser University took a fresh look. The premise was that maybe social isolation was the major factor. Was it the "cage or the chemical" that was causing the addiction?

To test this out, single rats were again placed in solitary cages and offered a choice of water or water laced with morphine, same as before. In contrast, a large group of rats were placed together, with the same beverage choices, in what was called a "Rat Park." Think of the most amazing resort: it had areas to play, to eat, to have sex. Soon there were lots of baby rats, too. So, there were jobs to do, other rats to look after—it was a very busy place. The findings stated: "the rats in Rat Park, called the 'Social Females' and 'Social Males' . . . are consuming hardly any morphine solution, but the 'Caged Females' and 'Caged Males' are consuming a lot."[21]

Due to the findings from the "Rat Park," that the drug, according to Bruce Alexander, "only becomes irresistible when the opportunity for normal social existence is destroyed," more people feel that the opposite of addiction is not sobriety; the opposite of addiction is connection. That prompts the question: Can human connection actually prevent the addiction in the first place? It may not be as simplistic as that—stress, ACEs (adverse childhood experiences, such as abuse, neglect, and other traumas), and genetics can all factor into addiction.

But in a society where people may feel caged by loneliness and disconnection and increasingly addicted to everything from our devices to whatever it takes to numb the pain, social connection is an important way to help.

Loneliness, though, is different from solitude. Some people seek intervals of solitude in nature or retreats (being alone but not lonely) to reenergize or gain insights.

No one, however, chooses to feel lonely. In fact, it has physical repercussions affecting stress levels, the immune system, inflammation levels, and sleep.[22] Put simply, unless one chooses to do an extended period of meditation in a cave, people need to be around people.

Touch Starvation Is Real

Yet in our overscheduled, device-driven, often overwhelmed lives, many people are finding they have less time to truly connect. Touch starvation, also known as skin hunger, is a fairly recent term to describe a lack of physical touch or affection.

Service dogs and pets of every variety are increasingly popular for many reasons, including comfort and companionship. Did you know that for a quick fix of caffeine and oxytocin (the cuddle hormone), there are now cat cafés and even dog cafés that let you pay an hourly fee to connect with a room full of adoptable pets?

Japan, the birthplace of many of these trends, also originated something called "cuddle cafés," where individuals book time with a "cuddler" to be held in their arms. These cafés feature a menu of services ranging from clothes-on cuddling to conversation to costumes.[23] And in case you are surprised, the idea is spreading. At Cuddle Up to Me, in Portland, Oregon, certified cuddlers offer hugs and a compassionate presence.[24] These sessions supply relief and companionship to people and hopefully serve as a building block for more fully formed relationships to come.

Across the board, in our hyperbusy lives, often relationships take a back seat to other "priorities." Though it's not something we set out to do, it can happen, more easily than we may notice. If you don't want to look back with regret, make a choice to reserve the time to prioritize meaningful connections now. Whether it's planned time with friends, regular dinners with family, or simply taking your dog for an evening outing, it will make life happier and help you thrive.

Connection Challenge: Think of how you like to connect to the people in your life and challenge yourself to find a little more time to be together. Do it today.

Taken one step further, we have the ability to make happiness contagious. When one person becomes happy, we now know that this can spread up to three degrees: your happy mood makes someone else happy, they go on to make another person happier, and that person increases yet another person's happiness level.[25] When your happiness ripples out to uplift three more people, you instantly become an agent of positive change. In difficult times, when so many are struggling, this has huge social implications. Did you ever even think that you could seed positive social change by attending to your own happiness? Imagine the ripple effect if more people actually took this on.

HABIT 7: MEANING, PURPOSE, AND SOUL (SOUL SUNDAY)

"What is my purpose?" is one of the most perplexing questions we can ever face. It can take a lifetime or it can take one conversation. In this story, it is resolved very quickly:

One day, a student asks his master the purpose of his life. She answers, "Only you can find that, but knowing your purpose is not found in your mind, but rather in your heart." She then posed a question: "If you knew, right now, that you were going to die tomorrow, what would you most regret that you had not accomplished?" He thought about it and responded that he would regret not making peace with his family and not creating his own center for learning. The master smiled and said, "See how you discovered it for yourself. Now it is up to you to go and make these your reality . . ."[26]

On the journey toward feeling a sense of purpose, what is your inner compass trying to tell you? There is a part of you that has all the answers. Sometimes the hints bubble up when you release your mind from a one-pointed focus and give it permission to randomly roam. Whether it's through noticing fresh ideas, the feelings in your gut, or the callings of your heart, this is not the time to "make it happen," but to allow inspiration to come to you. Give yourself permission to notice the signs.

To attune to the stirrings of your soul, it also helps to slow down. That way, you can be more in sync with how nature works. Instead of criticizing yourself for a lack of clarity or tangible results ("I should be further along by now!"), realize that there is a life cycle and everything has its season. Whether you find yourself in a period of big growth or in a lull when nothing seems to be happening, it is helpful to be aware of nature's rhythm.

Just picture it: Spring, when new plants tentatively emerge from the soil—this is a time of new ideas sprouting, new beginnings. Summer brings full-on growth and it's when ideas are a riot of color blossoming for all to see. In the fall, you harvest everything that had been planted; it's a time of reaping all the seeds you have sown. Then comes winter, when there's a period of hibernation and incubation, when things are not moving externally, but there is so much going on under the surface to prepare for what is to come. Though spring and summer may be more showy and colorful, each season plays a vital part and builds on the other. All of them work together in a system that has been perfected through the eons. Nature in all her wisdom.

Rather than fight with this natural rhythm, the point is to flow with it. Rather than relentlessly pursuing your passion and purpose, hold this pursuit lightly. What if instead of finding your passion, which can feel like a lot of pressure, you allowed yourself to just cultivate curiosity? What speaks to you in the moment? What do you want to explore? Sometimes one thing leads to the other, and that may have no relation to your original plan. But you may come out in a fresh new place. When you eventually look back on your life events, you can see how one thing led to the other, and even if you thought you were taking a detour, you learned exactly what you needed to move forward. Enjoy the journey without self-judgment. It will add joy to your life and bring you home.

A sense of meaning can also come in many forms. Many experience a sense of meaning through their spiritual practice or religion. It could be family that gives their life meaning, or the type of work they do. Some are motivated by the pursuit of justice or social causes. If you ask your mind to guide you toward your purpose before you go to sleep, you may wake up with fresh insights, or receive ideas in the shower, or see signs that pop out to you during the day. Sometimes the message on a billboard may jump out at you, or what is written on a passing truck. Sometimes a refrain from a song will speak to you, or a book may drop from a shelf in a library. There may be a headline in the news, or a phrase that you heard on TV that does not leave your mind. Inspiration is everywhere—be ready to receive.

Post-traumatic Growth

Sometimes the events in life, especially the painful ones, can point us to a greater sense of purpose. Regular challenges: like in relationships—(rejection), health (breaking a leg), finance (unemployment), or other unexpected curveballs usually, according to Dr. Martin Seligman, settle after a month or two[27] and leave people basically back where they were—they're coping.

But there is another level that we cannot bounce back from quite as quickly. When people are witnessing sudden life-threatening events: the ravages of war, a violent personal assault, the shocking death of someone you love, a mass shooting . . . that can cause PTSD, post-traumatic stress disorder. Results of this sudden attack on the psyche often include flashbacks, emotional numbness, and feeling jumpy, easily triggered, or isolated.

Did you know that, though this is not true across the board, there are a large number of people who actually come out of this acute stress stronger than they were before?

Post-traumatic growth, a term defined by psychologists Richard Tedeschi and Lawrence Calhoun, two psychologists from the University of North Carolina, Charlotte, offers another pathway. Both had been working for a decade with parents who had lost their children—a loss that could rip anyone or any relationship to shreds. They discovered not only how much the parents helped each other, but how in the middle of their own grief, instead of drowning in despair, they were moved to do something to help other families from having to face the same tragedy.

They wanted to work to change the circumstances that had led to their own child's death. They had a focus, a cause, a reason for connecting with others that was bigger than their own suffering,

The difference worth noting here is that they didn't just experience resilience through bouncing back to their former baseline level. With post-traumatic growth, these people change as a result of their unthinkable ordeal, but it is a change for the better. They become stronger, more determined, and more aware that their life has a new meaning. MADD, Mothers Against Drunk Driving, was formed after Candace Lightner's thirteen-year-old daughter, Cari, was killed by a drunk driver. Kris Carr made a film about her inoperable stage IV cancer; found ways to conquer the disease; wrote a *New York Times* bestselling book, *Crazy Sexy Cancer Tips*, describing her wellness solutions; and used her experience to start a movement.

THE SIGNS OF POST-TRAUMATIC GROWTH[28]

1. **Discovering new knowledge**: New opportunities and possibilities have emerged that were not there before. Inadvertently, a person becomes an expert in an area that had caused them great pain, and they want to learn everything they can.

2. **Closer relationships with others** and an increased sense of connection to others who suffer emerge. After a mass trauma—think of September 11, or mass shootings—some sociologists describe it as "democracy of distress." From all walks of life, people are compelled to help.

3. **Greater appreciation for life.** My dear friend lost her brother to cancer very young—now she has a greater appreciation for being alive and for the little things she might have previously overlooked.

4. **Deepening spiritual lives.** Kris Carr repositioned inoperable stage IV cancer as "Crazy Sexy Cancer" and is not only thriving but running a successful online wellness platform. Kris describes cancer as her teacher, her guru. She says that when she changed her focus, desperation led to inspiration and she learned how to really live.

5. **Feeling stronger.** There is a renewed sense that if I can get through that, I can face anything.

Post-traumatic growth works this way: first, people are consumed by the pain. "Why did this have to happen? It's too much." There's an urge to wallow, obsess, avoid, or numb the pain. It's easy to get stuck there, especially without someone to talk to, and many do.

There was a study done that challenged the participants to take an active role in their healing. Instead of the medical professionals telling them what to do or how to think about what they had been through, they were tasked with coming up with ideas to not only get them through, but to help them move on. They were challenged to take charge. David Feldman, Ph.D., psychologist and coauthor of *Supersurvivors: The Surprising Link Between Suffering and Success*, explains, "Trauma survivors who experience PTG [post-traumatic growth] acknowledge their own sadness, suffering, anger and grief, and are realistic about what happened to them. But in the midst of their pain, they're able to ask: 'Given where I am in my life, how can I build the best future possible?'" Some even ask: How can I prevent this from happening to others? . . . which leads to a greater sense of meaning and purpose.

ACCEPT + CONNECT + TAKE ACTION →
POST-TRAUMATIC GROWTH

More than just accepting what happened to them, "They feel it made them better human beings than they would ever have been without it. And it made them wiser and willing to take the risk of being more fully alive."[29]

Happiness is not the absence of obstacles; it is an inner reservoir that helps us handle whatever comes our way. When we recognize that our true nature is happiness, we are reminded that though life happens, it's up to each one of us to choose how we interpret and deal with whatever comes our way. Whatever we can do to amplify our joy sends more of it into the world. The seven happiness habits: mindfulness, gratitude, wellness, generosity, authenticity, social connection, and purpose support this energy with proven practices that allow us to reconnect with who we really are on the inside. Each of these science-based strategies adds to our toolbox of inner resources. They also help us handle any difficulty (or lesson) that life can dish out. Through practicing these habits, starting with even one, we build up our resilience to the point that we can navigate our vessel on the waves of change, with grace, with grit, and with confidence that we are always growing. We discover how strong we really are and how we have the capacity to come into alignment with who we are meant to be. Happiness is not just a state; it is our very nature, and if we happen to forget that because of the challenges that come our way, it is also a skill that anyone can learn. Be proud of yourself that you have started this journey. You are already increasing your awareness of the many practices you can use to empower your life. Start with one and take it on for a week; you are building a foundation for sustainable happiness and lifelong growth. Happiness and the ability to access your inner resources is your birthright. Good news: you are already on your way.

Sadness

Sorrow prepares you for joy.
It violently sweeps everything out of your house
so that new joy can find space to enter.
It shakes the yellow leaves from the bough of your heart
so that fresh, green leaves can grow in their place.

— RUMI

NO ONE EVER WANTS to be sad. Happy, of course! Curious— sure! Reflective—even that's okay, but sadness—no way. . . . Why would anyone ever want to feel down?

Much as we would like it to be otherwise, no one gets through their time on earth untouched by sadness. Life happens, people we love go away, circumstances change, and what we expect does not always turn out as planned. Have you ever felt overwhelmed by sadness, for a person, for a loss, for an unexpected situation? Did you do what most people think of—try to stuff it away and be calm and carry on?

What we don't often recognize is that sadness has another side. Instead of feeling sorry for being sad, let's focus for a moment on the things that sadness can provide. This is a bit of a stretch for most people, as we are used to looking at sadness in a negative light.

But if you allow yourself to feel it, and to let it hold you tenderly, sadness can serve as a shelter. It will clarify confusion, and in the most generous act of all, it will guide you out of its embrace. Sadness can prepare you for joy.

In this chapter we will look at the difference between sadness and depression. Many people confuse these states. We'll explore how to navigate sadness, as well as the scientific uses of this emotion. We'll also discover some of the hidden gifts sadness offers and finally look at its wisdom through the eyes of those who have nothing left to lose.

Honoring Sadness

As an emotion, sadness has a big range with levels from mild disappointment to heart-wrenching grief. Have you ever noticed that as the intensity of the emotion grows, the permission to express it diminishes? It wasn't always this way. In generations past, when someone lost a loved one, they were *expected* to grieve. Black mourning clothes worn for a full year let others know to go gently with them; their world had shattered and they deserved time to heal. With the cultural permission to be sad in public, they did not have to "move on" before they were ready or pretend that they had it all together. Sadness, like joy, was a respected part of nature's cycle, and a necessary stage in recalibrating one's emotional life.

The problem is, in a society that values the appearance of happiness rather than the reality of authentic expression, there is an unwritten pressure to deny the depth of our distress, to put on a neutral face, to put our best foot forward. "Better to be stoic than sad, better to be brave than distraught. Get back in the game. . . . Don't even talk about how you really feel—you'll be seen as weak, or worse yet, damaged."

We Are Not Talking Enough

There is an enormous stigma about sadness, depression, and mental illness in general. When depression escalates, it should not be swept under the rug. As a society, we need to find ways not only to get help, but to have healthy conversations about it. Dealing with depression is beyond the scope of this book, but there is a wide variety of resources available. It is always recommended to select a medical or mental health professional you feel comfortable with, who has specific tools for specific situations. It's all part of being proactive in all areas of life. The truth is everyone has to deal with hard feelings at some time or another. But how we face them is up to us. In an ideal world, we'd face the difficult sides of life together and do this out in the open.

Not only can we support one another, we can also influence those around us, in the same ways we are influenced by them. These days, it's common to hear the words "I'm stressed, I'm anxious, I'm depressed . . ." They are thrown around to describe everything from mild states of discomfort and melancholy to the actual experience of anxiety or depressive disorders. The word has permeated popular culture so much that even young kids (who may be hearing it from the adults in their lives) are running around declaring to one another that *they* are so depressed.

The problem is when we are using the word "depressed," we may actually be meaning we are sad. And there is a difference.

THE DIFFERENCE BETWEEN SADNESS AND DEPRESSION

Being sad is not a mental illness, but part of our vocabulary of natural emotions. Unlike depression, which can linger for no apparent reason, sadness is a normal human reaction to loss and to disruptive change. Sadness is a state that is triggered by an event that is hurtful, disappointing, and tumultuous—think of the loss of a loved one, a family member, a good friend, or a beloved pet. It could be caused by a sudden move, being fired from a job, an illness, unexpected hardships. . . . these are all understandable causes of sadness, and during a lifetime, it's something we all will have to deal with in one way or another. Though no one seeks sadness (we run from it!), it is a necessary emotion that gives us the space to process what has happened so we can navigate our way through to the other side.

Understanding and being with the sadness is key. When people pretend their sadness doesn't exist, it cannot be healed. That lack of attention can, over time, morph into depression. These days, though, rather than recognizing sadness as an aspect of life that comes and goes and serves a purpose, we increasingly tend to *interpret* our distress as depression.

Yet even though everyone experiences sadness, not everyone suffers from depression. Because our tolerance for emotional discomfort is almost nonexistent, we quickly look for a way out. We turn away from sadness, because it is too daunting to really peer into the issues that are causing this feeling in the first place. Preferring that the sad feelings disappear, we mislabel them as something else: "What's wrong with me? I wish this would go away, I'm feeling so depressed. . . ."

Depression, though, is not the same as sadness. It is more of a chronic condition and can seem to come out of nowhere or at times get triggered through an event. Here is a quick summary of the general differences:

SADNESS	DEPRESSION
Normal emotional state	Abnormal emotional state that affects emotions, perceptions, and behaviors
Feel sad about some event or situation	Feel sad about everything
Emotional pain fades as adjusting to loss	Depression can be chronic
Can still enjoy some things	Lack of interest in favorite things
Some variation in mood, can be distracted from sadness	In moderate depression, can have respites; in severe depression, mood feels unrelenting
May feel some normal guilt	Pervasive feelings of unworthiness, self-blame, self-contempt (I'm depressed that I am depressed)
Nondepressive sadness does not typically include suicidal ideation	Can lead to self-harming or suicidal thoughts

Unlike diabetes or a broken leg, depression cannot yet be diagnosed with a blood test or an X-ray. The cure for depression is fuzzy at best, and medicines are prescribed, often to treat the symptoms instead of the cause of the distress. The diagnosis is based on the severity of the reported symptoms. When these symptoms match up with the clinical description of depression— someone has to have experienced for more than two weeks at least five of nine designated symptoms—ding, ding, they get a pill.

In *The Loss of Sadness*, Allan V. Horwitz and Jerome C. Wake-field argue that the very way the *Diagnostic and Statistical Manual of Mental Disorders* (*DSM*) guides medical health professionals to make their diagnosis is flawed. Under the *DSM* classification system, symptoms such as loss of appetite, fatigue, and depressed mood direct the diagnosis, but there is no way to look into the *context* of these symptoms. Is there actually an internal dysfunc-tion? Or do the symptoms reflect a normal reaction of sadness to an external event, such as the loss of a job, a relationship breakup, or the death of a loved one? This distinction between sadness caused by a life event and sadness caused by prolonged internal dysfunction is not generally noted. And the *symptoms* can look exactly the same (exhaustion, lack of appetite, pessi-mism, etc.). This just means that when decisions are made on the symptoms alone, it could lead to a mistaken diagnosis of a de-pressive disorder.[1]

That is just the diagnosis stage. Then, whether patients re-ceive the right medicine or not is a crapshoot; unless brain scans or other ways of diagnosing depression are further refined, the process is trial and error.

That is not to say that the right medication is not helpful. For people who indeed have a chemical imbalance and require these medications, they are a godsend. That and cognitive behavioral therapy training are the recommended ways to deal with depression, and they can save lives. Even if depression is harder to detect on the outside, it is a serious and real disease that requires serious attention. If anyone feels the signs of depression, they should always speak to a mental health professional. Help is available.

Yet because it is so easy to write a prescription, there are many times when medication is used as the first strategy, without considering any other lifestyle shifts that can make a major difference. Are antidepressants being overprescribed? According to a *Forbes* article, antidepressants like Zoloft, Prozac, and Celexa are so widespread they have been found in the Great Lakes and in fish, probably because prescriptions are being filled by more than 12 percent of the population.[2] That figure may even be higher today.

Another Approach

Here's a thought, and I want to preface it by saying this is not true in every case, but it is worth considering. What if the issue is not so much with the individual person, but with the imbalanced lifestyle that we, as a culture, are buying into? Compound that with the loneliness and lack of purpose that so many people are experiencing, just by living on autopilot and trying desperately to keep up. To add to that, when we are ruled by our addiction to phones, we are literally giving away our power. One study, led by Jean Twenge, mentioned that, according to the CDC (Centers for Disease Control and Prevention), in a span of just five years, teenagers, particularly girls, had a 59 percent rise in depression, and suicide rose by a full 65 percent.[3] Twenge's study suggests that this is connected to the rise in phone use. When we resort to putting mindless convenience before heartfelt connection, we can end up feeling sadness or even depression and not even knowing why. We are moving away from the connection that matters most, the one with the deepest part of ourselves.

Do you ever feel like we are neglecting the human necessities, like time to relax and time to be with the people we care about and who care about us? The basics, like time to sleep, to play, to laugh and wind down? Do you long for more room to breathe, to dream about some intentions, and what about just doing . . . nothing?

JOURNAL CHALLENGE

In your **journal**, give each human need or want (such as re-laxation/sleep, caring friendships, family time, personal development, nourishing food, financial stability, meaningful work, recreation/health, spiritual connection, giving back, experiencing nature . . . feel free to add your own) a number (1 being "I'm very satisfied" to 10 being "URGENT—I need to do something NOW!").

Instead of finding fulfillment in the moment and feeling appreciation for the simple, poignant experiences life offers (some of which feel good and some of which are complex), how many of us are forever chasing a picture of a "perfect" life?

What if *society*, in its distorted priorities, had the greatest illness? Author Dr. Neel Burton points out how masses of people have been treated: "By encoding their distress in terms of a mental disorder, our society may be subtly implying that the problem lies not with itself but with them as fragile and failing individuals." The idea that when life is making you upset, just pop a pill, has become widespread. But if we continue to equate ordinary unhappiness with a chemical imbalance or mental illness, we may miss the actual lifestyle problems that are the cause of many of the conditions in the first place. The invitation is to put our attention into choosing better ways to adjust our lifestyle. Let's call it what it is. The system we live in, breathe in, work in, and try to love in is disconnected, and will become more so, unless we take agency in managing our priorities.

Dr. Rangan Chatterjee, star of the BBC program *Doctor in the House* and author of *How to Make Disease Disappear*, advocates that instead of saying to patients, "You have depression" and prescribing antidepressants, there are other approaches yielding even better results.[4] The lifestyle choices that people make can impact and even transform their health. He tells the story of a sixteen-year-old boy named Devon, who had tried to cut his wrists and was sent to him from the ER to get some antidepressants started. Since he knew the boy's family as well-balanced and caring, the doctor was hesitant to write the prescriptions and asked them to come back the next day. He proposed to Devon an experiment. What if the way Devon was using social media might be a factor in how he was feeling—would he be interested in reducing his exposure to see if that made any difference? Devon said he'd give it a try, agreeing that for one hour in the morning he would not go on his phone. When he returned seven days later, Devon said, "I'm still not great, but I'm less up and down during the day and I'm sleeping better." It was a sign of improvement.

The doctor asked if they could move it up bit by bit, and over the next few weeks, Devon increased the off-device time, ultimately not looking at his phone for two hours in the morning and two hours in the evening before bed. Gradually but consistently he started to improve. In the meantime, Dr. Chatterjee was reading about nutrition, and the next time Devon came in, he asked Devon what he was eating. It was the typical teenage diet of processed junk food and sugar. The doctor drew a graph showing Devon that when your blood sugar is going up and down with what you're eating, it's not just an energy problem; your stress hormones, like cortisol and adrenaline, can also go up, and that can impact your mood. Devon got the point, and when he asked what he could do, the doctor recommended ways for him to stabilize his blood sugar during the day with more protein and healthy fats, like nuts, to snack on.

Months later, Devon's mother sent a letter saying that her son was like a different boy, happy at school, engaging with his friends, and doing clubs on weekends. When reading the letter, the doctor thought, Devon had been at a fork in the road—he could have been labeled as someone who has depression—thinking there was nothing he could do, and could have been on antidepressants for years to come. Or he could have tried the lifestyle shifts and discovered that with his conscious choices he could impact his own health.[5]

While this may not work for everyone (as some do require medication), it is most promising that this approach is seeing so much success. With sadness often misdiagnosed as depression and depression at an all-time high (the number one cause of disability globally according to the World Health Organization), taking a holistic approach can make all the difference. .

Challenge yourself to make one small change in your lifestyle today. These four pillars Dr. Chatterjee points to are deceptively simple:

- **Relax** and connect with loved ones—connection counts
- **Fuel Up** by eating more protein and nuts to help regulate blood sugar levels and mood
- **Sleep** to recharge your system—this is more important than you may know
- **Move** your body more—exercise effectively improves your mood

Choose one area to start and make one small change. Track how you feel the first week, and then track the changes over time.

Dr. Ellen Vora, holistic psychiatrist, takes this one step further by exploring the environmental factors that are linked to depression. These include inflammation, originating in the gut, which causes some people to feel depressed. She recommends "cultivating a diverse ecosystem of beneficial gut flora" and eliminating inflammatory foods. Gut health affects body and mind. Thyroid conditions, she has observed, are often undiagnosed, and for some, can lead to panic disorders and brain fog. Hormones are a whole other area, and hormonal imbalances may also be a contributing factor to feelings of depression, as can a lack of certain vitamins and nutrients.[6] These can all be looked into.

How we choose to spend our days is also enormously important: less "busyness," more nature, less addiction to devices, and more human connection, less chasing what we don't have, more gratitude for what we do—we all know this. The reminder is that you have more options than you may realize to deal with what ails you. Be your own advocate.

JOURNAL CHALLENGE

In your **journal**, come up with one action you can do today. Over time, small shifts lead to big changes and to creating better habits to help counteract both sadness and depression.

But there is more to the story: What if a small amount of sadness is actually a good thing? Though we all try to escape it, could sadness actually be an advantage in certain situations?

How Sadness Helps with Memory, Judgment, and Leadership

Professor Joseph Forgas at the University of New South Wales, in Sydney, Australia, has conducted several studies to determine if mild sadness can be a helpful state instead of one that most people want to avoid. He concluded that in specific circumstances, mild sadness (not depression) can help us be more discerning and more able to read people accurately, and it even can fuel greater tenacity.[7] Here's what he discovered:

SADNESS CAN MAKE YOUR MEMORY SHARPER

In one study participants had to recall the details of objects they had seen in a store. It found that on the rainy, gloomy day, the kind that can make people feel down, they remembered more details and with greater accuracy than they did on the cheery sunny day. Conclusion: if you want to absorb and retain all the details, a pensive state is better than a euphoric one.

SADNESS CAN HELP WITH SOCIAL JUDGMENT

Who is a more accurate judge of people? The experiment had observers look at a video of people accused of theft. Though the subjects in the video all denied it, some were actually stealing movie tickets, while some were not. The observers who were considered happy could only detect if someone was lying 49 percent of the time. The observers who were "experimentally put into an unhappy, sad mood" before watching the videotapes had a much different result—they could actually discern the ones who were lying 62 percent of the time,[8] 13 percent higher than their happy-mood counterparts. Conclusion: people in a sadder mood can make more accurate judgments.

SADNESS CAN INCREASE MOTIVATION

When participants in a study were shown either happy or sad films and then given a challenging task, filled with tough questions, the results were quite different. The happier group (as a result of watching the happier film) spent less time on the test and got fewer answers correct. The group watching the sad film (and feeling sadder) put in greater efforts and ended up getting higher results. Conclusion: whereas happy people might be less motivated to modify their situation (if it ain't broke, don't fix it), sadder people may be motivated to do a better job.

SADNESS IS USEFUL IN LEADERSHIP

Can leaders who deliberately display happiness or sadness affect the performance of their teams? Victoria Visser conducted research that can help anyone in a leadership position, from parents to CEOs.[9] Participants had to complete two tasks—one was more analytic (completing a sudoku puzzle) and the other task was more creative (doing a brainstorming exercise). The team leader gave the instruction to all the participants, but half the time his face and voice reflected happiness, and half the time his tone of voice and expression were not happy.

When people were engaged in the creative tasks, the happy leader motivated better results. Participants performed the creative task two hundred times better for the happy leader than for the unhappy leader, which is not surprising—they were lit up; they were inspired. Happiness is contagious. What is interesting, though, is that participants performed the analytical task four hundred times better when the leader showed signs of sadness. This change in performance was directly correlated to whether the leader seemed happy or unhappy. This suggests that leaders should think about their goals first and then choose an emotional approach to help them move people in that direction. Conclusion: happiness, as a leadership style, boosts creativity, but unhappiness or sadness can be surprisingly effective for motivating analytical thinking.

The Gifts of Sadness

While we're on the topic of the uses of sadness, how can it further touch our lives? In many ways, this emotion is a harbor in a storm and can actually help move us from a place of sorrow to a place of potential, and yes, even joy. Psychologist Tim Lomas assigns personas to the different ways sadness can show up, but I have framed them in terms of the hidden gifts that sadness can provide.[10] Sadness as a gift? Yes, it is possible! Here are all seven:

1. Gets You out of Harm's Way

The first gift of sadness is that it helps you get out of harm's way. If you are in a toxic situation and the sadness is so great that it prompts you to overcome inertia and make a move to safer surroundings, that sadness is a catalyst for action. Just as burning your hand on a stove instinctively forces you to pull away, feeling searing pain in your heart, at the breakup of a relationship, for example, may also force you to disengage from what might have become an unhealthy dynamic. Just like an animal would find a safe perch or hibernate to be out of harm's way, people have the same needs. Sadness creates the urgency to move you toward a place of refuge and to find shelter in order to recover your strength. If not for sadness, you might have stayed in that situation longer than you needed to. In this way, sadness can set you free.

2. Activates the Power of Tears

Sadness also evokes tears. These are evolution's signal that the person crying could really use a little help. Most people when seeing someone in tears are moved to want to lend a hand. Maybe that's why humans still have tear ducts. Crying is also nature's way of releasing pent-up emotions—most people feel so much better after a good cry. When hormones such as oxytocin and prolactin are released, they elicit feelings of contentment and comfort.[11] Crying is not a sign of weakness—it is a sophisticated and complex system to relieve stress and get help now.

Cry. Forgive. Learn. Move on. Let your tears water the seeds
of your future happiness.[12]

— STEVE MARABOLI

In times of grief, especially from the loss of a loved one, crying is more important than ever.

When Sheryl Sandberg lost her husband, Dave, it was a seis-
mic shock that no one had expected. He had died from a cardiac
arrhythmia caused by undiagnosed heart disease. While dealing
with her grief and her children's, a good friend, psychologist, and
professor at Wharton, Adam Grant, reached out. He suggested
that expressing the pain, instead of pushing it away, would help
the whole family not only heal but become more resilient. The
conversations deepened and they cowrote *Option B* to help others
find strategies to respond to life's upheavals.[13]

One useful option, he explained, is to choose to express what
you feel. If you feel like crying, whether in the car or in the middle
of a meeting, do it. If the kids have to go outside with a friend or
speak to a counselor to let their feelings out, that actually speeds
up their healing. Like physical exercise, the more you do, the
more strength you discover you have.

While Sheryl's instinct was to try to bring up positive
thoughts (and distract from the tears), Adam suggested a coun-
terintuitive approach: focusing on worst-case scenarios. You
might be thinking, "What could be worse?" Adam answered,
"Dave could have had that same cardiac arrhythmia driving
your children." Imagine losing all three at once. The point hit
home.

3. Gives You the Space to Reflect

Another benefit of being true to your needs is that you can carve out time to look at the situation and finally ask yourself the questions you never had the time to reflect on. Tears can also wash away the illusions that may have kept you unknowingly stuck. After mourning a loss and starting the healing process, there emerges a clarity that was impossible to see while enmeshed in old unhealthy patterns. You now have the time, space, and perspective to ask new questions.

JOURNAL CHALLENGE

In your **journal**, take a moment to answer:
- How do I want to respond as I move forward in the future?
- What could support me right now?
- What does this situation tell me about what I want or don't want?
- What made me feel trapped—what will I do now?

People who experience sadness may also feel disillusioned—but that is not bad. Though the truth of a situation can be painful (he cheated on me, she's all about herself . . .), it also gives you the wisdom of experience. The lessons learned may feel harsh, but you will not have to make them again. Sadness can be the birthplace of knowledge, and knowledge is power.

4. Opens the Door to Our Shared Humanity

Sadness serves as a doorway to compassion. By recognizing that everyone suffers sometimes, we don't feel as separate from others who are in the throes of upheaval. Instead, this shared sense of suffering compels us to reach out and help (think of the massive outpourings of compassion and generosity after a natural disaster)—we are bonded in the human journey.

Who doesn't feel heartbreaking sadness when a loved one passes, and who hasn't felt the burn of rejection, loneliness, or disappointment? We are truly on this wild ride together—some get the lessons earlier, and some later, but throughout all of time, sadness is and will always be one of the great equalizers. Whether you have millions in the bank or are just getting by, whether you have a huge family or simply a pet to love, we all feel sad at times. In recognizing that not one member of the human race is immune to pain, we discover that we are part of something much greater and more timeless than our self-oriented lives.

5. BRINGS US CLOSER TO THOSE WE HAVE LOST

I mentioned earlier that sadness has different levels, from disappointment to grief. Losing a loved one is one of the most intense levels and can take years to mend. Although it is said that there are five stages of grief, each person travels that road at their own pace. No one can dictate a formula or a timeline; some bounce back more quickly and some need the soothing balm of time—this is personal to the core.

This type of sadness is not a depressive disorder, but a normal passage. I have a friend, Diane, who lost her mother, and at the funeral and in the days after, her primal cries filled the room. When some of her family members, who were embarrassed at this tsunami of emotion, tried to shush her, entreating her to tone it down, the attending clergy had a few words to say. Well, it started with a few words, but ended as an impassioned speech on how he wished every mourner could be as connected to their emotions as Diane. He described how he had to help pick up the pieces much later on with the mourners who were quiet and stoic—they carried the weight of their grief much longer. But the ones who could let it out, grieving loud and proud, could traverse through it faster. Again, this is not a race, and each person has their own timeline, but this is a reminder that being stoic is not necessarily the best way.

Grieving does not have to mean a loss of love. It's an active expression of the love we still feel and a way that we maintain a connection with our loved ones, now departed. Tim Lomas explains, "One could argue that it (grief) is not a loss of love per se, but rather an expression of love . . . love in the presence of its 'target' manifests as joy, and in its absence manifests as sadness."[14]

Taken one step further, some people believe that upon death their loved one is gone forever; yet in time, some see signs of their presence in new ways: "Whenever that bird shows up, I feel like it's my dad sending me a message." Just because someone has crossed the veil does not mean that the connection is over. For some, the energetic bond can feel even stronger. Everyone will decide for themselves what interpretation they like best.

6. Helps Us Experience Greater Joy

There are three things that prevent us from coming back to joy. Psychologist Martin Seligman calls them the three Ps. The good news is that they have to do with our beliefs . . . which can change.

1.   **Personalization**: the belief that "it's entirely my fault." Chances are that this is not actually true. Many factors

(such as personal histories, environment, health, open-mindedness, etc.) converge in most situations. Don't carry a burden that is not yours to bear.

2. **Pervasiveness**: this is the belief that "it will affect *every* aspect of my life." The tendency is to bucket everything together into one mushy bowlful of gloom. Separate the ingredients. It is not *all* bad. For example, if you just went through a breakup, remember the positive relationships that still support you; focus on other areas of your life that are working.

3. **Permanence**: this is the belief that "these overwhelming feelings will last forever." When emotions are high, we tend to believe they will always be that way. Remind yourself that whatever you are facing, even the most challenging situations feel less intense with time—we are wired that way.

JOURNAL CHALLENGE

In your **journal**, think of a challenging situation through the lens of these three Ps. What aspect can help you carve out a new perspective?

What if the more you experienced sadness, the greater your capacity for joy? We can no longer take the happy moments for granted but embrace and enjoy them more fully because we now know the opposite. Just as the darkness creates a canvas for the rays from a flashlight, so can sadness be the canvas for joy. Kahlil Gibran says it beautifully: "The deeper that sorrow carves into your being, the more joy you can contain." Only when we are touched by sadness can we truly value the many facets of happiness. So that even in the most difficult of circumstances, there is hope—sorrow helps us experience greater joy.

7. ALLOWS US TO KNOW THE TRANSCENDENCE OF LOVE

Have you ever loved someone so much, you thought you just couldn't bear it if they were gone? When you look at a child or loved one sleeping peacefully, it can open your heart to the immensity of your feelings . . . and it may also trigger fear or sadness to think that it could suddenly change. "What if they die, what if they are no longer in my life, what if . . ." There is an intense vulnerability that we crack open when we commit to such a profound and timeless love.

> To love means opening up to that fate, that most sublime of all human conditions, one in which fear blends with joy into an alloy that no longer allows its ingredients to separate.
> —ZYGMUNT BAUMAN[15]

Fear, sadness, joy, and love can meld together in a breathtaking awareness of the preciousness of life.

By understanding how we are all, to a degree, subject to the whims of fate, we can appreciate more deeply the fragility and impermanence of life and the idea of losing that love to the unknown. At the end of the day, to love so deeply is one of the greatest gifts we can ever give or receive.

Sadness and Regrets

Knowing the gifts of sadness can bring a new perspective to old troubles. But one of the most pervasive types of sadness has to do with regrets: "I wish I had handled that differently, I wish I had been more open, I wish I had been more bold. . . ." Though the regrets are different for everyone, at the end of our days there are universal themes. Bronnie Ware worked in palliative care for eight years and sat by the bedside of those in their last weeks of life. She heard these themes again and again and chronicled the top regrets of the dying.[16] These wake us up to look at our priorities through the lens of those who don't have the time to shift theirs. We do. Which ones would you be willing to act on?

- **I wish I'd had the courage to live a life true to myself, not the life others expected of me.** Is there anything sadder than letting yourself down? When you have a dream, and you are healthy enough to go for it, celebrate and make the most of your precious time.
- **I wish I hadn't worked so hard.** At the end of the day, the project, awards, even achievements matter less than those you share them with. Choose people over pursuit—that's one thing you will never regret.
- **I wish I'd had the courage to express my feelings.** When you hold yourself back to not rock the boat, you end up compromising not only your priorities but also who you genuinely are. That's when feelings can fester and turn inward, causing a deep-rooted sadness. Speak up, speak out—not only does it get easier, but you will gain respect from yourself as well as others. It's also good to express

love when you feel it. You are aligning with your true nature; it doesn't get better than that.

- **I wish I had stayed in touch with my friends.** Though we
  like to think of ourselves as independent, the moments of
  connection and friendship are what we remember most.
  These are the currency of life. Don't presume you have
  endless opportunities to give the people you love more
  time. Either theirs runs out or it will be yours—today is a
  perfect day to show you care.

- **I wish that I had let myself be happier.** When we realize
  that happiness is a choice, we can create the conditions to
  allow more of it to show up. Ask yourself if there are parts
  of you that want to come out and play. Then do it now—
  don't wait. This is a win-win-win.

JOURNAL CHALLENGE

One way to do this is to write a letter to yourself in your
journal from the point of view of your inner coach, or if
you prefer, from your very best friend. It might go something like this, "Dear (you), I know you are going through
a rough patch right now, and you have every right to. It's
important that you feel what you are feeling and pay attention to where it shows up in your body, too. But this is what
you need to do next . . ." Imagine your wise coach or closest
friend is giving you some pointers on one action you can do
today or this week. Allow yourself some quiet time and tune
in—the answers may surprise you.

Sadness will take its course, and you *will* cycle back to feeling better. If you want to accelerate that process and not get stuck in rumination, tune in to your inner resources.

Another thing you can do is make sure you are not always alone. We can get caught in a cycle of thoughts that's hard to break. To change your perspective, go for dinner with a friend from time to time, or take an outing, see a concert, take a hike in nature. Being together is good medicine. It reminds you that this too shall pass, and you are not alone.

Sadness is a part of life, and it makes joy all the more poignant. It's important to know both sides, because when we shut out sadness, we also close down our capacity for joy. They are like both sides of a coin; each one is necessary. Sadness is not the enemy; observe its lessons so that you can move on. It is a portal to our next level of growth. Use it to clean house, clarify who you are and who you want to be. It will release old energy, guide you back to your own inner wisdom, and connect you with what is most important in your life. Sadness helps you make room for joy.

Desire

Desire is the starting point of all achievement.

— NAPOLEON HILL

WHEN YOU THINK OF desire, what comes to mind? Is it desire for success, desire to learn, sexual desire, or desire for independence? Whatever we are wishing for, desire ignites a fire that moves us forward.

So what is desire, anyway? It is defined as "A strong feeling of wanting to have something or wishing for something to happen[1]; a conscious impulse towards something that promises enjoyment or satisfaction in its attainment; sexual urge or appetite; or something longed for."[2]

JOURNAL CHALLENGE

When you were growing up, how was desire explained to you? Jot down your thoughts in your **journal**.

Some would say it is the opposite of apathy; it makes us feel alive. And yet some philosophies look down on desire. From an early age, we are warned not to desire too much. "Who are you to think you can do that? That's just not possible. Don't get too into it—you need more balance. You're setting yourself up for disappointment. You're becoming obsessed!"

Does that mean we should push down our desires, deny our intuition, and learn to play it safe? The only thing that guarantees is atrophy; if we're not flowing with life then we can become like stagnant water. It also suggests that we never come up with any new ideas and that we stay small. Is that what we are here for? No! This life is a grand adventure—we are not supposed to exist and then just die—there is huge potential in each and every one of us. When we experience desire, there is a spark that is ignited. We are energized, we want to grow, learn, and connect. How we channel that desire either sets us up for the fulfillment or leads us to a lesson. Both are incredibly valuable options that would not be possible if we stayed stuck in apathy.

In this chapter we'll explore the differences between hope and desire, the nature of desire, and what happens when desire gets extreme. That leads us to the difference between desire and passion, unpacking the two types of passion, and ultimately exploring how both open the path to purpose. Desire and passion are powerful forces, especially when we know how to direct them in a way that is aligned with our inner directives and with what we value most.

The Difference Between Hope
and Desire

Hope is one of the most misunderstood of all the emotions. It doesn't mean that we are in denial about the challenges in front of us or that we look at life through rose-colored lenses. It is the state of mind where we make the *choice* to look at life through a positive lens rather than a negative one. With eyes wide open, we are deciding to put more of our attention on what we want and what can emerge.

To even set ourselves up for this mind-set, we have to make a choice of what to focus on. Since what we put our attention on grows, do we stay on autopilot and immerse ourselves in the intricacies, intrigues, gossip, and gruesome stories at our fingertips, or do we make some other choices and take control? As we ingest information, just as we do food, are we going to gorge on junk-food news, or put our vitality first and take in the ingredients and the information that keep us feeling vital and inspired? This takes discernment, as left to our own devices, we are for the most part addicted *to* our devices. But just being aware that we have a choice gives us the opportunity to decide how much social media we will mindlessly take in and how much time we will reserve for real in-person connections and for people who really matter. This is all about owning our time and attention. This is also about taking back our connection to what we value most and checking in with our inner compass. When we are aligned with that, we sense the possibilities and can better guide our mind and our energies to create the conditions in which hope can naturally grow.

To be clear, I'm not saying that we should never watch the

news again or deny that bad stuff does happen. Just living life brings disappointments, challenges, and obstacles. We cannot and should not pretend they don't exist, but at the same time, that does not mean that hope has to disappear. In times of hardship, the sense that we are connected to our true natures and that there are better days ahead is more important than ever. It can ground us when everything around us is unstable, or when things take longer than we'd like. There is a bigger plan, and if we can stay open, we will be in sync with it. Martin Luther King Jr. said it beautifully: "We must accept finite disappointment, but never lose infinite hope."

Why Hope Matters

We all need hope for a positive future, as it both lifts our spirits and allows our minds to settle. One study that tracked college students for more than three years found that "hope was even better at predicting academic achievement than intelligence, personality, or previous academic achievement."[3] It turns out that hope is a mind-set that increases both your results and how you feel on the way to achieving them.

But as a vehicle that can move you forward, how important is it really? One research study asked the question: What gives you the best mind-set for greater well-being and success? Scientists Magaletta and Oliver compared three. The first vehicle was optimism: having positive expectancy that a future situation would work out, even if you were not in control. The second vehicle they looked at was your personal belief that you could succeed, that you could master what was in front of you, also known as self-efficacy.

The third vehicle was hope and, as a vehicle, hope turned out to be significantly better than the others. Why? Because hope, according to psychologist Charles Snyder's Hope Theory, includes the *will* to get there, as well as having different pathways to reach your goal.[4] You want to do something and you create a plan to carry it out. While optimism allows you to think that a situation will work out, hope helps you harness your willpower and suggest strategies to move things along.

Hope also translates to having greater productivity in the workplace, a surprising 14 percent more, according to Shane Lopez, Gallup psychologist and author of *Making Hope Happen*.[5] In an analysis of forty-five studies that looked at more than 11,000 employees, hope boosted productivity more than intelligence, optimism, or self-efficacy. Since it is not related to intelligence or income, hope can really level the playing field.

Hope gives you the best mind-set for well-being and success, and it boosts productivity. It is high time to give hope the recognition it deserves!

Hope Versus Expectation

Where hope points us in a direction of what we want for ourselves or others, expectation includes an attachment to a specific outcome. Not only do you hope for something, you expect it to happen. . . . If you achieve the expected outcome (you got the raise; you won the game), then you are satisfied, and life is good. It is almost like a longing in you is filled . . . temporarily at least. The problem is if your expectations were not met, whether about a job, health issue, or relationship, then you could easily become hard on yourself. (What did I do wrong? Why can't things ever work out?)

Some people look at expectation another way. They believe that when you've worked as hard as humanly possible and given everything you have to a project or goal, you deserve success; expect it! If you're in sports, and you've trained to the max—expect to win; if you're studying for an exam, and you've covered all the details possible and know it cold—expect to get that A. There's something powerful about devoting yourself fully to a goal, and there is no doubt that it will move you forward. At the same time, it doesn't account for the uncontrollable factors in life, like unforeseen accidents, health issues, or challenges in general.

A better way to gear up is by putting in the hours (preparation is a good thing) and *aspiring* to the best possible outcome. The difference is that by aspiring toward a goal rather than expecting it, you break free from the "all or nothing" restrictions of expectation. You get to experience more flexibility and breathing room. Instead of being stuck with one fixed picture of success, you have many more ways to move toward *feeling* successful. I love the saying "It could be that, or something better. . . ." When you are not in a rigid position, your options open further, plus you get to actually enjoy the journey.

One note—when expectations do not work out, consider what you have discovered through the process. Is there something you would do differently next time? What inner resources would you tap into? Would you take a different approach or consider new things when making your decision? Sometimes, things happen for a reason . . . you are being redirected to something that suits you more, that expands you in new ways and that can make you more attuned to where you need to be. When things don't work out as planned, you are always learning and through that growing stronger. Hope is not abandoned; it is just preparing you to stretch to where you need to be. As the saying goes, it's not rejection; it's redirection. There is always a bigger plan. Instead of fighting change, flow with it.

What Is Desire?

Both desire and hope move us forward toward our goals, but on a spectrum of one to ten (ten being the most intense), hope would find its place in the center at around five, and desire would be between eight and ten. Desire has more energy, more urgency, and more juice.

There is a primal element to desire. The ancient Hindu Rig Veda, written about 1500 BCE, states that the universe began not with light, but with desire. Desire is described as "'the primal seed and germ of Spirit.'"[6] That spirit is in all of us. It's what makes a baby pick her/himself up again and again when learning how to walk. It's the urge to ever expand to new horizons. As a species, we have evolved to desire what strengthens our survival—we are wired to stand up against those who threaten our loved ones, to find food and shelter, and to bring in the next generation.

Desire also gives us motivation to rise to our potential. Have you ever faced a challenge that seemed really tough, but something inside of you told you that you wanted to do it; you had to do it? Think back to your first job. You had no experience, no track record to fall back on, but you knew that you wanted to have the opportunity. Maybe it would open some new aspect in your life, maybe it would give you more independence—whatever the reason, you wanted it.

JOURNAL CHALLENGE

In your **journal**, recapture a time when your desire helped you face a challenge and get through it. Desire helps you stretch beyond your limits, go into new territories, and have the perseverance to try again when the unexpected happens.

It's important to frame your desires in terms of what you want, instead of what you don't. "I want to be energized and alive as I build this opportunity" is so much better than "I don't want to mess up the opportunity in front of me." It carries a stronger energy that helps it take shape. If you visualize what your desire looks like and how you will feel while in the process of building it, you are easing the way for that desire to be fulfilled. Elite athletes use visualization in this very same way. Studies with basketball players have proven that this simple technique helps them perform better than those who did not use it.[7]

Nothing is static in life, and new desires are constantly bursting forth within us, moving us to engage with others, find our flow, and get in the game. When we consider that the opposite of desire is apathy, it's easy to see how being out of touch with our desire could keep us isolated and cut off from life. People without desire can feel like they are drowning in resignation and dying a slow death. Desire is the spark that stirs expansion, creativity, and growth. Virginia Woolf put it beautifully: "I have a deeply hidden and inarticulate desire for something beyond the daily life."

There's a physical aspect to desire as well. Did you know that desire activates the neurotransmitter dopamine in the brain? Emma Seppälä, author of *The Happiness Track*, states that "anticipation of a desired outcome makes us feel good. . . . We experience anticipatory joy."[8] That is because dopamine is released in the brain to signal a reward. So, just looking at the object that we desire, whether it is a mouthwatering meal, a new toy, or a great pair of shoes, triggers neural signals that are associated with the release of dopamine in the brain. Have you ever planned a vacation in advance, researched the places you would visit, the restaurants you would eat at, the beaches where you would swim? This is a proven way to lift your mood. Stanford University researcher Brian Knutson found that even thinking about, indeed anticipating that thing we desire, like that future vacation, makes us happier. This desire-triggered anticipation also helps us complete major projects and goals, such as marathons or big moves. It fuels our drive and determination and helps us get to the finish line even if there are obstacles in the way.

> You can have anything you want if you want it badly enough. You can be anything you want to be, have anything you desire, accomplish anything you set out to accomplish if you hold to that desire with singleness of purpose.
>
> —ROBERT COLLIER

Desire is not wishy-washy—it's a potent emotion that is intent on getting results.

Extreme Desire

Within that, however, are built-in risks. Eastern religions warn us of the dangers of attachment. The craving for more and more material objects is a good example. How many clothes are enough to feel attractive? How many likes on social media will show us we are accepted? How much money in the bank will prove that we are secure? How much achievement will it take to combat the feeling of emptiness that says we will never be enough?

People who are tired of the "race to nowhere" and are seeking solace in spirituality may even get fanatical about the rituals and practices they are learning. For some, these rituals can take on increasing importance, even to the point of obsession. When we replace the addiction to acquisition with the addiction to experiences (adrenaline junkies) or to personal development (self-help seminar fans), we are just substituting one compulsion for another. But if we are *aware* of this human tendency and intentionally choose an integrated approach in which we decide our priorities based upon what we value most, we move closer to where we'd like to end up. This is a process.

The challenge with this often unconscious longing for more is getting caught in the Cycle of Desire. Here's how it works: you have a desire, you satisfy that desire, you feel immediate happiness, pleasure, or satisfaction, then that feeling fades. Rinse, repeat . . .

It's kind of like chocolate. You get that extreme craving for something sweet, and you have to have it. So you eat the chocolate. It tastes delightful and makes you happy . . . but the feeling doesn't last. Positive psychologists call it hedonic adaptation—you get that blast of elevation but return right back to where you were, and then . . . of course, the craving returns, and you need more of whatever it was that satisfied you temporarily.

As described in the *Project Happiness Handbook*, "After the pleasure of having the object fades, we desire something else. The idea here is that happiness that depends on external objects or attainment of immediate desires will only bring temporary satisfaction. Then when we find ourselves wanting something new, which we often do, we repeat the process. We end up creating a never-ending cycle as we constantly search for more objects and increasingly intense experiences that satisfy us temporarily."[9]

Anytime we find ourselves in the mind-set of "not enough" is when we are most susceptible to marketers who would sell us the latest pair of jeans, magical skin potion, or energy drink. It's not that we need it; it's always the desire to feel more complete within ourselves . . . to banish forever that feeling of separation, lacking, or emptiness: the hole in the soul.

Trapped in the pervasive pursuit of more, we are losing connection with appreciating the little joys, subtle beauty, and opportunities for awareness in this very moment. Desire, in this scenario, is trying to give you an important message: beyond all the noise, when you take a moment to look deeper, what you are really longing for is the feeling of returning to yourself. In the words of Eckhart Tolle, "All cravings are the mind seeking salvation or fulfillment in external things and in the future as a substitute for the joy of Being."

So let's talk about the joy of being. Have you ever felt like you had a surge in your energy? You felt clear, connected, and alive. In that moment you were linked with your true nature, the part of you that is peaceful, joyous, and knowing, the part of you that is with you always, just below the static of everyday life. You probably connect with it in nature, listening to music, in meditation, or in special moments. Call it your inner knowing, call it source, call it your core values—whatever name you choose, you feel aligned.

Some people use the analogy of a nozzle or a valve.[10] We are the valve, and we are connected to a massive hose, similar to a fire hose. The fire hose represents pure, clear life-force energy, which we allow or hold back depending on how we adjust our valve. When we are more at ease, the valve opens up. When stress takes over and we feel disconnected, the valve closes, as does our access to all of that clear energy.

It's often when we pause and detach from the hamster-wheel stresses that we can begin to notice all the good *already* in our lives. This is an easy way to open our valve so that the clear energy can flow to us and through us. We recognize the small things—the little moments of gratitude or a meaningful conversation when we really feel connected. These remind us of who we are and also of what is important at the end of the day.

It feels so good to be a conduit for this wonderful energy. And as we learned about the boomerang, when we talked about happiness, what we send out returns to us. You can make sure your valve is open so you can access this amazing energy and boomerang even more your way. Here are some simple ways:

- To energize the body, take a few belly breaths, go for a walk, or catch a yoga class. So often we walk around literally in our heads. It is both enlivening and grounding to activate our bodies. In doing this we open our valve so more energy can flow through.
- To level up mentally, bring some gratitude into your mind, listen to some inspiring music or a podcast, read a great book, or write in your journal.

JOURNAL CHALLENGE

You can pose a question in your **journal**, from the "you" sitting in the chair to your inner nature, nozzle open, energy flowing. The question could be, "What do I need to know right now?" Write for a page or more and see what your inner nature wants to tell you. You may be pleasantly surprised.

- You can also change your environment by calling a good friend or stepping into nature. Having a social interaction or an interaction with nature calms the nervous system and promotes hope and resilience. These are all within your control, and you have them in your toolbox to help open your valve anytime you want.

Desire and Passion

Desire can give you the motivation toward your goals, but passion can make you unstoppable. This is especially true if it connects to your core values and your purpose. Desire helps you move forward, and passion dials it up even more. Passion has many faces. It can sweep you off your feet, ignite a fire in your soul, or drive you off a cliff.

Passion emerges out of what feels like a need; it's even more intense than a desire for something you want. You can even be passionate about wanting to achieve a desire. In that headspace, you know you will go all out, full engagement, single-minded focus. Watch out, world!

Passion, according to Dr. Robert Vallerand, author of *The Psychology of Passion*, is "a strong inclination toward a particular object, activity, concept or person that one loves (or at least strongly likes), highly values, [and] invests time and energy in."[11] When we are passionate about something, we want to immerse ourselves in that activity. Hours can feel like minutes. It makes us feel alive.

Two Types of Passion

Did you know that there are two types of passion? The first is harmonious passion, which enhances your life and allows you to live it more fully. You are able to spend time on what you love as well as decide when to call it quits so you can also enjoy some quality time with friends and family. The second type is obsessive passion (which is very close to compulsive desire), and it seems to control you.

This type of passion is so captivating that it takes over your thoughts and your time to the point that you don't want to stop what you are doing. You are in the flow—why break it? The downside, though, can be severe. Some athletes, when they overtrain and sustain serious injuries as a result, know where this feeling can end up. In regular life, obsessive passion is at play when you find yourself being a workaholic, bingeing on videos, or indulging to excess in anything you enjoy. Though it feels good in the moment, there is a point of diminishing returns. Sure, you'd love to watch seasons one and two of a captivating show, but there's that nasty alarm in the morning, and you actually do have to get to work! Or you may be working such long hours that your family feels neglected and estranged. Here's the test: if you can stop the activity when you choose to, then you are in the clear. If you're swept into it to the point that other aspects of your life are suffering, then use that information to course correct.

It's how we handle our passions that makes a difference in whether they help us or hurt us. According to Dr. Vallerand's studies, passion is not just for the select few; 85 percent of people have at least one passion. Many have more. Think of your passion(s). Are they harmonious, or are there some that are leaning toward obsessive? Here is a breakdown of both sides:

HARMONIOUS PASSION	OBSESSIVE PASSION
Is controlled by you; can stop when you want to.	Controls you and monopolizes your time
Increases productivity and enhances other aspects of life	Leads to workaholism and burnout and risks damaging other aspects of life
Increases energy and keeps you vital	Depletes your energy and makes you run-down
Allows you to prioritize how it integrates into your life	Takes over your life priorities and becomes the one focal point
Leads to well-being and satisfaction that promotes closer relationships	Leads to conflict that undermines close relationships
Increase in positive emotions, health and well-being, and social connections.	Increase in negative emotions over time: you can end up suffering and may lead others to suffer with you

If you notice that your passions are borderline disharmonious/obsessive, here are a few actions you can take:

- Slowly add in other fun passions to dilute your primary passion's hold on you. If you're obsessively passionate about dance, add yoga (substitute your favorites). If you're into ruminating about one person, make time for some other friends, too. Look at the passion through a longer time frame; in the span of all your years on earth, this one activity or person really does not define who you are. Hold it more lightly, and if possible bring in some humor and perspective.

- Check into your whole ecosystem: family, friends, work, community, sports, and spirituality. This passion is actually one part of the pie—how does it fit into your life now, and how would it feel even better if all of the parts of your life could work harmoniously? Take one step in that direction.

- Passions, like desires, cannot be forced. As a child, I took weekly piano lessons. When my parents nagged me every single day to practice, any joy from playing the instrument dissipated into thin air. It was no longer something I wanted to master; in fact, I dreaded it! When people get to make their own choices about what they desire or are passionate about, then their curiosity can get reignited, the excitement for learning more gets activated, and any progress through one's own efforts can be exhilarating. If you are trying to ignite someone else's passion, give them the space to try a few things, then allow them to decide on their own. Allow them to find their thing; that's when enthusiasm erupts naturally.

Activating Your Purpose

The best part of tapping into your desire and passion is that both can lead you toward your purpose, your raison d'être, the sense of why you are here. This is a question that we all ask at some point in our lives, some earlier and some later.

The thing about purpose is that no one can tell you yours. It has to come from the wisdom of your heart, and it is personal for each one of us. One of the best ways to get closer to that inner knowing is to ask yourself some directed questions. Here are a few to get you started:

1. **What makes you feel most alive?** What are you passionate about that makes time disappear? When you hear musicians say "The song wrote itself" or basketball players talking about being in the zone, there is something beyond the mind that is active here. What activities or pursuits bring you to that place of alignment? Schedule more of these into your week. Even if they do not coincide with your purpose (if you love to sing, it does not necessarily mean that you will choose singing as your job). But the joy you feel will take you out of day-to-day worries and help you free up your mind so you access your intuitive wisdom and listen to the callings of your heart.

2. **What tears at your heart?** What social issue or personal experience makes you want to turn the pain surrounding it into purpose? If witnessing or undergoing something painful makes you want to use all your energies to correct that situation so others don't have to suffer, you are there. If you want to start a nonprofit for a particular cause, if you aspire to be very successful so that you can support a cure for a disease, if you choose an organization to give your time to because it is addressing a problem that you are concerned about,

you are already moving in this direction. This pathway to purpose is very meaningful and strong. It gives you the tenacity to overcome many challenges and evokes a deep connection to your "why" and your core values.

3. **What is your *ikigai*?** This is a Japanese word that means your reason for being. *Ikigai* includes joy, well-being, and a sense of meaning and purpose. Sounds good, right? But how can we find it? Here are some clues:

   • If you love it and you're great at it—that's your passion.

   • If you're great at it and you are paid for it, that's your profession.

   • If you're paid for it and the world needs it, that's your vocation, your calling.

   • If the world needs it and you eat, sleep, and breathe it, that's your mission.

   The sweet spot where they all connect is your *ikigai*. If we spend about eight of the twenty-four hours every day working, it just makes sense to choose work that leads you toward your *ikigai*. The good news is that people change jobs so many times during a lifetime (current reports in the United States range between seven and ten changes) that if you keep your eye on the prize and your intentions front and center, you can move in this direction. This leads us to the next question.

4. **Are you a renaissance person with multiple callings, or more of a specialist with just one?**

JOURNAL CHALLENGE

In your **journal**, reflect on the areas that call you and why. Some people know from an early age that they want to be, for example, in the medical field helping others, or their passion is fashion, or it has to be about making things. Some are born teachers. They already know what satisfies their core needs, lines up with their values, and generally feels right.

Others find it harder to answer the age-old question, "What do you want to be when you grow up?" Some people are endlessly curious and find themselves enamored with certain disciplines, eager to study everything there is on the topic, but when they put that passion into the real world, it loses its luster. And soon enough, there is another area that looks fascinating, that compels them to study everything they can about *that* particular topic. It is great for a while, but then this new attraction appears. Some might say, "Why are you always chasing shiny objects—can't you just focus on one thing?" There is a good reason, and Emilie Wapnick, in her TED Talk has coined a name for this type of person. If you have multiple interests, many desires, and sequential passions, you can be called a "multipotentialite."[12] You are most likely very good at:

- Idea synthesis—as innovation happens at the intersection of two or more fields

- Rapid learning—as you're not afraid to try something new, your skills are transferable
- Adaptability—as you can pivot to meet the needs of the market

The good news is that this rapidly evolving world needs these skills just as much as we need specialists. In fact, every team should have a mix of both types to get the best results. So whether you have found your purpose or are moving toward it, don't box yourself in. You have more to offer than you know.

5. **Gratitude leads to giving, which leads to purpose.** What are you grateful for? Robert Emmons, a pioneer in the field of gratitude, and William Damon, a leading expert in human development, found that people who had gratitude for the little things in life were more likely to try to "contribute to the world beyond themselves."[13] When we see how others make the world better, and how it enriches their lives, too, it is very inspiring, even contagious. Gratitude from others, which emerges when we share a skill that helps a cause, can also lead to a greater sense of personal purpose. What makes us happy is the feeling of putting our capabilities into action, and when it has the double benefit of helping others, it increases our sense of purpose even more.

Are you a good connector, good at organizing, strategy, team building? If you have a gift for decorating and know how to throw a great party, these are all valuable skills for event planning. You can contribute your time and experience to an organization that wants to make a difference, or even to someone in your neighborhood who could use a leg up. Everyone can be of service. Look for opportunities to help. When you use your powers for good, you'll discover that what you seek is seeking you. Your purpose will find you.

Hope, desire, and passion are powerful drivers to move you toward your best life.

Hope, when harnessed, leads to greater well-being, a more resilient mind-set, and greater productivity.

Desire ignites your potential and gives you the juice to reach for your goals. When you align your desire with what you value most, your life takes on more meaning and you create opportunities to grow into who you were meant to be.

Passion is like an inner fire that activates your joy. When engaged with your passion, you feel life flowing through you in wonderful ways. When you keep passion out of obsession, it will enhance both your energy and your relationships.

The good news is that hope, desire, and passion all contribute to sparking your purpose, your reason for being, your *ikigai*. Explore what you want to focus on and what gives you joy. Remember to keep your valve open to see the goodness all around you and all the potential within you. It is never too late to meander toward your purpose. Every experience, if approached with curiosity and awareness, gets you closer. This time is rich with opportunities. . . . Let hope, desire, and passion guide you toward what you want in life, while liberating the best within you.

Fear

The very cave you are afraid to enter turns out to be the source of what you are looking for.

— JOSEPH CAMPBELL

LET'S FACE IT—WE LIVE in a fear-based world. Just watching the news is enough to make anyone not want to leave their bed. In a culture where charging hard and being "strong" are highly prized, acknowledging our fears is not a badge of honor. Fear is not an emotion that people want to announce to the world.

But fear, at its best, switches on an innate capacity to react more quickly so we can escape dangerous threats. You could even say it's because of fear that the human species is here today. So why do we have disdain or even shame about this emotion; why do we tend to reject or suppress not only the fear itself, but the message it is trying to tell us? Doesn't it deserve some respect, too?

The perception that feeling fear is a weakness undercuts its potential, as fear has always been designed to protect and serve us. When a person feels fear, it doesn't mean that they are weak *or* that they are strong—it means that they are tuned in, awake, aware.

There is great resourcefulness available when we acknowledge the fear, see it for what it is, and then take action. It is when we cover up our fears or push them to the back of some dark corner in the mind that they can fester and grow and take on a life of their own.

Because we are all dealing with so many stressors, whether they come from the outside world or from inside our minds, it's important and even vital to look at this emotion with fresh eyes. As much as we'd like to push them away or simply press delete, these fears are tools that the ego uses to try to keep us safe—they serve a purpose. Fear is an essential signal, warning us to pay attention to our inner messages.

So, given all its bad press and how intense life can be, consider this an opportunity to relearn how to work *with* this emotion. Imagine if we could use our fear as fuel—we can. Imagine if we could intuitively get the gift that fear offers, and so avoid future situations that could threaten our safety, not to mention our sanity. Fear has much to share. Can we be open enough to take it in? In this chapter, we'll explore why fear exists, the different types of fear, including some of fear's paradoxes, and how fear can be your friend. We'll also look at what happens when fear goes underground and at some useful strategies to make the most of this underappreciated emotion.

Why Fear Exists

Fear is part of our ancestral arsenal. Throughout evolution, the species survived because people were able to tune in to the signals of fear. At its best, fear is an instinctive response to a dangerous situation. Whether it was a predatory animal lurking in the distance, a thunderclap warning of a major storm, or the sight of people fighting in close proximity, these were signals to fight, take flight, or freeze.

We just have to look in the animal kingdom for examples of how different animals react to the fear of danger. Just like humans, it's fight, flight, or freeze. Tigers, for example, will mark and defend their territory when they feel threatened; they'll *fight* when danger approaches. When villagers near Bali's Mount Agung volcano noticed snakes and monkeys streaming away from the mountain and into the villages, some thought it was a sign that the volcano would erupt soon,[1] and it did! The animals, fearing danger, intuitively took *flight*. When the American possum is frightened, it will *freeze*, meaning they play dead ("playing possum"). Fight, flight, or freeze. We are not that far from our four-legged friends, who demonstrate that all these responses can be lifesaving in times of danger.

Fear is a powerful emotion. When it surges in, it makes it hard to think about anything else and forces us to focus our full attention on the threat at hand. This emotion commands you into the present moment, so that you can get a sense of where you are in relationship to what you perceive as danger. You become more alert[2], your reaction time quickens, and your senses are fully activated so that you can take your next move. The body, in all its brilliance, mobilizes, too. You may experience trembling, rapid heartbeat, or tightness in the chest. All the systems not absolutely necessary for fight, flight, or freeze have been designed to shut down. Even the blood vessels in your gut dial down (which most people know as butterflies in their stomach)[3], in order for the blood to be redirected to the outer extremities, like arms and legs. This is so you have the power to quickly make your move if you have to.

Knowing the Faces of Fear

Fear comes in many forms, from mild uneasiness to full-on terror and so many states in between. If we were to look at the spectrum of fear, it would progress **from uneasiness, to apprehension, to worry, distress, anxiety, alarm, panic, terror, right up to horror.** Fear can also be expressed through emotional states such as **self-doubt, feeling isolated, helpless, agitated, jumpy, overwhelmed, insecure, unworthy, excluded, persecuted, or exposed.** Quite the range!

JOURNAL CHALLENGE

To get to know your fears better, take out your **journal** and:
- Pick several words from the paragraph above that you relate to
- Point to the situations that bring up those feelings
- Describe a potential shift to move you forward; for example:

TYPE OF FEAR	SITUATION	SHIFT
Apprehension	I had to talk in front of the group and got so nervous I forgot everything.	Practice over and over in advance until it feels natural. Now it is something I enjoy.

Not being enough	I compare myself to everyone all the time.	Explore and appreciate what is unique about me, instead of trying to blend in/seek acceptance from others

Fear is not among the warm and fuzzy feelings we seek, but what we don't often consider is that this emotion is part of every human experience, and it holds lessons for us if we pay attention. By becoming familiar with our go-to types of fear and some ways to deal with them, we begin to take away their sting. We also develop our own strategies, which can be useful when we want to help others deal with their fears, too. By naming the emotion, we can look at it more objectively, rather than getting swept up into its energy. Dr. Dan Siegel calls this strategy **"Name It to Tame It."**

Classic Fears

Now let's explore some of the classic fears (noting that anxiety has its own chapter and phobias are beyond the scope of this book). **Consider if there is one or maybe a few that stand out for you, and add these to your journal page.**

The following are potential thought starters to encounter the fears intellectually and emotionally, as well as some ways to look at them before facing them head-on. This is about taking inventory of your fears and the potential ways you can shift them. The more you know about them, the less they can hold you hostage. See which ones relate to you.

FEAR OF LOSS

1. The fear includes **losing a loved one**, like when you love someone so much you can't imagine life without them. This applies to romantic or family relationships, friends, mentors, even beloved pets.

   Shift: Let this fear bring you into the present moment so you value and take advantage of the time you do have together. This can be a powerful perspective adjustment that will help connect you more deeply than you thought possible.

2. Fear of loss also includes **job worries or financial concerns.**

   Shift: For greater peace of mind, realize that we cannot control all of life, and often we can only see part of the story. But we can derive lessons from every situation we encounter. The fear of financial instability is one of the greatest motivators to move out of our comfort zone and stretch to an expanded version of who we think we can be.

3. Then there's the **fear of losing opportunities**: when you make a decision to take one path, you'll miss out on what the other could offer (opportunity cost).

   Shift: Instead of being on the fence and going into analysis paralysis, there is great relief in making a decision. After that, you are in the game and can course correct as you go along.

4. You may also think you are **running out of time** to achieve what you were dreaming of.

   Shift: For a happier life, where you don't drive yourself crazy, substitute appreciation for expectation. Be grateful for the gifts, talents, and life experience you already have, and realize that imposed deadlines are stories that keep us stuck. Life is dynamic—so are you!

FEAR OF CHANGE

5. **Fear of failure:** You may be starting a new job, and there is a fear of discomfort—a lot of hard work is involved; are you ready for that?

    Shift: Your next step is always your choice. Hard work, tenacity, and caring about what you are doing makes you stand out from the crowd. It will also open doors.

6. And what **if the whole thing doesn't work**?

    Shift: Is anything guaranteed in life? It may not work exactly as you planned it, but nothing is ever wasted. When you look back, you'll recognize how it enriched your life and led you to your next stage. Rather than look at the negative—imagine how you would feel if it did turn out well—step into that.

7. Maybe you'd like to **leave a job or relationship**. Will you find something better?

    Shift: Check in with yourself to see if your job or relationship supports your values and aspirations. Does it help you live as your best self or can you do something to make it so? If not, life is as big as you can imagine it. Explore opportunities, reach out, and take the first step.

8. There could be a **fear of moving**. Will you make friends?

    Shift: If you are open to people, they will be open to you. If you greet someone new not with suspicion, but as an old friend, chances are they will respond in kind. Try it for a week and see what you notice.

9. You may think you're not a good enough friend, parent . . . you can fill in the blanks.

   Shift: All you have to do is try your best, be present, and put your heart into it. Your heart speaks louder than words.

10. Let's not forget **fear of success**—what happens if everything works out beyond your expectations—will you be able to handle it and will people treat you the same way?

    Shift: Number one—you are already successful. Be proud that you are a good person. You deserve to live fully. Self-sabotage is the body's way of protecting you from something you had been afraid of in the past. If you are taking the next step, it's because it is your time. Be tender with that as you are now ramping up. The truth is as you shine, you give others permission to do the same.

FEAR OF REJECTION

11. It is so easy to **feel as if you're "not enough."** Every ad is a reminder to buy something to be "more impressive." What to do? In your **journal**, write down a few thoughts that can change your perspective.

    Shift: Don't buy into the hype. There will always be someone more or less (powerful, creative . . . fill in the blank) than you. It's not about comparison—it's about claiming your unique values, passions, and gifts. These are your superpowers; don't undervalue them or yourself. When you express your inner nature, old fears have no relevance.

12. It feels **dangerous to show any vulnerability**. But you can get so tired constantly putting up a mask.

     Shift: Masks are exhausting. The strongest people have the courage to be vulnerable and to live fully. It's about having the confidence to show you are human. The funny thing is that it gives others permission to be real as well.

13. You may be doing well on the outside but are plagued by insecurity. **Imposter syndrome** is real.

     Shift: Yes, it is! Imposter syndrome describes people who cannot internalize their accomplishments and who are afraid of being discovered to be a fraud. According to research, 70 percent of people have felt this way.[4] Realize that your accomplishments do not define your worth. Trust in your overall competence. And practice savoring the small everyday wins. Gratitude for the little things puts the so-called big things in perspective.

14. You may find it **challenging to accept praise** or even acknowledge your accomplishments in case others are jealous.

     Shift: As long as *you* know you are doing your best, that's the greatest acknowledgment. But accepting a sincere compliment is good, too. Learn to say thank you and take in the moment. At the same time, don't let either praise or criticism go to your head. What matters is not what people say, it's how much you are connected to your core values.

FEAR OF HARM

15. If you **see life as dangerous** and view people as out to take advantage of you, you may shut down emotionally or become numbed out.

    Shift: Every relationship teaches us something— whether it is what we value or what doesn't work. Be discerning, but don't close yourself off. Embrace the lesson, support yourself, and notice how strong you are getting.

    When you send out a vibration of fear of being harmed, you are energetically making that more dominant. Instead, focus on what you want, not what you don't want. Choose thoughts of being supported and empowered. Remember the people *you* are there for when they need an ear, and know that they are there for you as well. Spend time with people who remind you how strong you really are.

    Reflect on one time that you confronted a daunting situation, and you faced your fear and made it through. That quality is in you still.

FEAR OF DEATH

16. Many people have a strong **fear of death**, especially if it represents a fear of the unknown, emptiness, the void, or the end. This is a primal fear.

    Shift: The prospect of death is never easy. It is unknown territory, except for those who have near-death experiences. This happened to my father, and it brightened his view of death immensely.

Dr. Sam Parnia, author of *Erasing Death*,[5] conducted the largest research study of near-death experiences. All patients reported looking down at their bodies on the operating room table from above (as my father had). They could also make reference to the exact conversations the doctors and nurses were having as they looked at them from above. One might say that these conversations were just hallucinations, but not so, as they were consistently validated by the doctors and nurses who confirmed the details the patients had reported. According to Parnia's research, "The mind, the self, the thing that makes us who we are [also called *the soul*] is actually able to continue even though many of them [participants] have reached the point of death."[6]

There are religions, including Christianity, Judaism[7], and Islam, that believe the soul also exists in other realms, and religions such as Hinduism and Buddhism include reincarnation. Psychotherapist Dr. Brian Weiss makes a strong case for reincarnation as he chronicles multiple past lives in his classic book *Many Lives, Many Masters*. Everyone will determine their own interpretation of what happens after death—it is highly personal.

But even scientific evidence is now revealing that the death of the body is not necessarily the end of the line. The words of Albert Einstein concur: "Energy cannot be created or destroyed, it can only be changed from one form to another." Some people report feeling the energy of their loved ones nearby, even after they have passed. In many ways this is a comforting way of looking at the world.

With that in mind, then why is death so harrowing? We generally tend to think of death as a traumatic experience. But what if dying was not as terrifying as we might think? Recent research from Kurt Gray, associate professor of psychology at the University of North Carolina at Chapel Hill, reports, "When we imagine our emotions as we approach death, we think mostly of sadness and terror. But it turns out, dying is less sad and terrifying—and happier—than you think."[8] He compared blogs from people who were dying of cancer with blogs from healthy people challenged to *imagine* they had just a few months to live. You'd expect the terminally ill group to be full of doom and gloom, but this group actually used more positive words like "happiness" and "love" (and fewer words like "anxiety" and "terror") than the group imagining their deaths. The real terminal patients had come to feel a greater gratitude and peace for their life, perhaps because they knew it was waning.

Some strategies to deal with the fear of death include this challenge: If you made the choice to live this year as if it were your last, who would you reach out to, and what would you choose to do? Make a bucket list and intentionally fill your time with positive experiences. When you are designing your days to include meaningful activities, life satisfaction rises, and the fear of death is far less likely to be as dominant in your mind.

A gratitude journal also helps to emphasize the preciousness of each day. Even little graces, conversations, and observations take on greater magnitude when one becomes aware of the impermanence of life.

On a more practical side, those who put their affairs in order are often less afraid to die, as they know that even if anything unexpected happens, their wishes will be honored.

The fear of death is an invitation to control what we can, explore a spiritual or philosophical foundation that resonates, and then choose on a daily basis to live and love fully. Even the fear of death cannot engulf us when we are focused on sharing love. This becomes the greatest legacy of all.

Paradoxes of Fear

We have seen that fear comes in many shapes and guises. Have you ever felt you had one type of fear going on, just to have an opposite aspect show up almost simultaneously? Another way to look at fear is through the conflicted feelings that this emotion can bring up. Sometimes, for example, we have a fear of failure ("I need this to work to support my plans"), but hidden in that is a fear of success ("If this works out too well, I may alienate those closest to me"). We may fluctuate between both extremes depending on the situations we are facing. Here are a few different ranges in which fear can show up. Can you visualize each one as a line of energy? Which end are you closer to?

JOURNAL CHALLENGE

Take out your **journal** and replicate the lines below. Where would you position yourself in each example? Put an X on the spot. Depending on what's going on, you may find yourself at one side one day, and at the opposite side the next, or somewhere in the middle. This can even happen within the span of fifteen minutes! Fear can take you on a roller-coaster ride. Yet we don't often look at ourselves in this way. Notice any insights you gain about your fears and your preferences. You may be surprised at what you discover.

Fear of success   Fear of failure

Fear of uncertainty/   Fear of complacency,
trying something new   being stuck in a rut

Fear of being swallowed   Fear of not
by others' needs   being needed

Fear of standing out/   Fear of playing it
going full-out   safe/small

Fear of commitment   Fear of being alone

Fear of not having   Fear of being bored
any time

(cont'd)

←————————————————————————————→

Fear of being hurt in   Fear of never taking
a relationship   a risk on love

←————————————————————————————→

Fear of not being   Fear of being
seen/visible   made fun of

←————————————————————————————→

Fear of freedom   Fear of boundaries

In this small exercise, you are getting to witness your unique fears: old ones, new ones, maybe some that have been in hiding. By getting these fears out of your head and onto paper, you are freeing valuable space in your mind so you can discern which are the fears that protect you, the fears that guide you, and those that don't serve you at all. Even knowing this changes the game: Awareness gives you choices. Choices give you power.

How Fear Is Your Friend—
the Positive Side of Fear

Fear can provide the focus to help you collect yourself, harness your energy, and make your next move. To ease into this, there's only one thing required, and it's not something that comes naturally to everyone. It entails paying attention to your fear rather than second-guessing or squashing it. It involves being with it, honoring your instinct, and letting the answers come to you. In the height of fear, when you ask yourself "What's my next move?" listen for the clues. You will get them quickly, usually in directives like "run, hide, fight, scream, be quiet, trust yourself, you got this . . ."

Fear will *work* for you, but you have to respect it and tune in to its message. A word of warning—this is not that easy in this day and age. If anything, there is constant pressure to disregard the instinct of fear. The adage "No fear" has taken on a life of its own. From a young age, children are taught "Don't be afraid; don't be a baby."[9] As adults, we hear "Be unstoppable—the only thing we have to fear is fear itself." Note to self: maybe it's time to stop pushing down our fear and instead listen to the signals it is sending.

Here's a question: If fear enters your mind or body, in reaction to a clue in your environment, does that mean you are a coward? The answer is a full-on "NO!" On the contrary, it means you have the actual good sense to pay attention to your biological instinct, your genuine gut feeling, instead of overriding, ignoring, or censoring it even from yourself!

Author and educator Karla McLaren puts it well: "Fear is not cowardice; it is the protective mechanism inside you that knows you're not adequately prepared for whatever is coming next. Fear stops you—not to immobilize you, but to give you the time you need to gather yourself and your resources."[10] Simply said, fear is not cowardice; it is caution.

When Fear Is Suppressed: What Happens When Fear Goes Underground?

By suppressing or belittling fear in order to appear confident, considerate, or courteous, there may be a price to pay. In his notable book *The Gift of Fear*, Gavin de Becker, a danger analyst, explores the difference between fear, worry, and anxiety.

Fear is involuntary; it is the body's warning system that something here and now is a threat—so pay attention! It is safety-oriented and responsive to immediate dangers. The classic example is a woman waiting for an elevator late at night. It opens and there's a strange man inside. She gets an uncomfortable feeling in her body, but her mind steps in to say, "It's just an elevator ride. I don't want to shut the door in his face. That would be just rude." She goes in, against her gut feeling. He moves too close to her in the elevator, and she feels his hot breath on the side of her neck. She gets off at the very next floor, saying to herself, "I had a feeling . . ."

The point is she did have a warning sign; her gut sensation was trying to give her a message. Although nothing happened, she did not honor it—she opted for politeness and got on the elevator. When fear is flowing, it tries to send warning signals; but it's up to us to pay attention. How many times have you had an odd feeling about a situation—maybe you had an inkling that a deal was too good to be true, or maybe you felt upset after spending time with someone and you couldn't quite figure out why?

JOURNAL CHALLENGE

In your journal, jot down one situation when you listened to your instincts, and one when you ignored the red flags. Now list the outcomes for both situations.

The truth is, there will always be a protocol of accepted ways to act so you "don't rock the boat." But this is the perfect time to let go of what other people want and put yourself first. Think of yourself as an animal in the jungle—what instinct is trying to come through? Be fierce enough to respect it and give it its due. That way you can react decisively and in alignment with your inner guidance. You already have an internal safety system. This is an invitation to recognize that your instincts are there for you, like a wise presence inside, just waiting for you to pay attention.

Keeping the circuits open to those intuitive warnings is more important than we may know. By consistently dismissing the instinctive fear messages and telling ourselves "not to be afraid" or "they are just letting off steam, not to worry," we are literally training our brains to disregard and eventually disable those signals that are there to serve us. Women in abusive relationships may even try to tell themselves that it is a badge of honor to dismiss their feelings of fear.

Eventually, when we downgrade and ignore our fears, that powerful built-in safety system, which has been repeatedly overridden, ends up becoming weaker. Unlike the animal that deals with their fear instinct head-on and then returns to a calmer place, as we repeatedly ignore and rationalize ourselves out of our fears, the internal security system breaks down and the signal becomes so faint we can barely hear it at all.[11] Unless true fear is recognized as the ally it is, it cannot protect you from real danger.

How Changing Your Beliefs
Can Change Your Life

Sometimes we inherit beliefs from those around us. You've heard the expression "Kids don't miss a thing"? Even from infancy, we learn by watching those closest to us. The brain's mirror neurons influence children to empathetically feel what their parents feel, as if those emotions were their own. As young children, usually under seven years of age, we can take on attitudes and beliefs from those around us, such as parents, caretakers, or close family. This applies to fears as well.

In his renowned book *The Biology of Belief,* biologist Bruce Lipton states, "The fundamental behaviors, beliefs, and attitudes we observe in our parents become 'hardwired' as synaptic pathways in our subconscious minds. Once programmed into the subconscious mind, they control our biology for the rest of our lives . . . or at least until we make the effort to reprogram them."[12]

When parents unknowingly brand their children with messages like "don't walk ahead, you'll be kidnapped" or "you can't do anything right" or "don't bother me now—why can't you see I'm busy . . ." or whatever the negative words may be, a child's subconscious brain takes in the message that they are not safe, not important, or not good enough as part of their identity. These old hurts show up as fears or feelings of unworthiness and can shape how people see themselves and their potential for years to come.

When we suppress what is uncomfortable, it stays trapped. Dr. Candace Pert, author of *Molecules of Emotion,* explains, "When emotions are repressed, denied, not allowed to be whatever they may be, our network pathways get blocked, stopping the flow of the vital feel-good, unifying chemicals that run both our biology and our behavior."[13]

We can stay stuck on autopilot, with the subconscious mind and its embedded negative tapes running the show. Or we can be *with* the fears, feel where they rest in our bodies, and invite them to the surface so they can be released. These disowned or "shadow" parts of ourselves want to be acknowledged. They point the way to what is ready to be healed.

If the wound is the place where the light enters you, we then have the opportunity to turn that wound into wisdom. What has it taught us? Where is it guiding us, and how can we use that insight to empower our life and perhaps make a difference for someone else, too? Sometimes our fears can point us to our purpose.

Strategies for Change

I have chosen five strategies to help you: learn self-compassion, how to make it safe for your fears to emerge, how to release old fears, take baby steps to desensitize yourself to fear, and finally how to take full-on action. Each addresses a different aspect, and together they equip you to know yourself better, be gentler with your tender parts, and be fearless when you need to be. One caveat: these tools are geared for everyday fears. To deal with severe forms of fear or anxiety disorders, a mental health professional can help in more direct ways. That said, try each one and see which resonates with you the most. You will find a different type of relief in each technique. Then repeat your favorite daily for twenty-one days, which is the time it takes to embed a new habit. By practicing intentional activities, you change the neural pathways in the brain. Some may be able to see a shift in less time, depending on how close you already are to releasing that belief. Be easy with yourself. It has taken years to formulate these fears—give yourself some breathing room to let them go.

1. Perfectionism and the Power of Self-compassion

Perfectionism is a social fear of being judged, and it is growing. We live in a society that celebrates how people appear on the surface, the myth of popularity, and the adulation of celebrity. These days, getting your picture posted on social media is often seen as more importantly than heartfully experiencing what you were feeling in the first place. How people "represent" their lives has become more important than energetically being present.

One research study reveals that socially prescribed perfectionism among college students is escalating at an unprecedented pace, along with all the mental health issues it brings, including anxiety, depression, social phobia, and suicidal thoughts.[14] We don't talk about the fact that we have willingly enrolled in a system that puts salt into that wound on a daily basis. It's time for some discernment. It's time to look at what is working for us. And it's time to prioritize our focus on pursuits that support us, not tear us down.

Unknowingly, we have been seduced into the cult of comparison, setting ourselves up even further for feeling like we just don't measure up. Most people, no matter what their income level or education, no matter their accomplishments or accolades, carry some fear of not being good enough. There is too much pressure to be "on your game" all the time.

Brené Brown makes an important distinction. She explains that striving to be your best is one thing. Perfectionism is a different animal. It is enmeshed with the belief that "if we live perfect, look perfect, and act perfect, we can minimize or avoid the pain of blame, judgment, and shame."[15] In that way fear serves as a shield—on one hand, it is trying to keep you safe; on the other hand, it is also keeping people from getting close.

Perfectionism is being stuck in the fear of what people will think. It could tie back to the childhood need to behave in a certain way in order to receive love and acceptance from a parent. Perhaps life was unstable and you had to be the one who took care of things; you became the caretaker or the responsible one at a young age. Or maybe your parents wanted to brag about your accomplishments to their friends in order to make themselves look better. In any case, who you are on the inside was not recognized nearly as much as what you did on the outside.

In adult life, people who are perfectionists measure themselves on their accomplishments, attention to detail, and ability to get things done. There is nothing wrong with healthy striving, but the challenge for a perfectionist is to be gentle with yourself, avoid the "it has to be perfect or I am a total loser" thinking, and allow the process to unfold. As the saying goes, "Done is better than perfect."

Dare to try new things and do them badly; get messy; be a learner in life. Instead of not starting something new for fear of not knowing enough, you will always move forward when you try to grow. There is great freedom and even amusement in this!

Perfectionists get trapped when they measure themselves only on how well they are at "doing." There is no joie de vivre here as it can too easily become an insatiable drive. Because even with serial successes, there is always another goal, another mountain to climb; it is never ever enough.

So if you are a perfectionist, and I consider myself a recovering one, be aware of your self-talk. How many times a day do you unconsciously put yourself down? Have you noticed that some of the internal messages can be so cruel you would never dream of saying them to anyone else? It could range from "Bad hair day," to "those pants look disgusting" to "This isn't working . . . I'm done." The self-directed arrows are not about a skill that could be improved; it's that *you* don't measure up. A method some people use is to put a hair elastic around their wrist and snap it when they catch themselves in self-critical mode. But do not use that newfound awareness to say "Oh, there I am again, putting myself down." Instead, celebrate that you are waking up from mental habits that would keep you stuck.

The antidote to perfectionism and the inner critic's barrage is a healthy dose of self-compassion. This helps you bounce back faster than chasing down self-esteem, which still bases your value on doing "better" than those around you.

That addresses the head; now what about the heart? What about the part of you that feels upset and afraid to take the next step? Self-compassion also invites you to lighten up. Kristin Neff, a pioneer in the field of self-compassion, points to the three parts:

- **Mindfulness**: This helps you come into the present moment and not overidentify with what is bothering you.
- **Common humanity:** Rather than making you feel isolated, self-compassion focuses on our shared humanity; everyone everywhere goes through rough patches. Sharing our real-life challenges actually cuts across all boundaries and brings us closer.
- **Self-kindness:** Practice self-kindness instead of self-judgment. Try treating yourself as you would a dear friend. What tone of voice would you use? What soothing words

might you say? Consider putting a hand over your heart and saying, "(Your name)—it *is* a tough situation, and it's perfectly normal to be afraid. . . . You will find a way to get through it; you always do." Calm rather than condemn. It is like a wise part of yourself is helping the part of you that is scared or confused. You learn to accept yourself as someone who is just doing their best to navigate the ever-changing landscape of life. You begin to notice all the things you have discovered about yourself along the way. You understand that mistakes are also useful in providing a powerful lesson—they guide you forward so much faster than if you had retreated into your comfort zone. Rather than tell you that you are stupid, they remind you that you have the courage to try something new and you are growing.

Failure is the key to success; each mistake teaches us something.

—Morihei Ueshiba

Now, if you're among those who think that this practice would make you unmotivated and guarantee your couch potato status, studies prove that the exact opposite is true.[16] In this increasingly stressful world, grit is not enough to keep on going for the long run. Perseverance at all costs leads to burnout. If you want to bounce back more quickly, this tool must be in your toolbox. Instead of being a critic, be a coach. Self-compassion will build your emotional resilience over time, not to mention make you happier, more productive, and more confident.

2. Holding Your Fears Softly: "The Peace Process"

When fears come up, we have the choice to befriend them and utilize their protective focus to get through to the other side . . . or to numb them out with binges of TV, food, exercise, work, sex, drugs, whatever keeps you from the unresolved emotions that are emerging to be healed. This reveals the biggest fear of all—to actually feel your feelings.

When you open the door to welcoming all your emotions, one thing is key: go gently; this has to be a safe zone. Fears are fragile; they need a soft touch. It's not instinctive—most people tend to be incredibly hard on themselves, often without realizing it. Proceed lightly. You are now bringing sunlight to the darker places and honoring your fears with tenderness.

Imagine a baby who is sobbing. Similar to a baby, your fears are crying out to you to notice them, listen to them, and give them your attention. You would not lock a baby in a dark basement; it's the same with your fears. You want to make it safe for them to emerge. Just like a baby, they may need to be held, comforted, and allowed to relax in your caring presence.

Christian Mickelsen has developed a process that is a gentle but powerful way to deal with fears. Called "The Peace Process,"[17] it bypasses the mind by addressing the feelings embedded in the body. The body, which stores all types of memories, including traumatic ones, is used as a pathway to release fear. There are seven steps. Choose a fear you have, probably not your most intense one as you are learning the process. You can do this again with the bigger fears once you know how it works.

Think about the fear, let it come to the forefront of your mind. Remember that you are in a safe place and that the fear can't hurt you, then focus on feeling it in your body. These steps will help you through the process:

1. **Find the feeling:** Because feelings can be felt in the body, think of your fear and notice where it shows up in your body (most people identify the heart area, the throat, or the gut, though it could be anywhere).

2. **Stay present:** Keep your attention on that part or parts of your body. Do not try to solve the issue in your mind or numb it out with food, phones, or other go-to addictions. You can do this!

3. **Accept that feeling:** Instead of suppressing it, let the feeling come up for air. Like you would a hurt child, try to send it some care, some love.

4. **Focus on where the feeling is most intense:** In that feeling lodged somewhere in your body, there's one spot that has the most charge, the most intensity. Put and keep your tender attention right there.

5. **Let it breathe:** When you focus your care on that area in your body, the feeling may move or get more or less intense. Invite it to get bigger and witness how it changes. Mickelsen compares it to an oil candle. He states, "The fuel needs oxygen to burn, but once it's burned out it's over. Your attention is the oxygen and the feeling is the fuel. We never know how much fuel is in there." So it requires you staying with it and providing the presence to help it to run its course. It could be seconds or minutes or, rarely, a few hours.

6. **Connect with peace:** Let the feeling grow and move around, keeping your loving attention on the part that seems to be most intensified. Eventually you'll notice that the fear will dissipate, and the feeling of peace will be stronger than the feeling of fear. This usually occurs in five to ten minutes. Sometimes it can be more, sometimes it will go faster—stay with it.

7. **Find lasting peace:** After the fear has subsided, you will feel a neutral feeling, which is a sense of peace. Test that you've cleared the fear entirely by thinking about the issue you were releasing. See if you are feeling anything but peace, and if so, repeat the process again. Depending on how deep-seated the feelings are, this may be a gradual process with several layers to get through. But every time you do it moves you to greater freedom. Soon, you will notice that you feel less entrapped by the fear that was keeping you stuck. You are giving yourself breathing room and the green light to go forward and bring out the best within you.

3. Saying Thank You and Releasing Your Fear

By thanking the old beliefs for doing their utmost to keep you safe and then releasing them for something better, you are creating space to embrace a more aware and updated version of yourself. For example, replace "Don't trust strangers" with "I enjoy connecting with wonderful people." Swap "I'm afraid to be myself" with "The people I want to spend time with appreciate my unique approach to life." Trade "I'm afraid I won't succeed" with "I learn and grow with every experience."

JOURNAL CHALLENGE

After you identify what fear you want to release, open your **journal** and describe the fear. Write down how it protected you in years past, and thank it for being there in its intention to keep you safe. Now you are ready to let it go.

Here is a body-centered (somatic) visualization to help you release it. Imagine you are giving the limiting belief or fear a color. Now visualize that color collecting in your body, and then moving down your torso, down your legs, through the bottom of your feet, and into the center of the planet, where it dissolves. It's easy, like a magnet is pulling it out of your body. Then visualize a golden sun, with your new insights, excitement, and positive energies coming into the top of your head and moving down inside your body, filling you up top to toes with a warm serene feeling, completely replacing any trace of the color of the old belief. Enjoy the sensation of warmth, lightness, comfort, and peace. Sit with this for a moment or two. Then open your eyes. You are now prepared to put your focus on positive change and to go forward to experience the best of your life. You can repeat this anytime.

4. START SMALL: HOW TO DESENSITIZE YOUR FEARS

There's a reason that, as a child, you start riding a bike with training wheels. You are taking action, but in a way that makes you feel safe. For this strategy, you create a plan, think of the finer details, and begin with little actions[18] to help you gain momentum. Action is the antidote to fear.

If you have a fear of public speaking, then get together with one good friend who does not judge you and will be kind no matter what they have to say, and speak in front of them. Did you die? No! It probably went better than you had anticipated. Onward! The next step is to practice. The more you repeat an activity and notice that nothing bad happens, the more it desensitizes you to fear's grip. Using the example of public speaking, you'll begin to feel more at ease each time you rehearse it in front of others. Then you might challenge yourself to speak in front of a small group. Soon you will be ready to try speaking in front of a bigger gathering. Then maybe take a course or join a Toastmaster chapter. With slow, deliberate actions, you will prove to yourself that little steps lead to big strides.

5. THE FIVE-SECOND RULE – GETTING INTO ACTION

The Peace Process eases the way for buried fears to be released from the body, making it safe to let the fear dissipate. But what about the fears (not the anxieties) that we are already aware of, that live front and center in the mind? George Patton said, "There is a time to take counsel of your fears, and there is a time to never listen to any fear." Fears of trying something new, fears of shining too bright (don't ever listen to that one!), fears of sharing your ideas in a group, fears of going over to talk to someone new . . . these are fears of basically overcoming inertia to finally get out of your comfort zone, which may be increasingly uncomfortable because you know you want more!

This brand of fear does well with another strategy to get you unstuck. Developed by Mel Robbins for getting you past your old habits, it's called the Five-Second Rule.[19] This is useful when there's something you know you should do, but you feel either scared or overwhelmed by the notion. The idea is that from the initial time you have an impulse to do something new, you have a five-second window before your old conditioning that would keep you stuck kicks in. Five seconds can flip you into action. The counting distracts you from the habit of hesitating, overthinking, and worrying. When you reach the number one, that's your cue to immediately, that second, MOVE! Think of a rocket taking off and use that same countdown, so in your mind, or even out loud, you actually say to yourself, "Five, four, three, two, one—GO!" By counting (to redirect the mind) and immediately moving (to activate the body), you interrupt the old patterns of hesitation. Based on the research, this allows you to take control of your prefrontal cortex, the decision-making area of the brain, and helps you build a feeling of having more control in your own life.

This deceptively simple technique will help you override procrastination, apathy, and old habits that keep you from progressing. Use this rule to ask for that raise, sign up for that class, finally schedule some time to take care of yourself, or have that tough conversation. When you do something in spite of your fears and activate your internal locus of control, you restore your faith in yourself, get stronger, and develop grit and a confidence that no one can take away.

These techniques will soften your fears and inspire you to take action now. Do these exercises and choose one you'd like to practice consecutively. It will help you see your fears in a whole new way.

Fears are there for a purpose. They can point us to our intuition and shift us back on course to be aligned with our true nature. Take a moment to acknowledge your willingness to look at all the parts of life. It is not easy to look at our fears. Recognize your courage and readiness to bring these aspects to the surface.

Now think of an image of pure shining energy that is covered with the shadow layer of fears. You are that pure energy, and the fears are simply a covering. They do not define you, nor are they who you really are. Think of fears as a part of yourself that feels separate and basically wants to return to the central core. When this shadow/fear layer feels safe enough to share its lessons, then the layer of fear can be released. When we learn from our fears, their energy transforms into wisdom. The sooner we can come to peace with our "shadow" (difficult or more painful) layer of beliefs, the sooner we can take the learning within the situations and move forward. When we intentionally explore these unsettling beliefs and release them gently, then we remind ourselves of our true nature and reconnect with the core essence of who we really are.

Anxiety

Our anxiety does not come from thinking about the future,
but from wanting to control it.

—KAHLIL GIBRAN

ARE YOU THE TYPE of person who feels pressure to pack all of life's responsibilities into your twenty-four-hour day: morning madness, work projects and deadlines, after-work obligations, taking care of the home shift, maybe online for more catch-up details, grab some sleep, and do it all again tomorrow? Or are you hanging in there with another version that runs at a similar pace . . . a.k.a. the fast track to exhaustion?

"Anxiety-fueled disconnection," in the words of Brené Brown, can set us up for a host of numbing behaviors.[1] You know the scenario: come home, grab some popcorn, a chicken leg, a piece of chocolate . . . because you're too tired to put a plate together and sit down, and mindlessly end up inhaling the whole thing. Or maybe you escape to the bathroom during the day, when the need erupts to have a quiet cry, then you put on a good face in order to keep calm and carry on? Can we agree that life can be anxiety-provoking?

According to the National Institute of Mental Health, anxiety disorders affect 18.1 percent of adults aged eighteen years and up, more than forty million adults in the United States alone. But did you know that, according to the World Health Organization (WHO), one in thirteen people globally suffers from anxiety?[2]

Yet, even amid all the tension, it's important to remember that we have choices.

There are some people who have learned to address and adjust the frenetic *behaviors* that lead up to anxiety. Maybe they have reached a point where the pace of life is no longer working for them, so they course correct to be more aligned with their values. Do you know of someone who says, "I only take emails, calls, or texts from nine A.M. to nine P.M., and everything will have to work around that"? Or who actually has the fortitude to take a digital detox day? Choices: burnout or boundaries. You may say, "That's impossible for my life and what I have going on," and granted, sometimes it's not as black-and-white as that. But never doubt that we can take steps in that direction. Sometimes small shifts can bring big benefits.

The good news is that both everyday anxiety and the more complex anxiety disorders are highly treatable; that in itself is encouraging. The reality is that everyone experiences anxiety from time to time. How we handle it is up to us.

Anxiety, defined as "fear in the absence of danger,"[3] usually involves some future-oriented scenario. What is not commonly known is that everyday anxiety is not necessarily as bad as people think. Anxiety can be a healthy response to situations like preparing to give a speech, writing an exam, or dealing with escalating tensions.

Life by its nature is stressful; anxiety happens, and the healthiest expression is when it comes and then it goes.

For both day-to-day anxiety and the more deeply rooted anxiety disorders, it is a huge advantage to understand what is going on both in our mind and in our body. When we are aware of what we are experiencing, we can then find the best ways to deal with that specific situation. Simply put, when we know more, we can do more.

In this chapter, we'll explore the difference between fear and anxiety, as well as worry and anxiety. Though the words seem similar, they actually point to different states. We'll look at healthy anxiety and take an overview of anxiety disorders. Finally, we'll provide proven ways to deal with this much-misunderstood emotion. Let's dive in.

The Difference Between Fear and Anxiety

Though we often lump them together, there is a difference between anxiety and fear.

The official definition is: "Fear is the emotional response to real or perceived imminent threat, whereas anxiety is anticipation of future threat."[4] Anxiety arises about situations that have not yet happened and can range from normal anxiety most people feel, such as before taking an exam, to the debilitating anxiety experienced in panic attacks. Fear, though it can relate to future events as well, is often an instinctive reaction to facing a threat in the *present* moment—think of it as an internal alarm that is there to protect you in a frightening situation. You see a car speeding toward you in your lane; you hear something that sounds like a gunshot; you slam on the brakes when a child suddenly darts into the street. . . . There is pressing danger, in real time, and you are geared to respond to that instinctive fear, without any planning, actually without even thinking about it.

When fear is suppressed, anxiety, which is more diffuse and harder to specifically pinpoint, can set in.

Katie's Story

Katie is a mom in her early forties who tries to do it all: work, take care of her children, and keep her household running. In recent years, though, her relationship, which appears all right from the outside, has become more and more difficult. Her husband, Mike, goes with her to school functions; they look like most other couples in the community, but scratching below the surface, there is no love, intimacy, or honoring of each other. Their communication is tenuous at best, and at unforeseen times, Mike will erupt into heated rants about finances, child-rearing, and who is responsible for what. Katie feels that he treats her with disdain, and his verbal eruptions are increasingly brutal and hard to bear, but she feels powerless to do anything about it. He never would lay a finger on her—in her mind, that would be crossing the line—but if she were to admit it to herself, the emotional attacks regularly cut right to the bone. Many a night she can't sleep and can't figure out why. She feels raw and bruised on the inside and would leave him, but what about giving the kids what they need to thrive?

Rather than listen to her instinct, which would have her

admit that on some level the relationship is toxic and she does not feel safe, Katie buries her anxieties of standing up for herself and setting some boundaries about what she will and won't accept. There's a vague rationalization that Mike might just leave her with nothing. After all, she's "invested her best years" in the relationship; why should she throw it all away? She tells herself, "Nothing's perfect—just keep it together."

So, month after month, and season after season, Katie tolerates the treatment and tells herself that it's not that bad. Sure, she feels kind of anxious, but reminds herself that Mike would never really hurt her . . . not admitting, even to herself, the open wounds she ignores every single day. Katie always seems to be worried about something, and she doesn't know what to do about it. But the anxiety is real and it's not going away—it's growing. She hears that some of her friends are on antidepressants, and they certainly seem happy. What does she have to lose? In the therapist's office, she explains that she no longer trusts her intuition or her decisions. The reasons she gives for the visit focus on the escalating anxiety. She has suppressed, even from herself, her deepest fears.

For Katie, anxiety is the red flag, an indicator for the fears she has suppressed for so long. Her anxiety has motivated her to seek help, and that is a huge step. But just treating the anxiety and stopping there is like applying a Band-Aid to cover a deep, festering wound. It may appear to be healing on the outside, but the toxicity is still below the surface. If Katie dulls her anxiety through medication and stops there, she may be able to numb the pain and make it through the days, but she is still not dealing with the root problem: her core fears and reservations within the relationship.

By recognizing her fears and finding the courage to see the situation as it really is, Katie would be in a better position—not to simply dull her anxiety, but to hear her guiding inner voice and seek proactive help for her core issues. The real opportunity is to connect with the genuine message within her fear in order to deal with Mike's outbursts in a more resourceful way and explore better options for herself and her family.

Katie is not alone. A lot of people cope in this way instead of getting to the root of the problem. Yet when she finds a supportive environment and trusted professionals to help her address her core challenges, she will discover that, in the words of Francis Bacon, "Knowledge is power," and she is stronger than she knows.

Even though it may be hard-earned, awareness is not only empowering; it gives you more choices. When you learn to trust yourself, listen to your instincts to set strong boundaries, and align your life with your values, anxiety loses its power.

The Difference Between Anxiety and Worry

Anxiety means many things to many people; it is also often confused with worry, so much so that the words can be used interchangeably. Pop quiz . . . are you worried before a new job interview, or are you anxious? If you are a worrier by nature, does that automatically mean that you have anxiety? Psychologist Guy Winch assigns some useful distinctions.[5]

Though the words "worry" and "anxiety" both express an uneasiness, how we experience these states can be different. Usually people worry about a specific problem (such as a bill that is due or getting to the airport on time to make their flight) but can be anxious when their concern is about something more vague and nebulous (like the economy or traveling in general). The reason is that a worry can usually be handled like a problem in need of a solution, like "I'll pay half of the bill now, and half next month," or "I'll leave for the airport fifteen minutes early in case there's traffic."

The anxiety about the economy or the downsides of travel is hazier and not within your control; there's not one solid way to address it. Worry is also caused by more realistic concerns than anxiety. For example, Winch states, "If you're concerned about getting fired because you did really poorly on a project, you're worried. If you're concerned about getting fired because your boss didn't ask about your child's piano recital, you're anxious." Anxiety comes up because it's more challenging to find a reasonable solution for such a vague and unsubstantiated concern; it is harder to have peace of mind.

With worry, once we pay the bill, or otherwise deal with the cause of the worry, the concerned feelings are over, but anxiety over things we can't control can be prolonged and much more acute. Whether the issue is a relationship, health, or something work-related, it can escalate to a point that it disrupts day-to-day functioning, making it hard to concentrate and be present, not to mention productive. While worry can usually be put aside to attend to time-sensitive matters, anxiety can become so physically predominant that it's impossible to get anything done. There's a good reason for this: worry usually is mental, related to thoughts; anxiety, on the other hand, is more physical, and experienced throughout the body.

Healthy Anxiety

But what if some measure of anxiety was actually a good thing? Though the word "anxiety" is often correlated with overwhelming stress, what we forget sometimes is that a little anxiety is not necessarily a bad thing. If you are pushing yourself out of your comfort zone, traveling to unfamiliar lands, starting a new career, or generally jumping into uncharted territory, it is normal to have some anxiety. It's actually a signal that you are stretching and challenging yourself. You are pushing yourself to see what you can accomplish. This means you are alive—it is a good thing. In the words of Søren Kierkegaard: "Anxiety is the dizziness of freedom."

It's also perfectly normal to feel either mentally nervous or physically anxious before a job interview or a major presentation. Anxiety will warn you to show up a little early and practice your talking points in advance. In planning a party or outdoor wedding, the overly optimistic person may not consider the chance of rain—"It's the middle of summer"—but you can count on the person with a temperament of worry and feelings of anxiety to have a tent at the ready if the weather turns. In matters of taking care of their health, those who are always feeling positive may not see the doctor or dentist for years, but someone with an anxious but conscientious nature would be on top of their regular checkups. When you need a lawyer to go over a contract, would you hire the person with the chillaxed, laid-back personality, or someone who taps into their healthy anxiety to comb through all the facts and go deep into the details?

What distinguishes healthy anxiety, like the type we all experience from time to time, such as when dealing with a deadline or a family emergency, is that the feelings come and then they go when the situation resolves itself.

Anxiety Disorders

With anxiety disorders, the intrusive thoughts do not subside; in fact, they escalate enough to interfere with work or school and especially with relationships. Where fear usually has a trigger, and worry often has a cause, anxiety can be much more vague. Though there's usually no specific present danger, there is the hazy expectation, even dread around a looming future threat that's sometimes even difficult to define. There are many factors that play a part, from brain chemistry to genetics to life experiences to learned responses. Quite often these originate in childhood.

ACEs

ACEs stands for Adverse Childhood Experiences. In situations when adversity is experienced frequently, for example, in households where there is emotional, physical, or sexual abuse, neglect, economic hardship, and parents unable to support their children in a healthy way, then anxiety and stress, instead of subsiding, are constantly at heightened levels. This toxic stress can produce trauma. Most people in the United States have at least one such experience, no matter their background. According to expert and author Dr. Nadine Burke Harris, "This kind of prolonged activation of the stress-response systems can disrupt the development of brain architecture and other organ systems, and increase the risk for stress-related disease and cognitive impairment well into the adult years."[6] Get your ACE score[7] using an easy ten-question quiz[8] in order to make yourself aware of your risk of chronic disease. With that awareness, you can intentionally build in practices that promote resilience. Researchers explain, "Think of it as a cholesterol score for childhood toxic stress." This is a worthwhile way to be on top of your preventative wellness. It is encouraging that this well-researched resource is now gaining traction.

JOURNAL CHALLENGE

In your **journal**, jot down a few actions that help you relieve acute stress. What is one new action you would be open to try?

Anxiety does not have a one-size-fits-all solution. Some anxiety is best addressed with a combination of therapy and medication, and some, more related to being overstressed, can be remedied by changing the *behaviors* that gave rise to the anxiety in the first place. Anxiety disorders[9] emerge when anxiety has grown to a point that it interferes with aspects of life. Here are the variety of types:

- **Generalized anxiety disorder** (GAD) makes it hard to identify the cause of the anxiety, and it's increasingly challenging to control the worry. Feelings of irritability or restlessness increase; it's tough to sleep or even concentrate.
- **Panic attacks** can lead to feelings of terror, pounding heart, difficulty breathing, nausea, sweating, shaking, or a feeling of impending doom.

- **Social anxiety** brings up intense fears of being judged, rejected, or humiliated by others.
- **Obsessive-compulsive disorder** involves repetitive activities, like washing hands, checking stoves, or walking in a certain pattern as a way to ease the anxiety.
- **Separation anxiety**, which can produce feelings of panic, occurs when a person or even an animal is separated from those who make them feel safe.
- **Phobias** have to do with specific fears of situations—fear of heights, fear of leaving the house, or fear of spiders, to name a few.
- **Post-traumatic stress disorder** (PTSD) is the anxiety that results from the experience of previous trauma, like in combat, sexual assault, or serious accidents.

An anxiety disorder is not a personality flaw or a weakness— it develops either over time or as a reaction to a specific life event. It's helpful to remember not to blame yourself for experiencing anxiety; so many people are in the same boat. The best use of your energy is to put a plan in place around how you will respond to it.

How to Deal with Anxiety

The good news is that anxiety is not a life sentence. All these feelings can improve with the help of a medical professional, and ideally a team of people with complementary approaches. Dialectical behavior therapy, or DBT, includes mindfulness to help people be present, regulate their emotions, and deal with distress. Cognitive behavioral therapy, or CBT, sometimes in combination with medication, helps people understand how their thought patterns contribute to feelings of anxiety and how they can change their thoughts to improve how they feel. New behavior techniques also help reduce or eliminate the symptoms of anxiety. Here are several that can be useful starting points:

1. **Be a detective**: Learn what triggers your anxiety.

JOURNAL CHALLENGE

When you feel anxious, jot down in your **journal** what is causing that feeling. It may be work deadlines, relationship issues, family, unexpected news. . . . Identify the cause and write it down, giving your level of anxiety a number on a scale of 1–10, with 1 being the lowest. If you really want to track it, set your phone alarm for three times per day for one week, and when the alarm goes off, jot down your anxiety levels. Notice if there are variations during the day; look for any patterns.

---

2. **Mindfulness meditation:** One of the strategies more people are tuning in to is meditation, which improves resiliency to stress and sharpens focus and attention, while reducing the body's inflammatory response and pain.[10] It is being taught in schools, corporations, and community centers, not to mention being available on a variety of apps, such as Headspace, Calm, or Insight Timer. Today, this is almost Stress Survival 101. There's more than one way to develop a mindfulness practice. While some people

respond to sitting meditation, others are much better off with moving meditation, like tai chi, yoga, chi gong, or even hiking in nature. Controlled breathing helps calm the body and mind and activate the parasympathetic nervous system. Progressive relaxation and guided imagery helps the body release tensions and relax—it's helpful to get to sleep, too. Biofeedback connects people to electric sensors to teach them to control their body's functions, like heart rate, blood pressure, and muscle tension.[11]

3. **Work with the body to heal trauma:** There are also somatic therapists to help the body release trauma. The idea is that the body has an innate intelligence, down to the cellular level, and each cell is connected to the others. Normally, if something disturbing arises, the body knows what to do to come back to equilibrium. Scientist Dawson Church points out that problems in listening to the body's cues come up when trauma occurs, as in a situation when people perceive their life to be in danger, something is too overwhelming to cope with, they feel powerless, or the situation violates expectations.[12] This is when the emotions and pathways of energy within the body can get blocked. This is when we "check out." It is hard to be fully present and engaged when part of our thoughts and emotions are still stuck in a past trauma. Here are some options that may be useful to explore.

   • **EMDR,** eye movement desensitization and reprocessing therapy, found to be helpful for PTSD and panic attacks, uses specific eye movements in conjunction with therapy to release emotional distress.

- **Cranial sacral therapy** works through the body, focusing on opening up the central nervous system and releasing restrictions that can cause pain or dysfunction.

- **Acupuncture** works with tiny needles to unblock the energy channels of the body, known in Chinese medicine as meridians.

- **Acupressure** does the same thing without the needles, and reflexology focuses on the feet or hands to release tension throughout the body.

- **Tapping** (also known as EFT: Emotional Freedom Technique) combines acupuncture and psychology to release old traumas and has been widely used.

- **Psych-K** focuses on changing underlying beliefs related to self-esteem, relationships, and physical health.

- **HeartMath** has more than three hundred validated studies, showing how people can move into a state called "coherence," where the heart, mind, and emotions are all aligned and stress is dramatically reduced. This is done through shifting the rhythms of the heart, which sends a different neuromessage to the brain.[13]

If you haven't tried these yet, see which ones you are drawn to and explore how any one of these can help you release trauma, re-center, and allow your body-mind connection to function in healthier ways. You will learn to place more attention on how to navigate through anxiety and trauma, rather than getting stuck there. The point is that there are many modalities that can and do help. You can create a personal toolbox of coping resources to help you take control of your life.

Having these resources at hand can make a big difference. One study from the University of Cambridge
followed women who were poor and those who were rich
to track their levels of anxiety.[14] It was not a shock that
the financially secure women had less anxiety. What
was surprising, though, was that among the women who
were poor, those who used coping resources were significantly less anxious. Author Olivia Remes elaborates
that the research showed that "The way you cope or
handle things in life has a direct impact on how much
anxiety you are experiencing—tweak the way you're
coping, therefore, and you can lower your anxiety levels."

4. **Build your team**: Have a go-to person you can talk to the
    minute you feel anxiety coming on. She/he can help you
    test your assumptions to evaluate how real they are, re-
    mind you that you cannot control everything, and offer
    some perspective about how important that issue is in
    the whole span of your life. Depending on the intensity
    of your anxiety, you may want to seek an experienced
    health professional who can work more quickly to help
    you get results.

5. **Don't forget the self-care:** Remember the basics: sleep
    is vitally important to recover from stress, and exercise,
    including yoga, walking/running, and chi gong, helps
    you maintain emotional equilibrium. Did you know that
    alcohol or caffeine can escalate anxiety and trigger panic
    attacks? Sugar, as tempting as it is, does not help either.
    Maintain your glucose levels with regular meals and
    healthy, protein-filled snacks. Sometimes a good healthy
    cry relieves a lot of stress in no time at all. Anxiety is

a state that involves the body as well as the mind, so don't take your one precious body for granted—help it help you.

6. **The 4-7-8 Breath:** Breath is used to re-center in athletics, childbirth, and martial arts. Dr. Andrew Weil offers this 4-7-8 breath as the most powerful antianxiety measure he has found:[15] inhale quietly through your nose for a count of four, retain the breath (don't exhale yet) for seven counts, then exhale slowly through your mouth for a count of eight. Do this for only four rounds. (Some people start with an inhale for four counts, hold for four and exhale for six—see which one you prefer.) This should be practiced twice a day. In the evening, it will also help you fall asleep. It is known to be effective in anxiety-provoking situations. Over time, with regular daily practice, be prepared to notice the difference. One and a half minutes per day can change your life.

7. **Change your state of mind:** When you notice the beginnings of anxiety and you are zooming into a vortex of negative thoughts, change your thoughts and your actions. If your thoughts are moving into future scenarios that are filled with negative outcomes, **bring yourself back to the present**. Activate your senses to notice how your body feels in the moment, where you are sitting, the details of objects on the surface of the table, hear the sounds outside the window, observe colors around you— be here now. You can also change your headspace by getting your body moving: go for a walk around the block and notice your surroundings; get some nature near you if you can. You can also turn on a funny video, which

might be the quickest way to break from the state of anxiety. By the way, if you find yourself turning to your phone for instant relief if you get anxious, try to be aware of that tendency and really tune in to the root of the problem instead of distracting from it.

8. **U.N.L.O.C.K. a more resourceful approach:** If you are experiencing panic, check out the symptoms with a doctor first. If the issue is not physically based, seek a health professional to work with you. They may suggest Dr. Helen Odessky's U.N.L.O.C.K. method[16]:

- **U**nderstand (intellectual): Understand the way your panic symptoms develop and subside and learn to recognize the false message that the symptoms are suggesting, for example, that you are going to die.

- **N**egate (mental): Challenge the negative beliefs that accelerate the panic. Are they really true or errors in your thinking? In your **journal**, jot down why they are false, so they can no longer pull you in. You are taking back your power.

- **L**everage your fears (physical): Get very familiar with the feared panic symptoms that accompany a typical panic attack. It could be rapid heartbeat, feeling dizzy, etc. Then replicate their effect (by sprinting in place or spinning in a chair) and patiently notice how your body will find its own equilibrium. By practicing this deliberate exposure to the symptoms and noticing that they do subside in time, you will have much less fear if they arise again. Your body gets to experience that the symptoms will pass, and you will be okay.

- **O**penness (attitude): Allow yourself to be open to the

possibility of change. Imagine a more positive out-come and try asking yourself, "What *if* it turned out better than I thought . . ." and write down what you would think, feel, and do in that scenario. Instead of living in dread, you are opening a space for positive change.

- **C**ompassion (heart-centered): When you are trying something new, there is a learning curve. When things don't go as well as you may have planned YET (they will get better with practice), how could you respond to yourself as you would to a child who is learning to walk? In your **journal**, write down your own phrase, like: "It takes courage to try something new, and it's okay to make mistakes—everyone does—keep going—you got this." This is a process; know you are on your way.

- **K**indle (behavior): Small shifts lead to bigger changes: In your **journal**, write down a list of activities that make you anxious—you may be getting through them but with much anxiety, or you may have decided not to do them at all. List the easiest activities on top, leading progressively to the most difficult ones. Start with the easiest, practice it over time, and prove to yourself that you can take on things that you had previously avoided. Then move to the slightly more difficult activity. You will learn what it feels like to trust yourself to move out of your comfort zone. Your confidence will get stronger as you see yourself progressively taking on more.

9. **Forgive yourself:** People who suffer from anxiety will often condemn themselves as defective—"What's wrong

with me; why can't I just deal with this?" Anxiety, as we have seen, is a human reaction that most everyone encounters to one degree or another at certain points in life. The question is, "How do I get some support to learn what tools I can call upon if I need them?" Putting yourself down will, apart from the initial experience of anxiety, make you anxious about being anxious—you don't need that! Instead, forgive yourself if you felt anxiety, forgive yourself if you had a panic attack, and forgive yourself if you couldn't deal with a social situation. There are more people than you know in this boat. You *can* learn how to row, and then you will be able to help others, too.

Through this chapter, you can see that there is a spectrum of anxiety: the beneficial type that helps you rally under stress and do your best, and the more challenging types that are a call to address the symptoms, then their roots. This may lead to exploring lifestyle changes and establishing boundaries that align with your values and help you thrive. You *can* make choices that serve you.

By using anxiety as your messenger, you will get more in touch with what your mind, body, and soul need, and with this information, you can support a new level of being true to yourself and make the decisions that help you thrive. Anxiety does not make you a freak. The reason so many people are experiencing anxiety is because the culture is anxious, the world is more anxious than ever, and we have not yet learned to manage our addiction to social media.

It takes intention and some effort to sift through the healthy anxiety and the kind that invites us to look deeper, maybe reconnect with our priorities and tweak how we are choosing to live. In that sense it is a clarion call to awaken to the fact that we can course correct, we can make choices, and we have more options than we may know. Anxiety is not a dead end—on the contrary, it is an invitation to grow.

Confidence

Because one believes in oneself, one doesn't try to convince others.
Because one is content with oneself, one doesn't need others'
approval.
Because one accepts oneself, the whole world accepts him or her.

—LAO TZU

CONFIDENCE IS AN OUTER reflection of an inner alignment. You know when someone has confidence; their presence speaks before they do. Have you ever met someone new and wondered, "Who is that person? They have such a great energy, such a spark, and they are radiating sheer confidence." And . . . have you ever felt that you could use a little more? But sometimes the desire for confidence and the possession of it can seem far apart. Maybe you want to reduce some of the stress you deal with but haven't felt like you could make demands to carve out the time; maybe in your job, you want to speak out more in meetings but have held back; maybe you want more closeness in your relationships, but it was never the right time to raise the subject. Or perhaps you have a dream you've been harboring in your heart, but it would take a leap into uncertainty to get going.

The good news is that confidence is not reserved for the lucky few. There is a source of energy that helps you feel more connected and confident, and anyone can tap into it. This confidence you exude is much more than stand up straight, shoulders back, chin up, and put a smile on your face; that is all external. The confidence we are talking about comes from the inside, and you cannot help but access it when you are at home in your skin, when you feel aligned with who you are, and quite simply when you are enjoying your life.

You might be thinking, "Easy to say, but how does this happen?" It's easy to get caught up in negative thoughts and beliefs that have been holding us back and forget to think of what *gives* us energy. When our mind automatically goes to what we don't like about ourselves or our situation, when we focus on how we don't measure up, or on how others have it so together, we are setting our energy in motion, but not in the direction that we would like. We are effectively closing down the valve that connects us to the clear energy we all desire, the energy that connects us to our inner resources, our joy, and our confidence.

Inner confidence is also described as feeling your power to take a step forward. According to Ohio State University professor Richard Petty, "Confidence is what turns our thoughts into actions."[1] This includes getting through both the mental obstacles as well as the challenges to get into action. Getting out of our own way mentally opens the door to gaining confidence from doing. When you want to be the architect of your own life, you need both aspects: feeling like you are *willing* to take a step forward (even if you have fears), then *acting* upon that and taking the step. The good news is that these can be developed. The more we practice a new perspective, habit, or skill, the better we become at it. We learn as we go.

In this chapter we'll look at both of these aspects: confidence from inner alignment and from learning something new. We'll explore the power of belief and the different mind-sets that either support or sabotage our lives. We'll cover the downsides of self-esteem and how women can deal with the confidence gap. Then I'll give you some tactical hints, including knowing your strengths, how to feel your confidence grow, and how to track its progress as it emerges. Greater confidence is absolutely available—here are some ways to accelerate your journey.

Belief

We've all heard the saying "Just believe in yourself," but what happens when you feel discouraged or disappointed in life or even in yourself? What if you've had a few things that have not gone your way and you feel a little stuck? When you want to see external changes, it's always good to start with internal shifts. One of the most powerful shifts to make is learning to manage your mind-set.

After decades of research, Stanford University psychologist Carol Dweck discovered that how we think about our talents and abilities is one of the greatest influences in how successful we are in the world, and this works for business, in school, for families, and relationships.[2] She explains that if we believe that our intelligence, talents, or personality are "fixed," that we're either naturally good at something or we're not (and if not, then why bother putting energy in that direction), that is called a fixed mind-set. Someone with a fixed mind-set would not be interested in trying something outside their comfort zone. It's not their "thing," and chances are, if it's that challenging, it's not worth their time—move on! Besides, if they really go out on a limb and go for it, it could make them look stupid, or worse yet, it could fall flat, and they would feel like a failure—who needs that? Better to go with what comes easily and stay on proven paths where success is much more likely. Unfortunately, this is a very limited way to live. If we succumb to the fixed mind-set because it is familiar, we are effectively strangling our potential by buying into an old limiting belief.

On the other hand, if we believe that intelligence, personality, and character can be developed, and potential *can grow* by putting effort into learning new skills, that's called a growth mind-set. Someone with a growth mind-set approaches fresh challenges with curiosity and as a lifelong learner. They do not put the pressure on themselves to do it perfectly—after all, they are just starting out. This gives them the courage to take risks in areas untried. If something is somewhat challenging, it is actually a good thing. They know that the more they practice and the more effort they put in, the more their skills improve. Edison made ten thousand prototypes before coming out with the lightbulb—he definitely had a growth mind-set. Challenges are just part of the journey—if some path doesn't work out, that doesn't mean it's the end. Take another route.

The exciting thing about these mind-sets is that once we get to know them both, we can more easily notice when a fixed mind-set is putting limits on our confidence. Imagine yourself as a detective saying, "Aha—caught you in the act, fixed mind-set. Is that what I really want? Will that perspective help me—NO!

It will actually keep me right where I am. I'm tapping into my growth mind-set instead!" That awareness brings us to a choice point, and in that way, it brings us back to our own power.

At Project Happiness, we teach these concepts even to elementary school–age children, by translating them into the language of kids. The fixed mind-set, the one that thinks you are limited and shouldn't try something new, is similar to the inner critic voice. For kids, it's called your "Inner Meanie."

The growth mind-set, which kids call their "Inner Friend," inspires you to stretch through struggles and encourages you, saying that even if you don't know it yet, you will progress—just keep trying. Teaching kids how to make the choice for this empowering mind-set puts them more in charge of their internal state. One teacher working with at-risk students stated, "When students realize that they have control over effort and thus the results they see, they are off and running."[3] We had a class of seven-year-olds telling one another: "Don't listen to your Inner

FIXED MIND-SET (INNER MEANIE)	GROWTH MIND-SET (INNER FRIEND)
If I try something new, I'll risk looking incompetent.	When I try something new, I'll grow.
Challenges are a waste of time. If it's not my sweet spot, why bother?	I put effort into challenges as they help my brain, capacity, and confidence get stronger.
If it doesn't work out, I'm a failure—I'll be humiliated for life.	If my strategy failed, I'll learn from it and try something new— the most successful people deal with challenges all the time.

Meanie; listen to your Inner Friend!" Whether you call it focusing on your growth mind-set or on your "Inner Friend," *you* can
make that choice just as easily.

We need challenges to grow, but according to the research,
those with a fixed mind-set are five times more likely to avoid challenges.[4] This is actually a bigger deal than it might seem. Jenny
and Alexa were in the same after-school soccer league. Jenny had
exceptional hand-eye coordination and impressive speed. She had
been the star center for a few years in a row. Alexa, new to the
area, was an average but enthusiastic player. You could see her
doing early-morning drills before the day started.

Halfway through the season, the longtime coach had to leave
town for a family emergency, and a young new coach came on
board. She was a fanatic about practice and drove the kids hard.
Jenny, the star player, didn't like it one bit, missed most practices, and showed up just for the games. She couldn't wait for the
old coach to return, which to her dismay, did not happen, as she
had to relocate to care for her ailing parents. So the team had to
adapt to the new coach. Jenny did not go to practice; Alexa was
consistent.

Over the season and into the next, something unexpected
happened—the girl who was average started getting better than
the girl who was gifted. It took everyone by surprise when Alexa
started scoring goals every single game. For the first time, Jenny
had a challenge: to put in more effort and rise to her innate potential or bow out—what would she do? As you may have guessed,
her interest in the game started to wane. She said it no longer
grabbed her, and she'd rather spend more time on other interests.

Though Jenny had made brilliant plays in the past, Alexa's
consistent practice made her stronger and much more skilled than

anyone could have predicted. Her confidence grew along with her experience, and this rippled into all areas of her life.

If everyone stayed inside their comfort zones, there would be no possibility for progress and no opportunity for positive change. Challenges open the door to capacities you would not have known you had. You find out what you are made of.

JOURNAL CHALLENGE

In your **journal**, jot down a time when you faced a struggle that challenged you beyond what you thought you could handle, but you made it through.

- Describe how you felt and what you learned through that experience.
- Also write down a challenge that you are facing today. What beliefs could help you shift your perspective on that situation?

You give yourself a huge advantage by moving into the mindset that sees setbacks as opportunities for improvement and effort as the driver of growth. Instead of listening to your inner critic, you will train yourself to listen to your inner coach. Confidence is a natural by-product of witnessing the results of your efforts. So is a renewed ability to trust yourself, to trust in life, and to feel the expanded energy of being at home in your own skin. That's what gives you a glow, a radiance, and an energy that draws in those around you. That's why some say confidence is sexy! With this way of thinking, you don't have to worry about confidence—it will emerge within you.

Confidence Versus Self-esteem

Having healthy confidence is sometimes confused with having high self-esteem, but they are really not the same. The tricky thing about self-esteem is that it depends on external success, and it is based on how you stack up against others. Here's how it works: When we are feeling successful, then the self-esteem is in great shape. Let's say we ace a presentation, do well at a sports game, or win an argument, and we judge ourselves as valuable— life is good. The downside is that whenever something does not go right, whenever we make a mistake or fail at a goal, we judge ourselves as unworthy; the self-esteem fizzles like a balloon losing all its air.

Self-esteem is also based on being seen as better than someone else. Most people don't realize that, with all best intentions, when they emphasize self-esteem, they are actually entering the land of comparison and competition. This applies to parenting, too. Every parent wants their kids to do well and have friends; this will give them the foundation for success in life. It sounds good, and if they bring home the As and are invited to the birthday party, their parents are happy and the child's self-esteem is stoked. But what happens if their grades drop; what happens if someone was mean to them that day? Is that any reason for the child to feel less worthy?

Instead of praising the grades ("You're the best in your class, you're a genius"), consider praising the effort put into a project ("I can really see you worked hard on that"). The point is to guide children to do their best and strive for learning, rather than the elusive "gold star." Instead of praising popularity, emphasize being a good person. Being a person you are proud of is far more important for long-term confidence than being admired by random people.

When we measure ourselves by factors that are beyond our control, like a job promotion, or the number of likes on a social media post, then we are giving others control of how confident we feel about ourselves. This prompts the question—is that the choice we want to make? When everything is perfectly in sync, all is well. But when any one thing goes wrong, the most anticipated results can blow up in no time flat. Being dependent on external circumstances is a setup for eroding confidence instead of building it up.

Amy Morin, in an article for *Psychology Today*, suggests that if you have to measure yourself at all, base it on things that you have a say in, not the external events of your life over which you have no control. When you have a solid sense of yourself and you feel good about yourself, you will be able to ride the waves of change. No matter if a project you are working on is delayed, if you are going through a breakup or job loss, you can connect to an inner knowing that you will get through it; you always do. She states, "Instead of chasing . . . self-esteem, measure your self-worth by who you are at your *core*.[5]

"Use a measuring stick based on factors you can control—not the external events in your life. When you know who you are— and you're pleased with the person you have become—you'll experience a sense of peace through life's inevitable ups and downs."[6]

Self-compassion Matters

This is where self-compassion comes in. Unlike self-esteem, which has us judge our worthiness based on how we perform compared to others, self-compassion reminds us that everyone makes mistakes. Accepting ourselves, imperfections and all, is key. Otherwise, we spend way too much time agonizing about how it "should" have been. Even if we did not do well in a situation, we are all worthy of kindness. When you speak to yourself as you would a good friend, you can bounce back from setbacks faster and feel better about yourself. This leads to a confidence that is sourced internally—and one that is better able to withstand life's challenges.

According to Kristin Neff, author of *Self-Compassion*, "If you're self-compassionate, you'll tend to have higher self-esteem than if you're endlessly self-critical.[7] You can have self-compassion even when you've failed miserably. It does not depend on being better than other people."[8]

Women and Confidence

> You were born with potential. You were born with goodness and trust. You were born with ideals and dreams. You were born with greatness. You were born with wings. You are not meant for crawling, so don't. You have wings. Learn to use them and fly.
>
> —RUMI

Some women are lucky enough to have inherent self-confidence or to have been raised in families that fostered this quality. But a recent study[9] of four hundred students showed that girls lose faith in their own talents by the age of six. Part of the study had boys and girls play a new board game. For some kids, the explanation was that it was "for children who are really, really smart" and for another group it was described as "for children who try really, really hard." The results? "Six- and seven-year-old girls were as likely as boys to enjoy the game for those who try, but much less likely to say they enjoy the game for smart children."

A BBC article quotes Professor Andrei Cimpian, who states, "Early on, society's stereotypes can create differences in trajectory. . . . It's disheartening to see these effects emerge so early. When you see them, you realize how much of an uphill battle it's going to be."[10]

Though these tendencies are showing up in childhood, the facts are that these days, more women are graduating from college than men. According to the U.S. Department of Education, women will comprise more than 56 percent of students on campuses in the United States, and that trend is expected to grow.[11]

So why are so few women represented in traditional positions of influence? We have talked about the glass ceiling for years, but can confidence and mental beliefs also play a part? In this current climate, there is more urgency than ever to address the issue, and greater numbers of people than ever who want to see change. In some industries, the contrast in conditions is not as significant, but in some it is shocking; just think of what female actors or anchorwomen get paid as compared to their male colleagues. Time to rebalance the scales. . . .

The good news is that there is a renewed energy to engineer a shift. In order to set a strong foundation, certain key pillars need to be in place. These are pay equity, leadership equity, and responsibility equity. Christine Lagarde, managing director of the International Monetary Fund, points out, "Globally, women earn only three-quarters as much as men . . . even with the same level of education, and in the same occupation."[12]

- **Pay equity** means getting equal pay for equal work—this is front and center.

- **Leadership equity** will happen through women having access to the highest echelons of power: by voting more women into offices and boardrooms, by promoting them in organizations and communities, and by encouraging education and awareness.

- **Responsibility equity** has to do with shared responsibilities in the household and instituting proper maternity and paternity leave and daycare. Currently, the United States is the only industrialized country that does not offer paid maternity leave. "In Sweden's efforts to achieve gender equality, each parent is entitled to 240 of the 480 days of paid parental leave."[13] On a recent trip there, I was pleasantly surprised at how many dads were out during the week, midday with their babies. Maybe we can learn a few things. . . .

In the meantime, in the United States, progressive corporations, many of them in the tech sector, are leading the way in offering generous paid time off for maternity leave (and in some cases, such as Netflix, paternity leave). Besides creating goodwill and reducing stress so that parents can be fully present during this critical phase, by having paid leave policies in place, these businesses avoid the cost of having to seek and engage new hires. This is a win-win on so many levels.

While we work toward advancing the infrastructure of society, it's equally important to look below the surface. There are widespread mental beliefs that prevent these changes from happening as quickly as we would like. Aside from some inspiring examples of women following their own wisdom and creating a new definition of success, there are ingrained ways of thinking that play a big part in the confidence gap. Here is a quick overview. Tick off the ones that apply to you or the women in your life:

- Successful women often downplay their talents. "I was lucky; I was in the right place at the right time; I have an exceptional team. . . ." They don't take credit for their brilliance or hard work.
- Women ruminate more than men, getting stuck going over and over the details on every aspect of a problem.[14]
- More women get trapped in the pressure to do things perfectly, which can slow down decision-making, and, in extreme cases, be paralyzing.
- An internal report at Hewlett-Packard revealed that unless women have all the credentials in a job description, they will not even apply, compared to men, who have the confidence to learn on the job, so will apply even when they can only fulfill 60 percent of the requirements. Tara Sophia Mohr in a *Harvard Business Review* article elaborates, "They [women] didn't see the hiring process as one where advocacy, relationships, or a creative approach to framing one's expertise could overcome not having the skills

and experiences outlined in the job qualifications."[15] They were stuck by the wording in the guidelines, thinking that by following the "rules," which led them to academic success, they could prevail in the more dynamic workplace. There is a tendency for men to turn self-doubt into anger and motivation, which leads to action.

- Higher levels of testosterone in men are correlated with greater risk-taking.

- Women can default to guilt: beating themselves up mentally primarily in two ways: I'm not a good enough mother; or I'm falling behind—I'll do some extra work at night. Often they go hand in hand.

- Men overestimate their abilities by 30 percent, according to a Columbia University study: "The main difference in women not being selected as leaders appears to be attributable to men's overconfidence in their abilities."[16]

- A study conducted by LeanIn.org and McKinsey states that though "Women negotiate for promotions and raises as often as men . . . they face more pushback . . . Not surprisingly, women are almost three times more likely than men to think their gender will make it harder to get a raise, promotion, or chance to get ahead."[17] Like Sisyphus, many women feel like they are constantly pushing the boulder uphill.

- Men are often promoted based on their future potential, whereas women advance because of their past experience.

Given these mental constraints, it's no wonder that it's harder for women to claim their appropriate place. Here are ten ways to foster greater confidence:

1. **Encourage girls and women** to strive less for being seen as "good" and more for being seen as having moxie, resilience, and grit. Authenticity over perfectionism. It is better to prize effort, tenacity, and resourcefulness rather than the qualities of being likable, attractive, or pleasing. The movie *Wonder Woman* ignited a viral thread of delight as women created videos of themselves embodying that badass but caring superhero. Women were recognizing that part of themselves on the screen.

2. **Embrace the superpowers** of empathy, emotional intelligence, and heart-centered leadership. These are huge advantages and will help you advance as artificial intelligence gains more momentum.

3. **Don't stay long in blame or rumination**. Pointing fingers at others or at yourself will not move you forward; it will keep you stagnant. Know what *you* stand for and make a plan. Then keep on going.

4. **When in doubt, choose action**. You already know enough to take the first step.

Don't be intimidated by what you don't know. That can be your greatest strength and ensure you do things differently from everyone else.

— SARAH BLAKELY

5. **Develop your tribe of supporters**, allies, collaborators, and groups that share your vision. Make the time to develop these relationships—they will sustain you.

6. **Use your voice + hard facts + passion** to drive change and embrace the idea of failing forward.

Keep on going! We need to accept that . . . we'll screw up royally sometimes—understanding that failure is not the opposite of success, it's part of success.

—ARIANNA HUFFINGTON

7. **Get the fuel from your core values** and use those as a foundation for how you handle conflict and for the decisions you make. You will have the courage of your convictions and sleep well at night.

8. **Confidence is a choice you can make**. Authors Katty Kay and Claire Shipman point out in *The Confidence Code*: "You're born with a set of genes, and that's basically your concrete highway. But during the course of your life, you can build bridges and tunnels and other roads around that highway . . . that basically can change the way you are."[18] You can always add skills and new pathways to build up your confidence. In any given situation, you can **have the intention to choose the confident path**, and by traveling it more frequently, it expands into a road. Neuroplasticity would agree. By reinforcing any neural pathway, it gets stronger and eventually becomes your go-to approach.

9. **Claim your talents and your gifts**. Look at what you have accomplished so far, instead of everything left on your bucket list. Take that in and savor it—it will energize the next steps of your journey.

10. **Trust in your ability to figure it out**. Your curiosity, combined with your intuition, focus, and drive is a powerful recipe for progress. It's time to bring your *perception* of your abilities in line with your abilities. By getting out of your comfort zone and aligning with your true nature, you trust in who you really are.

Knowing Your Strengths

In order to claim our talents and uniqueness, as we **move from the confidence gap into the confidence flow**, a valuable tool is getting to know our personal strengths.

If someone were to ask you, "What are your top strengths and how would you describe your character?" would you be able to answer? Each person has different degrees of twenty-four character strengths, such as creativity, bravery, kindness, teamwork, forgiveness, and gratitude, just to name a few. You can get your personal profile by taking the University of Pennsylvania VIA Survey character quiz, developed by Dr. Martin Seligman.[19]

Finding out our character strengths is the first step. For confidence, fulfillment, and happiness to rise, the challenge is to put our top strengths into *action* in our daily lives. Let's say one of your strengths was creativity and you were dying a slow death in a restrictive desk job: then creativity would be informing you that by ignoring that facet of yourself, you are missing a source of accomplishment and joy. If leadership was one of your character strengths, this is a signal that as you use your leadership even more, you will experience both deeper fulfillment and the confidence that arises from honoring your essential self.

> ### JOURNAL CHALLENGE
>
> In your **journal**, jot down your own particular strengths, how you are already using them, and some ways you can bring them out even more.

As you use your innate strengths in day-to-day life, you will discover that when you act in alignment with what is most important to you and your values, not only will others have trust and confidence in you, but you can experience a deeper trust in yourself, more joy, and more self-confidence—you are being true to who you are.

Of course, it doesn't end there. In order to expand your world and the confidence you have within it, it's important to get a sense of your best self—the best version of you possible. This is the you that is living up to your potential, using all the characteristics that you want to embody. It's the you that has the strength, the capacity, and the success bursting forth . . . on your terms. It is basically how you want to show up in the world.

Three Words

Brendon Burchard, author of *High Performance Habits*, offers another way to define the best of who you are.[20]

If you were asked to describe your inner self, what words would you use? If you were asked to name some qualities that reflected who you aspire to be, in other words how you want to show up to others, would they be any different? This exercise

JOURNAL CHALLENGE

Take out your **journal** and follow the prompts; you will want to look back at these words later. Here are the instructions:

Select three words that define the best of who you are and that will serve to guide your thoughts and actions in your personal life. At a core level, are you: bold, compassionate, enthusiastic, reflective, kind, creative, strong-minded, present . . . The list is as long as there are people. What three words best describe **how you aspire to be** in the world and why?

Next, select three words that describe **how you want to relate to others**. It could be to your family, coworkers, friends, strangers, anyone and everyone that you interact with.

Some words to prompt your thinking are: aware, fair, curious, uplifting, courageous, appreciative, playful, caring . . . The words you select will be unique to you. What three words describe how you want to interact in the world and how you want others to see you? Jot down why.

Then, select the three words that remind you of what has, and what will, **make you most successful** in life. What are your secrets to success? Some ideas: presence, perseverance, friendliness, vision, generosity, focus, humor, boldness. . . . What words will make you most successful, and why?

Finally, the difference between people who simply say the words and those who put them into action can come down to having a bigger reason to show up as your confident best self. Who or what is compelling you to keep on going because they depend on you? Is there someone who believes in you that

(cont'd)

> you have to show up for? Do you need to be at your best for
> a cause that touches your heart: maybe you want to end suf-
> fering, maybe you want to be a voice for those who cannot be
> heard? For whatever reason, you know that giving up is not
> an option. Have a strong "why."

asks you to think of words that reveal attributes you want to
bring out of yourself, how you want others to experience you, and
qualities that amplify your success in life.

If you want to get the maximum benefit from your words,
then program them into your phone as reminders. On the iPhone,
as you set the time for your alarm, you'll want to press the word
"label" and replace it with your three words. Now, every time
your alarm goes off, you are reminding yourself of your best self.
Hold the intention to step into it. Because people are dynamic,
these words can change as you do. You might want to revisit this
exercise every year, and see if there are any new qualities you
want to focus on.

When you decide that you want to be more confident and are
willing to put some effort into it, you are already on your way.
Here are a few steps that can help:

PRACTICE

Confidence grows with the inner work (know your triggers
and have a plan to deal with them) and is reinforced with action. Psychologists call it the confidence competence loop. The
more you practice the guitar, the better you get at playing it . . .

then the more confidence you feel in playing it, the more you want to practice. . . . Sure, repeating the scales can be dull, but these exercises help attune the ear and provide the foundation from which to create. The best athletes understand that by doing their drills, they are developing the confidence, mental strength, and physical skills to be at their best in the heat of action. Repetition brings competence. Competence brings confidence. Confidence allows you to try something new that you might otherwise be afraid to. When you reach out of your comfort zone and go for that challenge, anything is possible. Confidence on the rise . . .

Here's a challenge: For the next month choose one theme, a new interest, or something you are passionate about, put it in the calendar, and build it into your day or week.

> If you talk about it, it's a dream, if you envision it, it's possible, but if you schedule it, it's real.
>
> —TONY ROBBINS

PREPARE

If you are planning a big tennis match or any other activity where you want to draw on your confidence, take some time to prepare. This could mean anything from figuring out exactly what you want and why, to visualizing how well it could go. You may not know all the specific steps to achieving this goal, but start thinking of yourself as the person you desire to be on every level, physically, mentally, and emotionally. Visualize how you want to show up: your confidence, poise, ease, humor . . . whatever is most important to you. Add details to make this as vivid as you can. If you want to be a

_____, start seeing that in place. How would you feel, what would you see, what would you hear? It's most important that you open your valve to align with your expanded energy and then close your eyes and feel this in your body. Then you can start trying that on in reality, acting like you are already in that confident state.

That's your work on the mental level. Then bring in your pragmatic side. Anticipate the inevitable challenges, as there are always things that come up, and have a Plan B ready. ("If it happens this way, I can do that.") Every obstacle allows you to learn something new. Arthur Ashe says it well: "One important key to success is self-confidence. An important key to self-confidence is preparation."

Support Yourself

You will see that with your efforts you do progress. Sometimes, though, as you develop more confidence, get stronger or more focused as you work toward a goal, it can change the dynamics with the people around you who are used to seeing you a certain way. If they resent that you are growing into a bigger version of yourself, it's important not to buy into what others may think and to show *yourself* some love and support. Create a mantra that is meaningful for you: "I am strong and beautiful." "Life is opening for me—I am unstoppable." "I am growing every day." You'll think of what works best for you. Consider putting these messages on sticky notes in key places like the bathroom mirror or your computer, phone, or fridge.

To vibrate at the frequency of confidence and positivity, it also helps to keep your own levels high by daily meditation and gratitude. By something as simple as journaling a few things you are grateful for, as well as noting a few good qualities you saw in yourself that day, your sense of well-being and confidence will go up. You will also discover that your attention is less on what you are lacking and more on what you already have. You are enough, just as you are.

You may be tempted to compare yourself to others. Don't do it! Instead, realize that your uniqueness is what counts and surround yourself with just a few handpicked people who are excited to see your confidence emerge. We tend to have an affinity with those who are vibrating at a similar level of energy (your vibe attracts your tribe). Make an intention to be around at least some people who lift you up, and you will do the same for them. As you appreciate yourself more, focus on what puts a smile on your face, and align with what is meaningful to you, you cannot help but build your confidence in powerful ways.

Confidence and Change

As you revise old ways of thinking, reconnect with your inner nature, and make decisions based on your values and best energy, you will tap into an innate confidence that waits within . . . always. Confidence is who you are on your deepest levels, and it is there to be accessed and amplified. The great thing about confidence is not only does it help you bring forth your best self, it can help you use your powers for good.

YOUR CONFIDENCE + CARING + COMMITMENT = UNSTOPPABLE CHANGE

Wonder Woman (or insert your favorite superhero) has nothing on you.

With realization of one's own potential and self-confidence in one's ability, one can build a better world.

—HIS HOLINESS THE DALAI LAMA

Anger

Anger is just anger. It isn't good. It isn't bad. It just is. What you do with it is what matters. It's like anything else. You can use it to build or to destroy. You just have to make the choice.

— JIM BUTCHER

HAVE YOU EVER FELT so angry you could barely stand it? And then the thought of dealing with it was so daunting, it felt like the anger could burn you up, too? There is a quote by Seneca that explains it well: "Anger is like an acid that can do more harm to the vessel in which it is stored than to anything on which it is poured." When anger is not understood, it can rise to the surface, like lava through a volcano, in an explosion of epic proportions, potentially hurting everyone, including you, in its wake. There's also another direction anger can travel: instead of erupting outward, it can implode; that's when you suppress, deny, or otherwise bury the anger inside, which can be equally if not more damaging.

But anger has another side: it can be our teacher and show us the way to areas that need awareness, attention, and a new perspective.

Several years ago, in a private audience with the Dalai Lama, one of the students from a film that I had produced, called *Project Happiness*, asked the Dalai Lama a question on what to do about anger. The Dalai Lama became very animated and told us a story of two different ways of dealing with this potent emotion. The Dalai Lama had posed a certain question to two Tibetans to explore reactions to anger: "How do you feel about the Chinese?" He went on to explain, "One man, even before he spoke, his face became very red and then his cheeks were red. And then he said, 'Yes. I am very angry.'" The Dalai Lama contrasted this with, "On the other hand, there are some Tibetans, even though they spent many years, at least two decades, in Chinese gulag . . . a lot of problems, a lot of suffering, a lot of torture, but their mind stayed very calm. Although both are in a free country now, in India, some are still mentally not very free. Too much anger. Too much hatred. Those happier, more calm-minded Tibetan ex-prisoners, their mind, I think, is more free from these negative emotions . . . So the result is that these people are happier."

While the first man was never physically incarcerated, he remained a prisoner of his anger, and the actual ex-prisoners, who had risen above their anger, were now free not only physically, but mentally as well. Whether you deal with abuse or escape it, unresolved anger stays with you wherever you go.

The good news is that anger, like any emotion, serves a purpose. It is a signal that something in your world is not right: maybe a boundary has been violated; maybe you feel you are being prevented from getting something you really want; maybe you have been hurt so much that you cannot take it anymore. If handled thoughtfully, it can guide you to find a better way to live. At moderate levels, anger can help you push through an obstacle, manage pain, and connect with your courage. If you have ever experienced your anger in a way that challenged you to show up in a stronger and more determined way, you know that it is a powerful emotion, one that offers the advantage of insight, action, and drive.

In this chapter, we'll explore all the facets of anger, its downsides, the gifts it carries, and some practical strategies on how to work with it when it comes up. This is a potent emotion. Becoming more mindful of how you deal with anger is vital to learning how to actually use its power to help you move forward in your life.

Anger's Many Faces

First of all, let's take a closer look at how anger can show up. This is one emotion with an enormous range of levels. Think of a thermometer that goes from a lukewarm temperature to scorching. Anger begins with low-level annoyance and elevates to feeling resentment, frustration, irritation, indignation, upset, pissed off, furious, and even blinded by white-hot rage! It can vary by situation, of course, but where along this spectrum do you most often find yourself? Is there a specific scenario that brings this feeling up? The more you have self-knowledge around what you are feeling, the better equipped you are to handle whatever comes your way.

Triggers: Why Does Anger Come Up?

We all have situations that activate anger—no one is immune. It is simply a question of degree. Here are just a few scenarios when anger can emerge—some are lighthearted and some are connected to deeper wounds. As you read through them, notice if there are any that you can relate to:

There's the simple frustration of being stuck in traffic, or God forbid, having your phone or computer not work. . . . Your dog or cat may have done its business in the living room rather than outside. The news reveals yet another fiasco; not something you can control, but it sure is maddening. Exasperation shows up when you are running out of patience; no matter how many times you explain something, your relative keeps asking the exact same question. Sulking is when anger goes passive; this is not going anywhere, so why even try? Anyone who has been passed by for a promotion or has had someone close turn on them knows that it's easy to feel let down, resentful, or, in some cases, brutally betrayed. These feelings are especially searing when you have given your trust to the people involved.

Have you ever witnessed an argument where one person was loud and the other increasingly distant? The quiet one, holding a silent anger, is feeling withdrawn and in some cases numb. . . . He or she just doesn't want to, and maybe cannot deal. Aggressive behavior, on the other hand, often starts if you have been provoked or subjected to hostile interactions yourself—old wounds with fresh faces can make you feel the need to strike back to hold your ground.

If you think that's the end, oh no, there are more . . . in fact, you can find almost as many scenarios as there are people. If you've been disrespected or ridiculed, you might feel humiliation—that should not have happened! Jealousy is another way anger reveals itself—why do they already have what I desire?

When you notice yourself leaning toward bitterness and

indignation, that can come from feeling trapped in an unhealthy relationship or even violated. If your safety has been threatened, if your values have been disregarded, if your power is being attacked, it is increasingly troubling. Whether physically, mentally, or emotionally, a boundary has been crossed, and you don't yet see a clear way out. The emotions of shame and anger are both intensified.

There are so many aspects to this one emotion. Which ones resonate most with you?

Past and Present

Anger, like all emotions, can be triggered either by people, present situations, or past events. Most people have childhood beliefs that made such an indelible impression that they sneak in to color their relationships of today. Many of these influences come from our immediate family. Did a parent tend to express anger frequently, through passive-aggressive tactics, or did they suppress it and withdraw, only to have it come out another way?

As children, we all yearn for safety, and anger can be a very scary emotion to witness. Every child develops coping mechanisms to get them through, and these tendencies linger in one's body language and internal attitudes well into the adult years. It's normal to be easily triggered if someone you trusted, whether a family member, friend, or lover hurt you when your heart was open—you do what you can to protect yourself.

The bottom line is that anger, which is a strong response to a perceived hurt or threat toward you or others, is actually a call for help. No matter what age you are, it is an attempt to release emotional pain so you can feel less threatened, more secure, and more at ease. Beneath most types of anger is a pain point—that's why the anger erupts. But we can only transform what we are aware of.

Here is a powerful exercise:

JOURNAL CHALLENGE

In your **journal**, answer the question, "What was your way of dealing with anger as a child?"

Write down three situations when you remember anger coming up. You might look at three different ages. It could be that *you* were getting angry (at least for one example), or it may have been someone close to you. Then jot down, as much as you can remember:

- What happened in each situation
- How you tried to handle it
- How you ended up feeling
  - both in your mind (thoughts, fears)
  - and in your body (stomach tightened, heart racing, sweaty palms . . .)
- What you discovered

Take your time with this—you can go into as much detail as you want.

On another page, list three situations where anger has popped up in the past year or two, either yours (at least one) or someone else's. Again, include details about what happened, how you tried to handle it, and how you ended up feeling, both mind and body, and finally, what you discovered.

The next question to explore is if there are any similarities between your childhood reflections and how you process or witness anger today. Do your examples seem random, or can you detect a pattern?

Think of yourself as a detective—you are gathering trapped information so you can free up your energy to live your most vibrant life. Because the mind tends to look through a negative lens, sometimes called the negativity bias, just beware that you don't use this information to put yourself down ("It's hopeless, I should have handled it differently . . ."). On the contrary, this is a time to celebrate your courage for peering under the hood in the first place. The more you look at your anger, the less it will rule your life. This is true for every emotion. Your efforts today lead to your freedom tomorrow. This small exercise can give you many insights you can draw from.

Body Clues

We often think emotions are a mental game, but our bodies are giving us clues all the time. The earlier we catch them, the less they need to escalate to grab our attention. Anger is a perfect example, and Paul Ekman's work introduces the most common traits. You probably know them instinctively, but next time you see someone who is angry, check out—and it can be subtle in some people—how their inner eyebrows drop, their eyes start to glare, their chin may come forward, and their face or neck gets red.[1] When the anger is well under way, the lips or the jaw can tighten, too, with teeth displayed. Think of an animal before they attack. In case they need to be ready for a potential fight, the blood will automatically flow to the arms and hands. And of course, the heart rate increases, as does blood pressure.[2] We've all heard the expression "His or her blood was boiling." That's anger personified.

Unconscious Anger

To maintain boundaries and ward off danger, every being, whether human or animal, is equipped with this preprogrammed software that automatically kicks in when the body feels at risk. It's usually not even a conscious reaction. If a member of your family is in danger, you won't weigh in and ponder the pros and cons of protecting them—you just GO! Even in the animal kingdom, there are fights for dominance and displays of anger to establish who stands as the leader. Have you ever seen one dog sniff at another's food? Almost instantaneously there's the growl that lets the intruder know, "This is mine, buddy. Back off!" Animals don't reflect, they don't deliberate—they act.

From a scientific perspective, anger starts in the lower limbic area near the brain stem in the amygdala. When you are threatened or angry, the amygdala becomes super active, and like an emotional sentry that senses danger, it activates your urge to "fight, flight, or freeze." The intensity of anger takes over your ability to reason. Think of a little child screaming at the top of her lungs. That's when you are having an "Amygdala Moment." That's why anger can seem to take you on a wild ride, and it becomes hard to connect with the prefrontal cortex, the part of you that acts like a wise parent, helping manage emotions and make good decisions. Some describe it as "your brain is being hijacked." That's what's going on when people are in a "fit" of anger.

In this state, it's easier to say things or do things that you are likely to regret. Beyond having no filter, empathy can go out the window, kindness can disappear, and you literally can get swept up in a tsunami of emotion.

Contagious Anger

Have you ever walked into a situation where someone was so angry that you could literally feel it? Then when you got closer, the intensity of that anger was spewed over you, too? Have you ever gone to a new place expecting it to look a certain way only to discover that it was the exact opposite? Years ago, I was fascinated by the subject of peace. There was great passion around the topic as it was a time when people globally were protesting the Iraq War. You could not watch or read the news without seeing stories of peace rallies in cities across the country. So I decided to get a firsthand view and brought my then-nine-year-old daughter with me to the center of the action in downtown San Francisco. This was not a quiet rally; there were people chanting in every corner, flags and posters everywhere, and a pulsating energy that was getting louder by the minute. My daughter stayed close to my side. I do not support war of any kind, but we were both struck by the intensity of anger—unstoppable rage, actually—within those who identified as pacifists. Anger can catch on like a forest fire and entrap everyone in its path. In groups of every persuasion, when there is the perception of injustice, it doesn't take much to ignite mass indignation, groupthink, and even hatred. The precarious point is that when anger becomes contagious, depending on the issue it is addressing, even well-meaning individuals can easily get swept into the raging blaze and lose their connection to what it means to be an empathetic human walking on this earth alongside others who are also just trying their best to figure it out. But there is another way—we'll talk about that soon.

If we take a deeper look, anger is an attempt, and often a clunky one, of releasing unresolved pain, like hurt, sadness, and shame. Whether we realize it or not, we are carrying residue from past experiences, and it plays out in everyday circumstances. We walk through life easily triggered, or asleep because that is easier than actually being with the anguish that lies beneath the anger. How many people do you know who are walking through life numbed out—and using food, exercise, substances, or Netflix to get through the days?

The exciting thing here is that by listening to the messages of anger to course correct toward the best within us, we can work *with* this emotion and let it help us open the doors to more freedom and ease. But to harness this potential, we have to be aware of how it works.

So let's look at the two sides of anger that most people default to, before we explore the third path, the most transformational way, when anger can be our guide to a better life.

Most people approach anger in two ways: either expressing it on the outside or burying it inside.

JOURNAL CHALLENGE

In your **journal**, reflect on your usual reaction to anger. When we are on autopilot, these unconscious blueprints can repeat for years, as in bullying or abuse or other traumas . . . whenever one person takes out their pain on another. A simpler example is the story of the employee who gets humiliated at work, then comes home and kicks the dog.

Blame is also a natural way to cope with distress. Let's say you have been hurt or disappointed in some way. Can we agree that this is pretty much universal? Most people, to avoid a painful feeling, almost automatically go into blame or indignation— "they" caused the problem in the first place. "They" stopped you from going for your goal; "they" invaded your space; "they" crossed the line. Who wants to look at their own hurt feelings when they can distract themselves by pointing the finger away from the sensitive spots? And it may feel good to have the illusion of discharging the pain and getting it out of your system in one powerful explosion . . . but the core issues have not been looked at, and there can be a lot of emotional debris to sweep up afterward.

Some people think that unleashing raw anger is an expression of strength, and anger can feel liberating, even empowering, for a nanosecond . . . until the flying fit is over and the guilt sets in. But anger can feel good for that instant because the ego is reassured that it is still "in control." In truth, that "ego fix" is a learned way to avoid feeling the underlying fears.

For too long, we have been socialized to believe that anger is a more "acceptable" sentiment for men and boys to demonstrate than sadness or apprehension; better to be considered tough than a wuss. Up to this point, if we really look at it, men and women both have been trapped in a patriarchal system that has architected rigid and limiting roles for *all* genders. Men don't cry . . . really? So what are they supposed to do with their feelings of fear and futility? And is it actually anger they are experiencing, or is that the least risky way to mask feelings of sadness, unworthiness, or shame?

Past social norms reinforce that anger is a more manly emotion—generally people won't make fun of men or boys if they get mad . . . they are tough, maybe even cool. On the other hand, if women are angry and are loud about it, they can be called hysterical, out of control, or an angry bitch. This antiquated view of anger is a no-win for everyone. Harming anyone hurts us all. My hope is that this stifling system is starting to shift and this will not be a toxic pattern that the next generation and those to come will be burdened with. We can all influence the speed of that change.

Internal Anger

The second approach to getting rid of the unresolved emotions is by pushing them inward, stuffing the anger into corners of your mind, and suppressing any pain. If you have a mean or super-judgmental colleague who you have to work with, you can rationalize, "This is not life-threatening; I'll deal with it later; I should be compassionate." It sounds good, maybe even responsible and professional . . . but this is a very real red flag. There is the downside of not accepting how you feel. When we are deliberately suppressing the anger that is crying for our attention, we are ignoring, or even rejecting an aspect of our experience that wants to be recognized. You may notice you have more trouble sleeping; something is off. Imagine your body and your inner voice are trying desperately to give you a message. Squashing the emotion is like disrespecting not only the information your inner voice and your body are trying to convey; you are also rejecting those precious parts of yourself.

It is possible to even lose touch with what it means to be your authentic self and feel like you are an actor in your own life. Instead of appearing stoic and strong, you may actually be disconnecting from your inner guidance and putting yourself in a *more* susceptible position. That's when physical and mental aches and pains may start to show up . . . migraines, stomach or back pain, a feeling of uneasiness. So while suppressing the anger may seem to work in the short term, it can, over time, backfire in a way that leads to anxiety and depression.

Conscious Expression

Healthy anger: The good news is that it's not the anger that's the problem. Anger is just informing you that something needs to be recalibrated in your life. Just like technology is not the problem—how we use it determines if it helps us or hurts us—anger can also be used to make a situation better or make it worse.

Anger is a sign that something is coming up for attention, and both the body and the mind are trying to let you know. When you welcome your anger as a messenger and accept that it's okay to bring it into your awareness to heal, you end up stronger, wiser, and more resilient. By listening to the clues, you can act on them, deliberately, consciously, and skillfully.

Letting anger run riot can take out everything in its path. On the other hand, denying this emotion will only make it expand under the surface. But sometimes anger is just what is needed to deal with injustice or to right a wrong, and we don't want to keep it bottled up and festering. We need to use it skillfully.

So the *way* anger is expressed is the most important factor here. Is anger a useful strategy to get what you're after, or not? Is it opening the door to resolve an issue or just shutting people down? Is the blast of instinctive anger dishonoring you or others and inadvertently reinforcing a toxic pattern? Can the anger be used consciously to move you forward in a healthy way?

This means you are not suppressing or denying that your anger is there; you are acknowledging it. In perceiving the emotion, you are making yourself more conscious of it, and by doing so, the anger morphs from an instinctive reaction to actually entering what neuroscientist Antonio Damasio calls our "mindflow," where we can "construct responses that are different than the emotional ones." This is one way humans are different than animals—we are not limited by our instincts. **Instead of being caught up in our emotions, by perceiving/witnessing our emotions, our self, and the world around us, we can use consciousness to access more choices in how we respond.**

It is only through consciously handling the sticky situations and being with the emotion that is rising to the surface that positive change can emerge. Think of anger as alchemy: it can open the door to freedom and growth, and it's a shift that anyone can make.

One of the easiest ways to watch our emotions instead of being hijacked by them is through the breath. If you already have a meditation practice, you will have your routine, but if you are new to it, start simple. Sit on a chair and take a few slow deep breaths to settle yourself. Feel your feet on the ground and your seat on the chair. Your back is straight but not rigid. Then, take a conscious breath in, feeling the air come in through your nose and down to your lungs. If you put a hand on your belly, you will feel it expand. Count one on the inhale and two as you exhale. You'll feel your belly contract as you do. Count to ten (five full breaths) and repeat. ONLY do this for one to two minutes to start. That's what makes it easy to do every day. There's no wrong way to do it—this is a nonjudgment zone. When you get distracted, and everyone does, just come back to the inhale and count one. Thoughts of every variety will come and go—try to observe them and treat them as clouds that come and go. Next week, add another one or two minutes, and before long this will be a habit that you look forward to that gets your day starting well or ending peacefully. This is a no-pressure zone—start small.

Boundaries

One of the most important uses of anger is to restore boundaries that have been broken. I so appreciate the way Karla McLaren explains how the violation of a boundary can lead to anger, and that anger can lead you to restore your own energetic borders, stand up for yourself and others, and above all, remember who you are[3]. Boundaries are violated when someone enters your space against your will. There are levels of violation from mental disrespect to emotional harassment to crossing the line physically, including hitting or sexual abuse. Basically these are all power issues, where someone is using their power to diminish someone else's. By channeling your anger into visualizing a strong boundary, which is strengthened by your anger, you come to know what works for you and what no longer feels acceptable. From this more protected position you can then take action.

JOURNAL CHALLENGE

In your **journal**, consider if you have any boundaries that you may want to strengthen.

By consciously developing boundaries that align with your values, you give yourself the safety, comfort, and freedom to be who you are. By the same token, you have the ease to let other people be themselves, too; there's no longer the need to have them change to meet your expectations. You also choose not to enmesh with other people's boundaries; you can keep yours distinct. Then you can come from renewed strength rather than feeling like a victim of other people's agendas.

Another benefit is that by using anger consciously, you also create the conditions to not dishonor yourself or anyone else. You can be both assertive and compassionate. This anger is restorative and well considered and helpful to everyone involved.

Anger as Fuel for Social Change

Though anger often gets a bad rap, there are some situations when its potent energy is pivotal to protect those who have been mistreated. Some situations require that level of intensity in order to drive change. For Gandhi, Martin Luther King Jr., and the suffragettes, anger was the rocket fuel needed to address social injustice. They were able to use that energy and channel it toward improving conditions for the greater good. Sometimes called moral or social anger, it's all about shining a light on situations that are toxic and shaking things up to create a better world. Isn't it interesting that all these groups used nonviolent tactics? Unlike hate groups or corrupt political regimes, they made the deliberate choice not to let anger steamroll them into bloodshed. They were able to harness the intensity of the emotion to power up positive change.

That, however, is not easy! I recently heard Krista Tippett's fascinating interview of Congressman John Lewis talking about how he worked side by side with Martin Luther King Jr. and helped prepare groups of people to take part in the marches.[4] In the interview, he described how the participants actually got together days before the march to rehearse, as you would for a play, the most challenging scenarios that could possibly happen. They practiced responding with civility instead of getting sucked into the energy of those who would pull them down. They trained themselves not to match the hatred and hostility, even if people were screaming at them, spitting on them, or brutally kicking them in the ribs. How many people could show such control?

John Lewis and his fellow Freedom Riders did not suppress their anger, nor did they allow themselves to be triggered into violence, which would have had them immediately locked up and silenced. Instead, they used anger to fuel a deeply rooted motivation, to hone a clear intention, and to play their moves like chess masters so they could see their vision come to life.

Throughout the chapter, we've looked at the usual ways anger plays out and also some situations where it can be used to make us stronger individually and collectively. Now let's turn to more practical strategies to change how we deal with anger, both through questions to expand our perspective and activities to move the energy to a calmer and more empowered place.

Questions

SIMPLE QUESTIONS TO OPEN AWARENESS

A helpful way to recover from an "amygdala moment" and reactivate the thinking part of the brain—the prefrontal cortex—is to ask it some easy questions, such as: "Am I angry? How angry am I? What am I angry at?" It's deceptively simple but highly effective, as it moves us from being caught in the emotion to being able to pause and observe it. In that way, we come back to ourselves and have more choices.

CAN YOU NAME IT TO TAME IT?

When anger arises, the faster you witness it, the faster you can discover what's really going on and deal. Dr. Dan Siegel explains that when we can name what we are feeling by actually putting it into words ("I'm getting really angry now!"), we can create an opening for the upper part of the brain (cortex) to step in so it can literally squirt soothing neurotransmitters down to the lower brain area (amygdala) to calm it down.[5] Labeling your emotion gives you a biological pathway to return to a calmer state.

DO YOU HAVE THE FULL PICTURE?

Check in to see if you are really angry about what just happened, or if this feeling is actually an accumulation of all the people or incidents that aggravated you earlier that day. If you got out of bed cranky, that feeling can build on itself and intensify every encounter. Or, if you find out that the friend who blew up at you just discovered that her father has cancer, you probably would not be as upset with her. Consider what may have led up to an outburst, and that you don't always have the full picture.

AM I REALLY BEING THREATENED, OR IS IT MY EGO?

There are times when we magnify the perceived danger in an escalating spiral of emotion. It helps to do a reality check. Ask yourself, "Am I really in danger, or is it my ego that is feeling disrespected, rejected, or kind of scared? Am I being triggered because this is showing me a vulnerable part of myself that I don't accept or want to see?

Is the anger just coaching me to recognize the tender part of me that is tired of hurting? Must I get angry to regain control, or can I hold this part of me as I would a scared child?"

WHAT IF I FLIP THE SCRIPT?

Try switching around the statement "I'm mad at Mark" to "I'm actually mad at myself." Is there some truth there? Does a part of you feel like you let *yourself* down? Did you compromise, tolerate something, or give in when you would have liked to handle it in a way that was more authentic and empowering? The answer is to be gentle with yourself and know that beating yourself up just keeps you stuck. By simply being aware of and sitting with this dynamic, you are already moving through it.

IS THIS PERSONAL OR SYSTEM-WIDE?

Is the problem due to a conflict with one person, or is it a more widespread issue? In a family situation, is it a personal conflict between you and another family member, or are you dealing with deeply embedded belief systems (like guilt, shame, or scarcity) that have gone back for generations? In the workplace, is it an individual issue between you and your boss, or does the overall company culture pit people against one another? Ask, "Is this situation something that I can control or change, or is my best option to change my perspective about it?"

IS THIS REALLY MY PROBLEM?

Do you find yourself in a group of angry people? Do you really share the same values and feel strongly about what they are angry at? Is this something you deeply want to take on, or are you being swept into a fast-moving current? There's a Polish proverb that says, "Not my circus, not my monkeys." You have a choice.

WILL MY ANGER GET ME WHAT I WANT?

Anger is just a message that some aspect of your life needs course correction. How and when you express that anger can either make things harder or improve the situation. Ask yourself if expressing your anger in that moment will get you what you desire. Just because you are feeling anger does not mean that you have to act on it. If your boss pissed you off, do you have to blow up in his face—would that get you what you want? In the words of Aristotle, "Anybody can become angry—that is easy, but to be angry with the right person and to the right degree and at the right time and for the right purpose, and in the right way—that is not within everybody's power and is not easy."

It may not be easy, but the point is that it is entirely possible, and you can reposition anger as your ally. Imagine, on the simplest level, yourself saying, "Okay, anger—I see you. Now, what are you trying to tell me?" By listening to the message this powerful emotion is sharing, you will have a real advantage in knowing how to course correct so you can move toward your next level.

Strategies

Now, you may be saying, all that sounds good in theory, and I'm open to the idea, but what should I do when I am literally caught up in anger and it is holding me hostage? Here are some practical and proven strategies that can provide immediate help. The invitation is to see which ones resonate with you and try them out the next time that anger arises.

Disengage

When anger is rapidly escalating, the quickest solution is to walk away and say something like, "I need to cool down, let's talk later." By giving yourself time to re-center, you can get through your "amygdala moment," reengage with your calming cortex, and get back in the driver's seat. You can plan what comes out of your mouth and take care of finding the best solution to the issue. Note that if your tone is infused with contempt, you're probably not going to get anywhere. HOW you say it is as important as what you say.

Slow It Down

Psychologist John Riskind has developed a strategy to slow down your anger.

If you compare your anger to the speed of a car, at thirty-five miles per hour you are annoyed, at forty-five miles per hour you are getting irritated, at sixty miles per hour you are pissed off, and at eighty miles per hour you are enraged. Imagine you are putting your foot on the brake of a car to slow down your own reaction. Visualize yourself (and your anger level) moving from eighty miles per hour to sixty to thirty-five.[6] This way you not only avoid a potential crash, you actually create the opportunity to connect with the person in front of you, read their body language, and assess if this anger is even worth your time.[7]

Separate from the Trigger

Dr. Michael Levittan offers an interesting way to create some space so you can respond. Choose a level of how angry you are at this moment, one being the least amount of anger, and ten being the most. "Am I at six, or am I at nine?" Imagine putting your anger in a box with that number on the box, and seeing the box in front of you. This helps you recognize how you feel, separate the anger from the situation that triggered it, and pause.[8]

Now you are in a position to decide what you want to do with it. You've given yourself some breathing room and now have more freedom to choose your next step.

Get physical

Go for a run, walk it out, dance to some excellent music, and sometimes it helps to get in your room and scream (not at the person, though; that won't help you in your long-term goals!). The idea is to clear the adrenaline from your system and burn up the emotional energy before it burns you. Then you can regain your calm and carry on.

Breathe

Your grandmother was right. Taking some deep breaths can get you back to yourself. By holding the intention that you want to be calm, you can guide yourself back to the breath, even if your mind wanders. You might imagine yourself by the ocean and take a breath with each wave that comes in. Or try alternate nostril breathing, known as Nadi Shodhana, which is said to balance the two hemispheres of the brain.[9] In this way, you can prevent the spark of anger from igniting into a flame.

REACH OUT

Whether it is with a good friend or someone else you trust, find some time to let your feelings out. Let some pressure out of the pressure cooker. The point is to feel supported and at the same time see if you come up with new perspectives. You can also let your feelings out in a journal. We all have a wise self inside who is calm and knowing. Connect with that part of you to answer the question "What would you say to a good friend who was in that same situation?" You have more wisdom than you know.

FEEL IT TO LET IT GO

Where does the anger show up in your body? Is it a headache, your stomach in a knot, increased heart rate, or heat rising in your face? Rather than trying to make it go away, be with the feeling, as if you were taking care of a child who was hurting. Rather than trying to analyze it with your mind, just put your attention on the body sensations. You are observing the feelings, instead of being trapped in them. Soon you will feel the anger lose its charge and eventually dissipate.

WATCH THE CLOUD PASS BY

Emotions, as compared to moods, last for mere seconds. It's our thoughts that fuel them, enlarge them, and make them persist. See your anger as a dark cloud that may have cast a shadow over you but is in the process of moving past you. Anger is not who you are—it does not define you.

JOURNAL CHALLENGE

Write down three strategies for dealing with anger (from pages 188–191) that speak to you. Describe what upcoming situation you might try them in. Plan in your mind how they can help. If the situation arises, call on these strategies. Then take a moment to reflect on how they worked and why. You might want to explore something else next time or commit to implementing one of your favorites from the list. Experience by experience, you will become more aware not only of your triggers, but also how best to handle them.

To end this chapter, I want to share a story that is the most inspiring reaction to anger I have ever seen. If someone close to you had been shot, could you imagine yourself forgiving the shooter? Mary Johnson's twenty-year-old son was murdered by a sixteen-year-old who carried a gun. At the trial that followed, Mary said, "I wanted justice. He was an animal; he deserved to be caged."[10] As the years passed, Mary found herself consumed by hate and anger. One day she read a poem that inspired her to help other mothers whose children had been murdered. She knew that if there was even a chance of this coming to pass, she would have to meet with her son's killer, Oshea, who had been sentenced to twenty-five years behind bars in Minnesota state prison. Mary had to see for herself if forgiveness was even possible. "Unforgiveness is like cancer; it will eat you from the inside out. It's not about that other person. Me forgiving him does not diminish what he's done. Yes, he murdered my son, but the forgiveness is for me." In her first meeting Mary told Oshea, "I don't know you and you don't know me. You didn't know my son, and he didn't know you, so we need to lay down a foundation."[11] Mary began visiting Oshea regularly. Through that process, the anger and hate were gradually displaced by curiosity and even caring. When she discovered that Oshea would have no place to stay when he was released from prison, she arranged for Oshea to get an apartment in her own building. Oshea is now working at a recycling plant by day and going to college by night, determined to give back and to live up to the potential that Mary saw in him. He now speaks about forgiveness to large crowds in community centers and churches. And Mary wears a necklace with a picture of her son on one side and Oshea on the other. She calls Oshea her spiritual son, and they live right next door to each other. The effect of forgiveness is unforgettable.

START TO FORGIVE

Dr. Fred Luskin describes forgiveness as the feeling of peace that emerges in the present moment as you take your hurt less personally, take responsibility for how you feel, and become a hero instead of a victim in the story you tell.[12]

JOURNAL CHALLENGE

In your **journal**, write about one person or situation that keeps you stuck in anger.

* How has knowing this person challenged me to learn and develop?
* What insights do I have now as a result of interacting with them?

- Would I say that this lesson is complete?
- What would it take for me to be ready to move forward in my life?

Anger can be an instinctive volatile reaction or it can be a source of emotional information that focuses your attention to make you stronger, more determined, and more protective. Anger is one of the most powerful emotions, and using it wisely not only can make *your* life better, it can be a catalyst to move humanity forward. When people feel threatened, anger arises. When it is used consciously, it can restore stability, remove danger, and bring you back to your essential self, where you can feel secure enough to deepen your authenticity and come from love. Every insight you gain, perspective you expand, and activity you experience moves you closer to finding the advantages in each emotion and living more fully no matter what comes up. Trust that you are on your way.

Tolerance, Acceptance, and Empathy

When we know ourselves to be connected to all others,
acting compassionately is simply the natural thing to do.

— RACHEL NAOMI REMEN

TOLERANCE IS WIDELY REGARDED as something worth having, wouldn't you agree? Most people like to think of themselves as warmhearted, fair-minded, and wanting the best for others, and I entirely believe that to be true at the core level. Yet sometimes our behavior does not represent the values we espouse. What's up with that?

There is an underlying premise that we miss much of the time. Even though we are all connected as fellow human beings, there's a piece that eludes us in this outward-facing, sometimes crazy existence. We are all born as spiritual beings inhabiting a human body, and we are all fueled by the exact same life force. Think of a baby's first breath or the very last one before we return back to something greater. This energy is part of everyone and everything, and connects us all, whether we realize it or not. In this way, no matter if the place we are born into, the body we inhabit, the skin tones we are given have nothing in common, internally we are more alike than we are different. It's only when fear comes into the picture that it drags along the idea that we are all separate from one another and from the energy that gives us all life. This is not the truth, as this energy lives and breathes through all of us. But forgetting this level of deep connection, often as soon as we are born, we buy into the illusion that we are indeed separate.

But to take a more day-to-day view of what we are increasingly seeing, it's hard to ignore that the signs of intolerance and prejudice are in the air. Though we may want to see the best in people, all too easily the glaze of our unrecognized biases can blur our vision, prompting us to see life through the lens of separation. We end up noticing our differences rather than our similarities, and it's everywhere we turn. You've probably overheard statements like "I can't deal with those types, they are not our kind of people, so bigoted, so judgmental, too rough around the edges, too smooth, too awkward, too pushy, too (fill in your own adjective)," all meaning "They are not like us!"

This sense of separation is magnified every day. We just have to look at the media: for every one uplifting story that highlights harmony, there are countless others that inject alarm. Intolerance stems from fear of "the other" . . . the fear of being with strangers we don't trust, in situations that could be dangerous, in times that are insecure. This fear of danger brings out a tribalism that's rooted in our primal quest for safety. It's pretty simple: if we stick with our kind, we will be protected. This leads people to want to stay with their own groups and serves as a validation for "us versus them" thinking. We live in an era of sanctioned divisiveness, justified by collective fear.

This fear is pervasive and easily morphs into prejudice. Do you know anyone who is, shall we say, "highly opinionated"? This energy could revolve around politics, that's a given, but it could also show up around favorite sports teams, or the people they welcome as friends. Sally Kohn, author of *The Opposite of Hate*, comments in an interview that when she was researching her book, "Talking to neo-Nazis and talking to terrorists, people think their motivation is fundamentally good, by and large . . . No one thinks they're hateful. No one wants to be hateful."[1] Too often, people react to what they perceive as the hate of others . . . and then nobody wins.

"Prejudice" is related to the word "prejudge." Do you have a friend or coworker who often makes a judgment *before* they have the facts, before they have the full picture, and most important, before they truly know the individuals involved? Chances are that they are judging this circumstance according to past references (usually not even firsthand) that may not even relate to the specific situation. As we know, in an atmosphere of apprehension, hurt and hate can spread like a wildfire. People hate *when* they are hurt, when they are afraid, and when they feel separate from a sense of security that they will be okay.

In this chapter we will look at the two layers of intolerance: either for others or for aspects of ourselves. We'll look at the difference between tolerance and acceptance, and how to have more *self*-acceptance now. We'll also explore how tolerance relates to empathy, the various types of empathy, and how they can add a level of connection that deepens every relationship we encounter. Ready—let's go!

JOURNAL CHALLENGE

Sometimes it seems that a situation is the cause, and other times we judge a relationship that constantly presses our buttons. If you are being repeatedly triggered, there may be something unresolved in you that is getting inflamed. In the words of Dr. Shefali Tsabary, **"The thunders of your now arise from the storms of your past."** Here's the question: Could these judgments you're feeling also be messages about something *you* need to look at within yourself?

In your **journal**, write down all the thoughts that arise.

What Is a Tolerant Person?

Tolerance is defined as "sympathy or indulgence for beliefs or practices differing or conflicting with one's own."[2] Basically, we are willing and able to tolerate opinions or behavior that we don't necessarily agree with.

In a climate surging with conflict, it takes a strong-minded person to remain tolerant. It takes character, strength, composure, and confidence to make up one's own mind and not to be swayed by fear-based manipulations. When we realize that we all have the capacity to act with kindness or cruelty, then it becomes harder to spiral into a state of raging blame. A tolerant person can manage their emotions, not be run by them. We recognize them by their inner poise.

Tolerance for Beliefs

Imagine a world where there is respect for the spectrum of backgrounds, customs, preferences, and habits that make life both diverse and fascinating. There would be a celebration of differences: the colors, musical styles, culinary flavors, fashion, architecture, rituals, and sacred moments for all races and genders, especially as we move toward a more fluid and cross-cultural time. People would constantly be seeing new things, getting new perspectives, and knowing firsthand that our differences are not merely to be tolerated; they are to be celebrated.

This world would be about looking for the gems in others, not putting up walls in anticipation of the next attack. We would not be taught to fear "the other" but to do a gut check when we meet new people, no matter their background; we'd trust our intuition and inner resources and so stand unafraid to remain open-minded and warmhearted. In this world, we'd understand that we have much more in common than what would seem to separate us, and that our shared humanity is a core principle we choose to live by. An ideal world? Yes. But if we look inside at our core values, this is not that far removed from what most people want.

So how do we get to tolerance? We know that tolerance stems from expanded thinking, from opening ourselves up to new approaches, other ways of looking at things, and the spaciousness to have room for all of it. The expression "we agree to disagree" says it well, and skills like nonviolent communication can be game changers. Even if we don't see things the exact same way, I respect that you can have your own perspective, and you respect that I can have mine. We cannot expect to be of the same

TOLERANT	INTOLERANT
Accepts differences; we're all part of our humanity	Fear of differences; "they" threaten our safety
Inclusive thinking, open-minded	Us/them thinking, singular perspective
Nonreactive, emotions collected	Reactive, emotions agitated
Civility, "live and let live" attitude	Personal judgment, critical attitude
Wants the best for all	Wants the best for the group they identify with

mind in all things; that would be dull anyway, but we can come together on many topics like the importance of friends and family, the beauty of nature, the exhilaration of love.

Think of it as a tree. The leaves represent our differences: in eye color, skin tone, food preferences, holidays we celebrate, music we love, and so on. But the inner rings of the trunk are the human needs that we all share: to be loved, to belong, to be respected, and to be safe. At Project Happiness, we teach this to elementary school students—if a six-year-old can get it, then there is hope for everyone.

How Does Intolerance Arise?

Intolerance, according to the *Oxford Dictionary*, is the "unwillingness to accept views, beliefs, or behavior that differ from one's own." It is expressed through bigotry, and it can be hard to miss. But there is another side that is even more subtle. That side is judgment. No one likes to think of themselves as judgmental (it's righteous indignation!), but there are so many everyday situations that can be downright challenging. If you've ever felt frustration about a coworker who never gets an important point, even after you have explained it to them time and time again, you know what this is like. Maybe it's a friend who is late all the time, no matter how often you have explained how it bothers you, or what about someone in your family who is so whiny that you could swear they take delight in their own complaining? Perhaps you've been in a series of relationships that looked great at first but always reveal some startling flaw in the other person later on.

Yes, these all say something about the person you are judging, but at the same time, especially if it's a pattern, it may also be signaling that this involves a deeper part of you.

Judging Others and Avoiding Ourselves

When we judge others or notice that a person is constantly upsetting us, it can be a sign that we are projecting onto them an aspect of ourself that we have rejected or have no use for. Could it be that we are accusing them of the exact traits that we refuse to see within ourself?

Relationship experts Katie and Gay Hendricks describe it this way.[3] Say you have a fear of rejection from childhood. Chances are you either are not fully aware of this fear or you have pushed it aside. But even though your conscious mind is in denial, your subconscious is on high alert, always scanning the horizon for chances to work out this buried problem. Because of that, you'll enter a new relationship that activates this unresolved issue inside of you. On one level, some part of you understands this is a lesson that you need to resolve and goes to great lengths to do that.

The Hendrickses explain that even when a new relationship looks promising and this partner seems nothing like the last one, the unresolved dramas will play out—it's not a question of *if*, it is *when*. Once the blush of new romance has faded, you discover that s/he is not as emotionally available as you'd like. Whether it's their super-demanding job or awkward communication style, the end result is that you feel left out, rejected, replaying emotions from childhood. It hurt then, and it brings up old fears even now: "I can't help but feel so rejected, I'm worried about ending up alone." Since the underlying emotion of rejection is too uncomfortable to accept and deal with, it is much easier to criticize your partner ("There s/he is again, always doing their thing, never thinking of me or all the stuff that needs to be done—I'm so mad!").

The ego's solution is to push you to project your frustration and pain onto others, rather than dealing with it directly. Being intolerant of others is a signal that you may be secretly intolerant of some aspect of yourself. Some call it your shadow; it's that part of yourself that you have never been comfortable expressing . . . the part that is suppressed, buried, locked away . . . not dealing with that anytime soon! And that is exactly the reason why it shows up again and again in different forms.

What to do? Instead of replaying the dramas of unresolved emotions, the solution requires the courage to look inside yourself and receive rather than reject the parts that were hurt, frightened, or felt unsafe. By welcoming even the not-so-pretty feelings, you are learning to love and accept *yourself* at a new level. Although accepting yourself is a building block to loving and accepting others, this really has nothing to do with them—it's about you coming to peace with parts of yourself that you, up to this time, would rather not see.

Gay Hendricks recounts how at one point in his life, not realizing that he needed more love and acceptance, he ended up criticizing his ex-wife for being too critical and too emotional. He explains, "The truth was, I was out of touch with my own feelings. I wasn't 'sensitive' enough to what my mind and my heart wanted and needed. Therefore, I projected those unacknowledged aspects of myself onto others. I was secretly judgmental."[4]

Have you noticed that those who are the most judgmental of others secretly judge themselves the harshest, specifically that disowned part of themselves that they'd rather not see? In that way, intolerance is like a magic mirror, showing us what needs to be healed in order to live out the fullest and most loving expression of who we are. Here's an exercise to bring this to life:

JOURNAL CHALLENGE

- In your **journal**, in the first column, write down the name and traits of someone who bothers you the most. What is it about them—write down everything you can think of.

   Here's an example—"I have a friend who seems so helpless. I always have to help her out. She's argumentative, needy, demanding, and petulant." Write down what really bothers you about your person.

- In the next column, ask yourself if there are aspects of these traits that you have not acknowledged in yourself,

(cont'd)

perhaps a part of you that you have not been able to voice? In this example, there is a part of me that would like to have someone take care of me, too, and it would be fun to be able to rant once in a while instead of always being the one to find a solution. From this I can realize that while I am judging my friend, in truth I am projecting onto her *my* unmet need for support. It's a sore spot for me, and that's precisely why I find her so damn annoying!

- Finally, in the third column, describe one small thing you can do to move toward having your needs met. Make a call, a plan, an appointment? I for one can get some support, instead of always giving it, and befriend my own feelings instead of ignoring them.

The good news is that now that you are aware of it, you can take one action toward getting what you need to move forward. From an issue that was hidden, you now understand the dynamic and with that new knowledge can make the choice to take your next step. Try this—it may be awkward at first, but you are actively releasing energy that has held you back. It takes enormous effort to keep those old patterns in place. Notice how much more freedom you feel.

The Difference Between Tolerance and Acceptance

Tolerance has aspects of the Golden Rule: treat others as you would have them treat you. It is a "live and let live" mentality, regardless of what biases you harbor. It is also the basis for living in a civil society and bringing out the best in one another. Call it "Being Human 101."

Acceptance amps it up even more to include a warmth and a welcoming of the "other," being accepting of their choices, including how they choose to express themselves, how they identify gender-wise, and who they choose to love. We can also accept people's choices and not share their same perspective; that happens all the time. If a parent found out their daughter was dating someone from another religion, while it might not be a big deal for some families, it can be a highly charged issue for others. Yet the parents can still be tolerant of their daughter's new love and act in a way that is civil and polite.

But you can imagine how their daughter hopes for the person she loves to be not just tolerated but welcomed warmly into her family. Acceptance, more than just tolerance, makes people feel like they belong. It turns strangers into friends. The mind wants tolerance, but the heart longs for acceptance.

TOLERANCE	ACCEPTANCE
Live and let live. We can coexist.	Welcome to my world.
Treat others as you would have them treat you.	Not only do I treat you as I'd be like to be treated, I think you are okay.
On principle, I am tolerant of a group or an individual—this is an objective feeling rather than a personal one.	Acceptance is more personal: I accept you as you are, no matter what choices you make in your life.

Self-Acceptance

Another aspect of acceptance goes beyond accepting others; it is about accepting yourself. Self-acceptance is about appreciating the person you are right now, perfectly imperfect as we all are supposed to be, and 100 percent deserving of love. If you find yourself repeatedly putting yourself down, with the critic's voice whispering "You're too inexperienced, too tired, too fed up, too sad, too reactive, or too afraid to make a move . . . ," realize that just by being aware of that well-worn script, you can now reexamine the old beliefs that gave it power. Allow yourself to accept that all your facets are assets that make you unique (your strong legs power you to where you need to go, your strong will and ingrained tenacity make sure you get there). Accept how all your feelings are delivering valuable information. If you are a sensitive person, you have a greater capacity to love—that's an exceptional gift, certainly not a liability. Gather all these gems, and you will come to realize how many resources you have to work with in designing the life you deserve.

AWARENESS OF OLD SCRIPTS + SELF-APPRECIATION + ACCEPTANCE OF FEELINGS = SELF-ACCEPTANCE

Self-acceptance also influences how we handle the way life is unfolding. We are always facing new plot twists, and there are many times when what we expect does not show up as envisioned. That's when self-doubt can creep in and we can start to question the past decisions we've made. Are you stuck in a story that continues to diminish you, one where you feel foolish about past decisions or have regrets about the way your life has evolved? Is that, like a weight chained to your ankle, holding you back from stepping forward with a new dream, new idea, new inspiration? When you can't accept the past, it's hard to step fully into the future.

The antidote is to look at it with new eyes. Can you accept that you have learned something valuable throughout that process? With what you know now, would you approach something similar in a different way? Can you recognize that going through that situation has strengthened your clarity and resolve? Do you feel greater gratitude that you are now better positioned to make different choices, based on what makes you feel most aligned? By virtue of going through that situation, you now have new information and new strategies. The truth is the person you are now is not the same person that you once were. You may decide to treat people well or let something go not because of who they are, but because of who *you* are.

Perhaps you can see deeper into someone who had hurt you and recognize that they were in pain, too—it was not necessarily personal. This is when Don Miguel Ruiz's "Four Agreements" come in handy.[5] They remind us to:

1. Be impeccable with your word.
2. Don't take anything personally.
3. Don't make assumptions.
4. Always do your best.

Imagine if we just focused on Agreement 2: "Don't take anything personally." You never know what happened to someone that day, that year, or while growing up. How can we judge them? If people present themselves as intimidating now, imagine them as little children (literally visualize them as toddlers)—

everyone is trying to be accepted and loved. Each person you meet has something to show you. We learn as we grow.

If you can accept that even in the face of challenges things happen *for* you rather than *to* you, then you immediately give up the victim mind-set, reconnect with your strong core, and have the ability to look at your options with the greater insight that only experience can bring. Accept that life is your teacher.

Accept—then act. Whatever the present moment contains, accept it as if you had chosen it. Always work with it, not against it. Make it your friend and ally, not your enemy. This will miraculously transform your whole life.

—ECKHART TOLLE

Then choose to focus on thoughts that give you energy and hope, as well as plans that empower you, excite you, and reflect what you stand for.

How Tolerance, Acceptance, and Empathy Work Together

Tolerance creates a template (similar to the Golden Rule) for humanity to coexist, and acceptance fosters a welcoming spirit and brings us closer, but empathy can bring out the best within us.

Empathy is simply the ability to walk in another's shoes, to imagine what it would feel like to be in their position, and to look at life through their eyes. It also helps open understanding, dissolve divides, and create meaningful connections. Empathy is one of the cornerstones of emotional intelligence. Being aware of the emotions and states of others through recognizing their body language, expressions, and unspoken cues is a definite advantage in forging more meaningful connections. People who are empathic are less judgmental, less irritated, enjoy better relationships, and are generally happier. Sounds all right to me!

Types of Empathy

Empathy has different aspects, and to get the full picture, it's important to consider them all. *New York Times* bestselling authors of *The Yes Brain*, Daniel Siegel and Tina Payne Bryson, talk about the "empathy diamond," which explores the five facets of expressing empathy to help others and ourselves. When going through each one, think of a situation when you experienced this type of empathy and take a few seconds to remember how it touched you.

1. **Perspective taking:** Seeing the world through the eyes of another
2. **Emotional resonance:** Feeling the feelings of another
3. **Cognitive empathy:** Understanding intellectually another's overall experience
4. **Compassionate empathy:** Sensing suffering and wanting to reduce it
5. **Empathic joy:** Experiencing delight with the happiness, achievements, and well-being of another[6]

When going through each one, think of a situation when you experienced this type of empathy and take a few seconds to remember how it touched you.

1. PERSPECTIVE TAKING: SEEING THE WORLD THROUGH THE EYES OF ANOTHER

This is pretty straightforward—it has to do with imagining you are seeing through someone else's eyes—what would you notice, how would you experience your day, what would you be challenged by, and why?

2. EMOTIONAL RESONANCE: FEELING THE FEELINGS OF ANOTHER

According to Paul Ekman, author of *Emotions Revealed*, empathy can play out in two ways.[7] If you are feeling distressed when another feels pain (think of a parent whose child just got bullied), that is called **identical resonance**—you put yourself in their shoes and understand what they feel. In this judgment-free zone, you are highly connected to each other, feeling *with* them. One caveat: during that time, just be mindful not to take on all their stresses as if they were your own. Remember that your ability to help them will be compromised if you are disabled by their pain. You want to still maintain your own sense of self and your own feelings, while mindfully being fully present for theirs.

Reactive resonance is if you express pity or sympathy ("Oh, you poor thing—what can I do?"). You are expressing caring and concern, but because the distress is not shared, you are not really feeling *with* them. It implies a subtle hierarchy—you're in a good space and they are struggling.

3. COGNITIVE EMPATHY: UNDERSTANDING INTELLECTUALLY ANOTHER'S OVERALL EXPERIENCE

When your mind understands someone else's overall experience, it does not necessarily mean that you feel the same way.

Chris Voss, a former FBI kidnapping lead negotiator and author of *Never Split the Difference*[8] writes, "As a hostage negotiator, I could listen empathically to anyone, even terrorists, once I realized that understanding and articulating someone's viewpoint is not the same as agreeing with it."[9] This type of empathy is mental rather than heartfelt.

4. Compassionate Empathy: Sensing Suffering and Wanting to Reduce It

This brings in the element of action—not only do you understand what someone is feeling, you sense their suffering and care enough to want to actually do something to help. This heart-driven quality can be felt for one person, a group, or toward humanity.

5. Empathic Joy: Delight with the Happiness, Achievements, and Well-being of Another

You are happy when others get the promotion, achieve a goal, bring home a new puppy, find love, recover from an illness, and so on. Their happiness is your happiness.

Depending on the situation, you may draw from one type of empathy or another or even a combination. All these types of empathy play a role in having a meaningful and engaged life. When we learn to understand and share in the feelings of another, we act in ways that lead to better relationships, deeper friendships, and stronger communities. Empathy is one of the most powerful ways to bring us closer.

How to Bring More Empathy
into Your Life

The good news is that empathy is not a trait that we were born with or not. It is actually a skill that can be taught. Empathy is also a way to reduce bullying at the root cause, wherever it shows up: the schoolyard, office politics, or in everyday life.

Here are five proven steps to cultivate empathy that we have used in schools across the United States and many other countries—and they are good for any age. Anyone interested in emotional intelligence can benefit greatly by looking into these steps.

- **Watch and listen:** What are the words the other person is saying, and what message is coming from their body language?
- **Remember:** Was there a time when you felt a similar way?
- **Imagine:** Look beneath the surface and tap into how the other person might feel. If you were in their shoes, how would you feel?
- **Ask:** Check in with the person directly and ask, "In this moment, what are you feeling?"
- **Show you care:** Let them know you care through your words and actions.

This process leads us to tune in to what another person is saying through both words expressed and words unsaid. The body also delivers much information, provided we know how to read it. Extra bonus points if you notice: Is the person gazing directly or averting their eyes; if they are smiling, is it just through the mouth area, or are the eyes involved, too? Is the posture turning away or toward; is the body relaxed or rigid? Are the hands composed or fidgety? Is the stance wide or contracted? Even without the words, what type of energy is the other person communicating, and do the words match up with what the body is saying? Sometimes you can tell if someone is having a bad day just by the way they carry themselves and by the energy they bring into the room. Everyone can develop the capacity to notice these aspects, if we pay attention.

When we remember times we've ever felt a similar way, we tap into our own memory banks of experience. It doesn't have to be the same exact situation, but something with a similar emotional tone. If you say to yourself, "That kind of reminds me of how I felt when . . ." you are tapping into this aspect of empathy.

By imagining how that person must feel, we visualize what it would be like to see through their eyes. That helps us get a sense of who they are, what they want, and why it's important. We can imagine what led them to this place, how they feel on the inside as compared to what they portray on the outside. Pay attention to your gut feelings—this is where your intuition can play a vital role.

Asking directly what the other person is feeling gives them an opportunity to voice what is actually going on from their perspective. Do they ask you for help? Do they need to get out of the situation? Are there others they can count on, too? Whether they say a lot or very little, this is an opportunity for an important reality check.

The person who steps in and shows they care, whether by lending an ear or encouraging them to figure out the next steps, can help that person feel more supported, connected, and safe.

It takes courage to stand up for someone else, especially if there is group pressure to look the other way. This can make all the difference. Sometimes one kind word or empathic gesture can restore a sense of connection, dignity, and hope in a critical moment. The more we focus on empathy and use it in daily situations, the more others can pick up the cues as well.

JOURNAL CHALLENGE

In your **journal**, write down the five steps to cultivate empathy. Think of a situation where they might come in handy or reflect on a past situation where they could have helped. Allow yourself to coach yourself on some ways you will approach a challenging situation going forward.

Language of Empathy

There is a language for empathy that shows people you are there for them, and this too can be taught. Most people may think the best way to help another is by suggesting a "solution" to their problem or by presenting a silver lining ("Sure your house burned down, but at least you have insurance"). Although well-intentioned, that is usually not what they need most, and it may even make them feel worse. By truly empathizing and "feeling with" them, saying something like "That must be so hard—sorry you had to go through that. I am here for you," you help them feel the warmth of true connection, which is usually what they need the most.

We Are Interconnected

Dan Siegel emphasizes that teaching empathy is not just about looking at life through the eyes of another and understanding how they feel. That is one part. The other has to do with developing a brain that is oriented toward caring for other people. He further explains that this elevates our presence "toward living a life full of meaning, connection, and belonging to a larger whole."[10] The role of empathy in the brain is to remind us that we are not just single operators on this planet, but interconnected to everyone else as well.

In this chapter we have seen how tolerance, acceptance, and empathy work hand in hand to give us the structure, attitude, and skill set to architect a better world. They provide the pillars for a life full of respect, caring, and mutual support.

We are connected in profound ways. What would seem to divide us is actually what can bring us closer, as we recognize that so-called enemies are actually our greatest teachers. In our reaction to them, we discover the fragmented parts of ourselves that need some tenderness and care. They offer the lesson that we are all connected in our need for love and acceptance. We all have the capacity to develop these qualities within ourselves and inevitably influence those around us. This is my hope and call to action—that we can intentionally, through knowing ourselves and healing our own emotions, make the choice to bring out the best in ourselves and one another.

Thich Nhat Hanh says it beautifully: "We are here to awaken from the illusion of our separateness." If you are reading this chapter, you are already on your way.

Guilt and Shame

Guilt is the toothache of the soul.

—TOMMY COTTON

GUILT—NOBODY WANTS IT; REALLY, who would ever choose to feel this way? But what if I told you that guilt could be your silent supporter? No, I don't mean enemy, I mean ally. The sound of guilt is your inner wisdom's clarion call to help you reset your course. Guilt can be your inner reminder, a message from you to you that you may be steering away from your moral compass and acting in a way that is not in line with your core values. It gives you the opportunity to reflect on your actions and make a positive change.

In this chapter, we'll take a tour of guilt and its cousin, shame. Starting with guilt, we'll explore the best way to say you're sorry and what motivates different types of people to feel guilty. Discover where you stand. Then we'll move on to three types of guilt that can keep us stuck: unresolved guilt, survival guilt, and loyalty guilt. Guilt trip, anyone? You'll see some

effective strategies to deal. And if you think guilt and shame are
the same, you're in for a surprise. We'll dig into the difference
between these two emotions and introduce seven action steps to
navigate through these muddy waters so you can get out safely on
the other side.

The Upside of Guilt

Addressing guilt can be one of the quickest ways that you
can learn from your mistakes and move forward. If you have
behaved in a way that hurt someone, guilt has the power to get
you back on track. Simply stated: you did something you're not
proud of, you feel remorse, and instead of blaming others, you
want to clean up your act. You take this on as your responsibility (forget the blame game), and it is within your control to deal
with it.

Let's say you overheard some gossip about a friend. Instead
of confronting the gossipers ("Hey, what's up? She's just doing
her best") *you* spread the rumor to another group of friends as a
way to get closer to them. It's a human tendency. . . . But afterward, you feel upset with your actions. Instead of disregarding,
rationalizing, or burying that feeling, there is a part of you that
is yelling that hurting someone else, saying the wrong thing, or
saying nothing when you could have spoken up is not who you
are. It's not what you stand for, and it's not how you want to show
up in the world. That's actually a good thing: not only is your
conscience talking to you, you are hearing the message.

What to do? The solution is to course correct, and the
faster you can do it, the less guilt will dangle like a too-heavy

pendant around your neck. You'll feel a sense of relief as you make amends. Bonus points if you ask yourself "What is the lesson that this situation is trying to teach me?"

Most people would advise you to just say you're sorry. As children we were taught "Just say you're sorry; apologize and it will be over." But *how* you do it matters. To get the most benefit out of an already uncomfortable situation, when you do say you are sorry, it will help you move on and make a difference to the other person only if you mean it. One of the most direct ways is to really put yourself in their shoes. Imagine for a moment what they felt like and how the incident may have shaken their confidence and clarity. If you could imagine yourself as them, how would you have felt in that situation? With that insight and empathy, you can be sure that your message will be authentic and meaningful. Can't you always tell if an apology is real or if it's just empty words?

The good news is that it's never too late to say you are sorry. Though we all have guilt from time to time, people suffering from addictions may see it more than most. They have a certain level of experience in this area. It turns out that not one but two steps of the Twelve-Step Program have to do with making amends:

1. Made a list of persons we had harmed, and became willing to make amends to them all.
2. Made direct amends to such people wherever possible, except when to do so would injure them or others.[1]

The impetus to make amends can come years after the incidents that incited the feelings of guilt, and it doesn't matter.

The point is that you become aware of the people you have hurt, and you care. People are often so caught up in their own issues, so burdened by their own problems, that they don't fully realize they have done something that has hurt someone else. So having the awareness that something is off and the intention to do something is where it all starts.

From that new level of understanding, you can take action to apologize and so release your thoughts and energy from being stuck in the unfortunate things that you did. Now you know better.

Making amends takes it one step further than a verbal apology. It includes taking responsibility for the fallout and putting effort into trying to make it right. That action move could be repaying an old debt or repairing something that was broken. In an extreme case, if someone was responsible for a car accident that resulted in a fatality, they might decide to become an organ donor. Though they cannot bring back the life that was lost, they can potentially save another one.

This abiding intention works on two levels: first, through reflection and awareness, you are bringing your feelings to the surface. In that way you are stopping your own internal festering, and you are doing something that you can be proud of. Secondly, you are helping the healing process of the people you have hurt. Healing times two.

Whether you offer an apology or take action to make amends, you cannot control how or if others will accept your offer . . . but do it anyway. If you approach them sincerely, from your heart, that's all you can do, and knowing you have tried your best is good enough.

JOURNAL CHALLENGE

In your **journal**, describe a time when you felt guilty. If you made amends then, how did it make you feel, and how did it affect the relationship? If you have not made amends yet, are you willing to look at that now? What would be your first step?

What Motivates You to Feel Guilty?

Why does guilt even come up? Have you ever noticed that when you felt guilty over some incident, your friend might have seen it in a totally different way? People can approach the very same situation with very different mind-sets and perspectives. This leads to some deeper questions: What motivates us to behave in the ways we do? And how do we rationalize that behavior? Our *motivation* and how we justify it has a lot to do with whether we feel guilt in a given situation or not. What makes one person feel guilty doesn't even touch someone else. How are you wired?

Psychologist Lawrence Kohlberg[2] tackled this question through a research experiment he set up. Participants were asked about their reactions to a complex situation. See how you would respond to this dilemma:

Sam is beside himself because his wife is running a high fever, and it appears that she could die. He runs to the doctor in his small town, who suggests a special form of radium that one druggist has developed. Apparently, though it cost the druggist two hundred dollars to make, he is charging two thousand. Sam doesn't have near the amount required. He begs the druggist to accept the money he has on hand and the rest on a payment plan. The pharmacist cannot do it, as then he'd have to make exceptions for everyone. Desperate, Sam raises half the cost from his neighbors, but it's still not enough, and time is running out. That night, he decides no matter what, he has to get his wife the medicine. He does something he's never done before—he breaks in after the store has closed and steals the medicine, which reverses his wife's conditions and brings her back to health.

Most people might do the same thing, but according to Kohlberg, who asked thousands of people in his study not what Sam should have done but "What *motivated* Sam to do what he did?" the research study participants came up with six main reasons to justify Sam's action. These were sorted into three categories (listed below), basically explaining why people do what they do.

As you read through them, ask yourself which of the reasons below resonates most strongly with you.

1. Obedience: What we do is based on *personal* fears and desires, usually to avoid being punished or to get rewards.

This level of motivation revolves around what *you* decide to do, rather than the rules that society imposes. It was personally important for Sam to get the medicine for his wife. He didn't want to steal; that was not his nature. Though he probably felt guilty and tried his best to find another way, he felt forced into a situation where he had to take a stand. Besides, he had offered to pay the two hundred dollars, which was the real cost of the medicine, and the druggist had refused. Even though the druggist would probably call the police (the punishment), Sam had to act to save his wife.

Have you ever felt guilty because you decided to take on something that normally you would not even consider? What if your boss asked you to do something somewhat unethical?[3] If you felt an inner conflict, would you tend to go with what your boss asked of you (he might fire you otherwise), while knowing in your heart that something about it felt wrong? Or if this was a repetitive pattern, making you lose sleep and feel stressed out, would you check in with your values and say no? Anyone who has been in this situation has grappled with this type of guilt.

Rewards: Other people are motivated to do something because they want to enjoy the benefits and rewards, period. You might agree that if Sam was motivated by the incentive of enjoying more years with his wife, then that would be enough of a reason to do what he did. But doing something for your own self-interest can be complex, too. What about exaggerating your skill sets in a job interview or inhaling all the best chocolates from that brand-new box? Did you feel regret afterward, or can you justify your decision and feel good about it? Each circumstance is different, but one of the best things guilt can teach you is to check in with yourself.

As we explore motivation and doing what *you* desire, let's clarify that *self*-care is anything but selfish. It's actually quite the opposite. Taking care of your energy, whether it's physical, mental, emotional, or spiritual, is one of the most responsible things you can do. By replenishing yourself, you have more of you to share with others. When you are feeling less frazzled, you'll actually become more productive, too. Do *not* feel guilty about calendaring some time for you! Whether it's a walk, a run, a yoga class, or a power nap, whether it's scheduling time to read a book, meditate, or just do nothing at all, you need to allow yourself some time to decompress. Even an intentional fifteen minutes a day can make a huge difference. Book in this guilt-free time—it will refresh you, renew your energy, and allow you some precious breathing room. Hint: unless you put it on your calendar, it will be the first thing that you will compromise. Honor this revitalizing time just as you would a doctor's appointment. Think of it as preventative medicine for the soul.

2. The second category of motivation is driven by what *other* people think or do. Some people give a lot of value to social approval and some feel most at ease when abiding by society's rules.

Conformity: Let's say Sam knew that not only did he want to help his wife get through this, but if he did not steal that drug, his wife's parents and family would never let him forget it . . . ever. If you've been in a situation where you felt enormous social pressure to take a certain path, even if it was not your first choice, you will be familiar with this type of guilt. Social pressure is real. Groupthink is very persuasive. Giving in to it can sometimes feel like the path of least resistance, and because of that, the better choice.

Minding the law: On the other hand, there are those who stand by the letter of the law and who would condemn Sam for breaking it. The druggist would be in this category. He believes that if he had to make exceptions for every hard-luck story, he wouldn't even have a pharmacy to run. He firmly believes that rules exist for a purpose—they keep society running.

Peer pressure from family, friends, or colleagues is real. If it is used to lift people up for team building or, for example, to rally some friends to provide meals to someone recovering from an illness, that's awesome. However, if someone is putting a guilt trip on you to live by their values (like when and who to marry) or to impose other archaic "rules" that don't align with your values, then have a discerning eye. As the saying goes, "Don't let anyone 'should' on you."

Another downside is when peer pressure turns into bullying. Say someone at your school or workplace was being singled out for something you knew they did not do: Would your guilt tell you to step in and say something? Or would your concern about being the next one on the chopping block prevent you from doing what you thought was right? How about if you noticed someone doing something unethical at your job? Should you blow the whistle and report the injustice, or have your teammate's back and look the other way? Go for justice or go for loyalty?

Every situation is different, but these are interesting questions to ask. When it feels like a no-win situation and you think that the best path in that particular situation is to do something against your better judgment, remember to build in some self-compassion. This type of thing is not easy. You are doing your best to find an answer. The main question is what can you learn from the situation, and how, in the future, this knowledge can inform your life. If you allow it, as you go forward, your guilt can guide you to an action that flows with your values.

3. The third category of motivation has a moral imperative. Some people are motivated because of a higher calling: they stand for helping to create a system that honors individual rights, or follows time-tested universal principles, such as kindness or the sacredness of life.

Human rights: If Sam was motivated by this category, he would be thinking that there's no way he's letting his wife die just because the pharmaceutical companies and the law are standing up for such enormous profits. That is just flat-out wrong; everyday people need and deserve better care! And besides, his wife has a right to live—he would do it for her.

Universal ethics: There's also the universal philosophy that all life should be regarded as sacred, so society's laws are not the highest court in these types of situations anyway.

In reading all of these, do you think that you are generally motivated by personal desires, social constructs, or universal values? While all these motivations have their time and place, there are occasions when you can move up in category. If you have felt guilt for looking out for yourself only and did something to repair the hurt, you may find yourself opening to actions you could take to make it better for others, too. If you experienced guilt around social bullying, you might be motivated to take a stand to protect others from that same sort of thing. Guilt can be a magnificent teacher. As we integrate this emotion's lessons, we can become more attuned to what works not only for us, but for the greater good as well.

How Guilt Can Keep Us Stuck

There are two kinds of guilt: the kind that drowns you until
you're useless, and the kind that fires your soul to purpose.

—SABAA TAHIR

Guilt can call on your conscience and help mend personal relationships, but if it is not dealt with, it can expand to the point of keeping us stuck in an unhealthy place. Let's explore the three types of guilt to watch out for in relationships: unresolved guilt, survival guilt, and separation (or disloyalty) guilt. These forms of guilt are felt *within* a person, instead of from an external source. Each has its own spin and its own challenges, but with awareness, each can also move us closer to our best version of ourselves.

Unresolved guilt, the kind that lingers like a low-grade temperature, always below the surface, always making you feel encumbered, actually takes up space in your thoughts. Think of it as real estate that could otherwise be used for creativity, joy, and fulfillment. You may feel dragged down and not even know why. One way out is to face the situation head-on and use your best efforts to apologize and make amends. If unresolved guilt is ignored or suppressed, even if it is not addressed, both people involved know it, and it creates a tension in the room. Eventually, it will impact how we behave around a particular person, and in some cases it even causes friends or families to take sides. A sincere attempt to apologize and improve communication can do wonders to help move the situation along. But when people are more polarized, consider having a neutral person involved as a mediator. When you know you have tried everything you can, it's time to reclaim your life. Give yourself full permission to move on.

The second type of guilt, **survival guilt**, is what we feel when we have prevailed while someone close to us has perished. When parents lose a child in a car accident ("It should have been me"), when one person keeps a job while the whole department is laid off ("I'm a single person—I could find something else; they have families to take care of"), when a grad student studies in the United States while there is a bombing in her country and family members die ("How could I be chasing my selfish dream when my family is facing death?"), when one sibling is healthy and the other has a severe disability ("How come I get to have this life, and he will be in a wheelchair forever?"), the ones who are thriving can feel tremendous guilt. This is not something you are in control of. As Guy Winch notes in his book *Emotional First Aid*, "What makes survivor guilt especially hard to purge is that there are no actions for which we must atone, no relationship ruptures to mend, and no outstanding apologies to be rendered."

One thing that may help is to question who is really responsible. If there was social unrest, a natural disaster, or a debilitating disease, it's important to remember that though you wish there were a different result, you are not responsible for what occurred. One perspective that has helped me is that though often we cannot figure out all its reasons, life has its own master plan. The inevitable truth is that we are all going to die. But right here and right now, we are here for a reason.

Allow yourself the space to grieve, and if symptoms of PTSD (feeling easily startled, vigilant, on edge, and isolated)[4] emerge, get professional help. Try to remember that you are not alone, even if it feels that way.

It is hard to even make sense of it, especially when loved ones have been hurt or lost. The challenge is to eventually move from that place of personal sadness to open your perspective up to include others and ultimately use your energy to pay it forward.

One of the best ways of getting through the pain and dealing with the guilt is by living one's life to the fullest *in honor* of the one you have survived. After the mass shooting at Sandy Hook Elementary School, several family members who faced unthinkable loss turned their pain into action by creating Sandy Hook Promise, a national nonprofit dedicated to spreading awareness. "Our intent is to honor all victims of gun violence by turning our tragedy into a moment of transformation by providing programs and practices that protect children . . . and prevent the senseless, tragic loss of life."[6] No one dreams of being propelled to take on something like this. I'm sure the parents who lost their children would have preferred to have them still by their sides, rather than finding themselves compelled by a burning purpose to create positive change. But working to help others in honor of a loved one can help to make sense of the tragedy and foster a greater sense of meaningfulness. By helping others, we often heal ourselves.

The third category of guilt involves **separation guilt** and **loyalty guilt**, which are closely related. Separation guilt shows up if you feel guilty about leaving others behind as you move forward in your life. Should you take the new job even if it means you will be farther away from your parents? Should you go to a conference if your children have the flu? Loyalty guilt develops if living your authentic life threatens the values or expectations of family members or others in your community. If your sexual or gender orientation is not aligned with what your family expects, you might feel guilty even bringing up the topic. If you are an artist at heart and your family expects you to be a doctor, it can be debilitating to even think of how they could be disappointed.

Though it takes courage to have these difficult conversations, if your loved ones genuinely want you to be happy and can be less fearful of how outsiders may view their own status in society, your being authentic is always worth the risk. Just as you want the best for them, others can rise to the occasion and want the best for you. Guilt can be a portal to deeper connection.

If, however, embracing a new perspective is beyond your family's capacity at this moment, you could politely state that certain topics are off the table—they are not up for discussion, and you can decide not to get enmeshed if emotions escalate. Realize that you have done what you can to plant the seeds for later conversations, if there is an interest. In the meantime, though, if the dynamic becomes increasingly one-sided, you might decide to limit your time interacting with them. Above all, you owe it to yourself, your own future, and to those whose lives you will touch to be true to your essential self and to listen to your inner voice.

Guilt Trip Alert

As compared to the three types of guilt you experience inside, guilt trips are imposed on you from other people, from external sources. Have you ever felt like someone was trying to "use" guilt on you to simply get what they wanted? If you have escaped this human dynamic, you are one of the very few! Sometimes we can see guilt coming at us, but with master guilt-trippers, it can be subtle and sly and harder to spot. When a relationship is increasingly infused with feelings of guilt, or if you are being manipulated to act in ways that don't allow you to grow, it's time to look deeper. Here are a few red flags that signal that you are being drawn into a guilt trip.

Have you noticed that this one person makes you feel like no matter how much you try to please them, you cannot ever get it quite right? They may also compare you to others, with the unspoken message being that you are never enough. Are you being coerced to agree to certain conditions because "If you really cared about me, you would . . . ?" Or do you feel that you cannot say no as the other person would either hold it against you in anger or fall apart in sadness? Are they personifying the angry victim or the selfless martyr who has done so much for you? Finally, are your needs for independence, individuality, and joy perceived as less important in the relationship, and do you feel you have to compromise your authentic expression to keep the status quo?[7] Guilt trip alert!

If this is the case, consider that this relationship is all about manipulation, not true caring. Be aware of your own triggers.

JOURNAL CHALLENGE

In your **journal**, write "I feel guilty when . . ." and set some boundaries that either prevent you from being in that situation or help you navigate around it. This is the time to see the relationship as it is, not as you would like it to be.

Do not allow anyone to surreptitiously tear you down so you can fulfill their unresolved needs. This is the time to recognize the underlying dynamic and take a stand to grow into your best self. Do not allow yourself to be psychologically bullied. In the words of Eleanor Roosevelt, "No one can make you feel inferior without your consent."

The Difference Between Guilt and Shame

Where guilt reminds you that you made a mistake, shame tells you in no uncertain terms that you *are* the mistake. Guilt has to do with an action that did not fit in with your moral code and made you feel uneasy. It gives you the push to take control of and change your behavior. It leads to repairing the grievance, healing past hurts, and to building better relationships.

Shame, on the other hand, is the feeling that something is wrong deep inside. People experiencing deep shame feel flawed at the very core of their being. Psychology professor June Tangney, in her study of 550 fifth graders, followed up in eighth grade and again at age eighteen and found that experiencing shame early on makes life much more difficult later. Her research, exploring the different effects of guilt and shame, showed that the students who were more prone to feelings of guilt were less likely to self-medicate with drugs and alcohol and more likely to practice safe sex. For those who tended to feel shame, it was the opposite: they were more likely to drink at a younger age and have unsafe sex and were less likely to apply to college. As shame grew, their hope for a positive future withered as well. Tangney further stated, "When people feel shame, they focus on the self—they often feel powerless, worthless or exposed. When people feel guilt, they tend to focus on behavior. Guilt is more proactive."[8]

It also relates to empathy for others and taking action to correct mistakes, where shame invokes anger, self-blame, and isolation.

Brené Brown says it well: "Shame needs three things to grow exponentially in our lives: secrecy, silence, and judgment." Shame causes people to feel separate from others and often too embarrassed to reach out for help.

In a world where we are supposed to be "happy," shame is not a topic many people want to spend their time chatting about. This emotion is sneaky, often hard to detect, and it's something we tend to hide even from ourselves. According to Thomas Scheff, professor emeritus of sociology at UC Santa Barbara, "In modernity, shame is the most obstructed and hidden emotion, and therefore the most destructive. Emotions are like breathing—they cause trouble only when obstructed."[9]

Shame gives rise to addictions, eating disorders, and other attempts to control, numb out, or deflect the bad feelings. In contrast, guilt leads to healing addictions, taking action to rectify the past, and finding solutions for the present and into the future. Where shame furthers a feeling of lack of control over what will happen, guilt fosters a hope that "I can make this better."

GUILT	SHAME
I made a mistake.	I am a mistake.
I recognize my behavior was wrong.	Others can see through to my core flaws.
I feel remorse for my actions.	I feel bitter and blame others.
I reach out to others.	This is my business.
I look for solutions.	I self-medicate to cope.

This suggests that when we want to help get someone we care about onto a better course, it is more helpful to focus on the *behavior* that needs changing instead of making the person feel badly about themselves ("Next time, walk the dog as soon as you get home" versus "You're no good with pets; I can't trust you to take care of anything"). This can be an overt or subtle distinction, but it is a powerful one.

Action Steps for Guilt and Shame

Here are seven strategies to deal with guilt and shame and to help you release yourself from the shackles of old beliefs that make you feel less than who you really are. Each one takes a different approach to ease you to the other side. Find one or two that speak to you, or try them all.

1. APOLOGIZE WELL

Even with the best intentions, sometimes an apology is not well received. While you cannot control another person's reaction, you can know you've done your best to address it as completely as you possibly can. Here are five steps to help you cover all the bases:

- Don't interrupt. Let them explain what happened from their perspective so you can see it through their eyes.
- Let them know that you understand their perspective (no matter if you agree with it or not). Communicate, "I can see how it made you feel _____, and I understand why." You are validating their emotions.
- Express remorse for the pain they felt.

- Offer a way to compensate or atone for your actions; it shows you want to take full responsibility and do something about it. They may refuse but will appreciate the offer.
- Express that you understand how your actions violated the expectations and the steps you are taking to prevent that in the future. This will help rebuild trust.[10]

2. NOTICE YOUR THOUGHTS

One thing to remember is that you are not your thoughts. Thoughts and feelings come and go; they do not define your essential self. When you get to know your triggers, you can more easily observe them rather than just react. Mindfulness meditation[11] is another powerful way to help you regulate your emotions, relieve stress, and detach from your thoughts, rather than be swept up inside of them. Imagine you are looking at your own thoughts—when you can name what you are feeling, you come to realize that you are not what is passing through your mind.

3. ACKNOWLEDGE YOUR FEELINGS

In order to get through these emotions, they must be moved from the shadows by being shared. Choose someone you trust, someone who has empathy and who knows no one is perfect but we're all trying our best. Together, in connected conversation, you can release your feelings from the shroud of secrecy, try on a new perspective, and explore practical ways to move through. Be real about what you are feeling. Give voice to what has been uncomfortable to speak in order to reach the freedom you want. The most courageous thing you can do is to be honest and real . . . with yourself.

When we bury the story, we forever stay the subject of the story. If we own the story we get to narrate the ending.

—BRENÉ BROWN

4. BEFRIEND YOUR GUILT AND SHAME TRIGGERS

JOURNAL CHALLENGE

In your **journal**, identify one thing that makes you feel guilty. It may be an obvious thought or it may be one that hides out in the back of your mind. Then, create a plan to make amends. You and the person you connect with will both feel better. And if they can't receive it, know that you have sincerely tried to mend the situation, and you have planted a seed. Feel proud of yourself for that.

As far as shame, even though we don't like to admit it, everyone has triggers. In general, it has to do with not living up to an image of how it "should" be. "You should always be strong, you should always perform well, and you should make it look easy . . ." NO! These myths do not reflect real life and they keep us all feeling inadequate and disempowered. Anyone who has felt "not good enough" has had some dances with shame.

If you've ever beaten yourself up for having a hard time finishing a project, you also know that guilt or shame are not far away. It's like a cycle that can keep you stuck. You procrastinate, blame, or shame yourself, and it becomes harder to even get moving. But you do have some choices here. Consider breaking the goal down into small doable chunks and literally celebrating when you complete any part of it. Decide to give yourself a chance. Instead of indulging in the mental habit of self-blame, plan some ridiculously simple tasks so you can regain your own trust. You can turn that blame or shame around and witness yourself making progress—but start easy. The more you are aware of what triggers your feelings of shame, the easier it will be to counteract them.

JOURNAL CHALLENGE

Take a look at your shame buttons and jot them down in your **journal**. Write one small thing that you can do to take a step forward.

---

5. CHALLENGE YOUR BELIEFS

Reflect on some of the underlying beliefs that are driving you. Identify one assumption or narrative in your mind that is holding you back. Byron Katie, in "The Work" has created a brilliant way to cut through limiting beliefs. In summary, she challenges you to answer four questions:

- Is it true? In every case?
- Can you absolutely know that it's true?
- How do you react, what happens, when you believe that thought?
- Who would you be without the thought?

Use these questions and delve deeper into the finer details to understand how your thoughts are influencing your feelings about yourself and life in general.[12] This is a powerful way to examine the story you tell yourself, expose what parts of it are literally holding you back, and choose another perspective to propel you forward.

6. BRING IN THE INNER ALLY

Whenever there is guilt or shame, the inner critic will try to run the show. Remind yourself that we all make mistakes, we all have weaknesses. You are not alone (even if you feel you are) in going through a painful time; we all have to deal with our own versions. Researcher Jessica Van Vliet writes, "People start to realize that it's not just them. Other people do things that are as bad or even worse sometimes so they're not the worst person on the planet. They start to say to themselves, 'This is human; I am human; others are human.'"[13]

It's okay to feel what you feel. Self-criticism, though it may be a familiar default, just keeps us stuck. Remember that the actions we take are limited by our awareness at the time. We're all learning as we go. No one came into this world knowing how to navigate every situation—life is our teacher.

Earlier, we mentioned the technique of speaking to yourself as you would to a dear friend or to a little child. What would you tell your five-year-old self in order to help her get through the tough stuff? Instead of unconsciously scolding, you would intentionally try to soothe. Do that now. Close your eyes, put your arms around yourself like you are giving yourself a hug. Say your name as if you are talking to yourself. "That situation was hard—it felt so bad. But it will pass, and soon, you'll look back and see how it made you stronger. You'll get through this, too, love, you always do. . . ."

Also choose a catchphrase that you can tell yourself each time you notice the critical voice/negative ego creeping in. It could be "perfectly imperfect," "life is lessons," "you got this," or select another that speaks to you. Consider this as part of your tool kit when the inner critic starts to do its thing. Even if you don't yet believe it fully, you are taking charge of redirecting your thoughts into a better-feeling place. The more you practice self-compassion, the easier it will be to call on this highly effective way of moving forward. As Dr. Jeffrey Schwartz describes it, "This means that if you repeat the same act over and over— regardless of whether that action has a positive or negative impact on you—you make the brain circuits associated with that act stronger and more powerful . . . meaning that the brain will be far more likely to repeat that behavior or habit automatically whenever a similar situation arises."[14] Whenever you practice self-compassion, you are utilizing this dynamic to architect your best self.

7. CONNECT

Reaching out to others is not a sign of weakness. On the contrary, it's a sign of utmost courage: the courage to acknowledge I'm feeling vulnerable, flawed, imperfect. It takes a strong person to admit—"Hey, I'm human, and I could use an ear, a hand, or just a hug right now." Most people try to pretend that they can go it alone. Brené Brown explains, "The hard part of the one thing that keeps us out of connection is our fear that we're not worthy of connection."

The funny thing is instead of alienating others, it brings us closer. We are wired to connect. In our heart of hearts, we do want the best for one another. Everything else is driven by the defenses caused by hurt.

It is through reaching out to the important people in our lives, or to a faith in something greater, that we sow the seeds for self-love, which leads to self-confidence, to self-empowerment, and to claiming who we really are. Also, by accepting ourselves, in all our expressions, we can then accept others, and in a fundamental way, this contributes to a society grounded in tolerance, empathy, and love.

Action step: Set up a time to meet someone you can talk with today. Seeking a medical professional is not a sign of weakness; it's a proactive sign of strength. While these emotions can make you feel isolated, the antidote is to express your feelings and intentionally explore better ways of dealing with them with someone you trust. Be open to updating your story about how you see yourself. Sometimes one shift can open you to surprising new insights that open the door to positive change. Pick up the phone; send a message. Take one concrete action in that direction.

Summing up: just because you have had guilt, you are not doomed to be a guilty person. Just because you have felt shame does not mean that you are shameful. Guilt teaches us to realign with our values. Shame guides us to be aware of the buried hurts so that we can bring them to the surface to heal. Ultimately the energy of both these emotions when dealt with can be redirected to a new sense of freedom, power, and possibility. Let them move you to what is waiting to emerge.

Love

Love is the secret to the universe. It resides in the energy of a heartbeat, the majesty of the mountains, the smallest drop of dew to the vastness of the galaxies.[1]

— RANDY TARAN

LOVE IS AN ENERGY that connects us to one another, to animals, to nature, to the great unknown. It is a yearning to inhabit our true nature, the spiritual essence that transcends time and space, the part of us that knows no boundaries, that is limitless and profoundly at peace. This is our true nature, beyond the layers of personality, ego, or worldly woes. It is the calm core that prevails through good times, hard times, and even lifetimes. It is what we tap into in meditation, contemplation, and transcendent moments. As above, so below—we already possess this energy in each cell, just as it permeates all of creation. It is the binding force of the universe.

In a more pragmatic sense, love is a force "that brings people together: from the primal bond of mother and child, to friendship, romantic love, love for people, or love for something greater."[2] We feel it in the gaze of a beloved, and in the union of two souls. "We are born from love, into love and depart this world moving towards a reunion with love." We all just want to love and be loved, but in a spiritual sense we are already loved, and the number one reason we are here is to love. Can we take that in? What if it could really be that simple?

The essence of love also revs up our better natures; love activates the best within us and inspires us to share that with others. Can you remember a moment when your heart was so full that you wanted everyone to feel that way? Or a moment when you felt a deep communion with just one person? Love connects us in profound ways and moves us toward kindness, understanding, forgiveness, and transcendence. It reminds us who we really are. When people connect through the vibration of love, it ignites the feeling that anything is possible. It is the fuel of positive change.

Yet if you were to look at the culture through the lens of everyday language, the word "love" has another meaning entirely. And it can be intense! Being "in love" can be a roller-coaster ride. Have you ever felt your heart bursting with so much love that you could barely contain it? Or have you ever been so heartbroken at the end of a relationship that you had no idea how you could pick yourself up and go on? This type of love: the passionate, half-crazed, obsessed version, can and does hijack your emotions and take you for a wild ride. The chemicals released into the brain have a lot to do with it.

In this chapter, we'll explore the many sides of love, from self-love to unconditional love for others. We'll take a deep dive into romantic love and how the chemicals in your brain inspire, lust, love, and connection. We'll also explore the stages of love and what helps love go the distance. Then on to friendship, love for people, and love for something greater, and finally we'll give you some proven ways to have better communication and feel more connected. It's a fascinating topic—let's start!

Types of Love

How can one word carry so many meanings? Whether it's self-love, the love of a parent for a child, romantic love, friendship, love for humanity, or love for something greater, each kind of love carries a different energy, and each plays a special part in our lives.

Self-love

Loving others comes easier when there is a base of self-love. It is the foundation of any relationship and allows for untold possibilities. But you might say that is easier said than done. Yet "It's not what you are that holds you back, it's what you think you are not" (Unknown). Some people think self-love is about standing up for yourself, knowing your worth, getting the respect you deserve, and carving out your space. But what if that is not the whole picture? There is a more all-embracing way to look at loving ourselves. Let's take a deeper look.

We are all born embodying love. We all have the spark of divinity, creativity, and greatness within us. Depending on what we encounter, the habits we take on, the mind-set and vi-

JOURNAL CHALLENGE

In your **journal**, jot down a time when you have experienced each kind of love, and how it made you feel both in your body and in your mind. Is there one type you would like to have more of?

TYPE OF LOVE	NATURE OF LOVE	DESCRIPTION
Self-love	• Feeling connected to a positive sense of oneself (gratitude and appreciation for who you are). • Your true nature is love.	The foundation for healthy relationships.
Love of a parent for a child	• Child is dependent. • Connection through the heart.	A healthy expression of this love is unconditional.
Romantic love	• Early stages can be super-intense. • Creativity keeps it fresh. • Can have power dynamics. • The body is the vehicle.	Can flood the senses and be transcendent.
Friendship	• Aristotle equated it to "shared goodwill," because the friendship is useful and enjoyable and because the friend is a good person. • There is mutual respect. • Mental /emotional connection.	Real friendships uplift both friends. Sometimes friendship can become romantic.

(cont'd)

| Love for people | • Strong intention to care about the greater good—together we rise.
• One person caring about many.
• How can we create a world where everyone can thrive? | This can be through a cause that would serve most people best.
A cause that allows you to express love is ideal. |
| Love for some-thing greater | • Sense of communion with the mystery of life—through God, religion, or spiritual-ity, power of nature, energy of life.
• Can be accessed through the heart or the spiritual side. | Transcendent love: staring at a starscape, seeing a baby born, feeling the divine. |

bration we cultivate, we can rise to our potential or we can get stuck. Often it's a dance between the two. One thing is sure: the clearer we are about who we really are, the more we are aligned with our true nature, which is love.

Self-love is about recognizing our core essence: the strength, the beauty, the peace, and the purpose that we all possess. That is truly who we are, and we might feel glimpses of that in quiet moments, or when we are in the state of flow. We feel connected to something greater—we are not alone. The self-doubt, self-criticism, and self-sabotage are simply signs that we are separated from our true nature. We are believing the illusion that we are small, damaged, and frail—we are caught in the lie.

And it's easy—there's so much more in the environment to

tell us what we are not (not good enough, etc.) than to remind us of who we really are. What about befriending yourself, respecting yourself, encouraging yourself, and finding joy within yourself? Have you ever done something where you made yourself laugh, just getting a kick out of being you? Self-love is an invitation to come home. In the words of Steve Maraboli, "The most powerful relationship you will ever have is the relationship with yourself."

Learning to create the conditions where it's easier to love yourself may also mean getting clearer about what you want and selecting what is life-enhancing and what is not. Which people, jobs, beliefs, and habits serve you, and which have you outgrown? What type of energy do you want to embody; what type of vibration do you want to activate? There is something known as heart coherence,[3] where we can learn to intentionally adjust our heart rate rhythm to promote feelings of connection, calmness, and love. We are not victims of circumstance—we *can* affect how we feel.

It is no accident that the heart is the symbol of love. My friend James Doty, a Stanford neurosurgeon and author of *Into the Magic Shop*, explains, "The heart is where we find our comfort and our safety in the darkest of places. It is what binds us together and what breaks when we are apart. The heart has its own kind of magic—love."[4]

When we are aligned with the energy of love, we can remember that we are much more than the challenges we face, the fears we have, the beliefs we hold. This is also a reminder that the love, respect, and kindness we want from others must be something we give ourselves first. When we *recognize* our true nature, then we know it's not something we have to aspire to; it's already there. Self-love is the foundation of every good relationship. In the words of Ralph Waldo Emerson, "We must be our own before we can be another's."

Unconditional Love

This type of love between two people knows no bounds and is present no matter the circumstances. The love between a mother and child is a perfect example. As babies, we depend on a parent or caregiver to take care of us, to feed us when we are hungry, to help us to sleep. Part of being a parent is instinctive. People have been raising children for millennia, and even though there is no rule book, they usually can get by. The body helps. When the "cuddle hormone," oxytocin, is released during breastfeeding, it increases the bonding between a mother and baby. Unless there is a bout of postpartum depression or other emotional difficulty present, parents generally do a decent job. At the same time, it helps when adults can have the self-awareness so they don't inadvertently project unresolved issues (like "Life is hard, then you die") onto their children. They certainly do the best they can with the knowledge they have and under the constraints they face. It's a tall order—everyone is trying their best. We learn as we grow.

Another aspect of unconditional love is when you want the best for another and care less about how you benefit. You hear all sorts of stories of parents sacrificing so their kids can have a better future. You want the best for another person; no matter if you disagree, no matter if your emotions take over, there is an underlying bond that cannot be broken.

Romantic Love: How the Chemicals in Your Brain Inspire, Lust, Love, and Connection

Romantic love has its own character. How we navigate it is influenced to an extent by childhood experiences (feeling loved, worthy, belonging) as well as the hormones secreted in different parts of the brain. From the brain on down, we are designed to connect. Our biology evolved millions of years ago to keep the species going strong. Neuroscientist Lucy Brown and biological anthropologist Helen Fisher have identified three different brain systems for mating:[5]

- **Sex drive**—to see who is the best partner out there. This is where estrogen and testosterone kick in. Pheromones, an odorless chemical only recognized by a potential sex partner, are also released. Some perfumes contain pheromones to make the person wearing it instantly desirable. Musk, anyone?
- **Intense romantic love or attraction**—which prompts us to focus on one mating partner. Here adrenaline is activated, resulting in the heart beating faster and a single-minded focus on your potential mate. Norepinephrine and serotonin jump on board, and then there's dopamine, which causes a happy feeling and is also linked to addiction.[6] Are you surprised?
- **Deep attachment** is activated for long-term bonding (in order to stay with each other to raise the child). This is when oxytocin, the "love" or "cuddle" hormone, is released, during hugging, kissing, and sex. So are vasopressin and dopamine, which work to encourage partners to stay together.[7]

Sometimes I am in awe of the intricate systems at play in our bodies and in nature—this is one of them. While we think that feelings just come over us, Mother Nature, in all her wisdom, has provided a cocktail of chemicals to get us going.

The Stages of Love

This leads us to the stages of love. In movies, it's all about the first blush of infatuation, or passion, intense drama, and then who knows. . . . But there's more to this story.

FALLING IN LOVE

This is the breathless, everything-is-new, obsessed phase: "Will they text, what does that message really mean, am I hot enough, when will I see them again?" High drama, bordering on addiction. Fisher reports that "We know that the brain circuitry for romantic love follows the same pathway as all the other addictions do." Because it's linked with the dopamine-fueled reward system, you crave this person and can't stop thinking about them. Doesn't that explain a few things! This is a natural addiction geared toward survival of the species, and it is there on purpose. So if you feel "addicted to love," especially at the early stages, it is not a design flaw—it's part of the plan.

In the realm of the erotic when desire is the spark, then mystery, the exploration of the unknown, is a very important element. At the beginning of a relationship, you don't know each other well yet; everything is fresh and exciting. There is an automatic curiosity, a compelling need to discover new things about each other, both physically and emotionally. This highly charged atmosphere provides the oxygen necessary for the fire of desire to burn.

BEING IN LOVE

The relationship can quickly become the focal point of life. Have you ever had a friend who got into a romantic relationship and then was never free to meet, let alone have an in-depth conversation? They may stop seeing their friends or doing their regular activities, so that they are free to meet their new partner whenever the impulse hits. That's all well and good, but in doing that, they are also closing off a part of their life that nourishes them, not to mention provides a sense of personal identity. When one person (or both) in a relationship gives up a certain percentage of what defines them in exchange for "being good-natured" or "making things work" and brings less than their authentic self to the relationship, then the relationship becomes less than the sum of its two parts. That is not to say compromise is not important, but if you're in that situation, you don't want to homogenize or negate the unique characteristics you both bring to the table.

JOURNAL CHALLENGE

In your **journal**, reflect on the questions: Have you ever lost your sense of self in a romantic relationship? What strategies can you use to stay strong and loving at the same time?

Then . . . there comes a point when you take off the rose-colored glasses. When the early glow of thinking that you really "get" each other and that the new partner practically can walk on water starts to fade, something new comes in. You actually are able to see their quirks and idiosyncrasies. Depending on how much a person has idealized the relationship, they can feel anything from disappointed to shattered to pleasantly surprised. It may be better than they thought or it may be "What was I thinking?" Some people view this time as a challenge. "Even if they are somewhat annoying, we can work it out. (I'll train/change him/her!)" Work in progress . . .

That can be tricky. Being on a crusade to change someone else might just mean that there is something in you that you are not happy with. Maybe it's the ego's need to look a certain way, or you might feel that your partner needs to be strong in areas where you have not yet realized your own potential. At one level, most people know that we really cannot change anyone else—we can only work on ourselves and, most important, become a friend to ourself.

As we have seen, when we love ourselves, it's so much easier to love another. When we are tuned in to the energy of love, we become so much more open to see the loving nature of those around us. We can see beneath the surface and tune in to that part of them. There's greater acceptance of one another. There's joy, commitment, and deeper connection. There is also a foundation of mutual respect, friendship, appreciation, and trust. You genuinely like each other's company, and just being together feels good.

Of course, conflicts will arise. Being in a relationship is the fastest way to learn the lessons we are here for. But with self-love in place, and through seeing others with the lens of love, it is so much easier to work through whatever comes up and emerge stronger, wiser, and ready to take love to a deeper level.

Thirty-six Questions to Increase Closeness in Relationships

Another way that people can get closer is through a series of questions designed to speed up the process. Would you agree that by knowing someone on a personal level, by sharing your values, vulnerabilities, dreams, and aspirations, you can build a better foundation of understanding and trust? Normally this whole getting-to-know-each-other phase unfolds gradually; it's a process and it takes time. What if you could do an experiment, and through this organized system, accelerate the whole process?

Based on research by psychologist Arthur Aron, Edward Melinat, and others, here are thirty-six questions to help deepen a relationship.[8] Only take this on if you are curious, ready, and eager to have a thought-provoking conversation. These questions have been used when people (lovers or significant others, friends, or family) want to know each other on a deeper level. Some might think these questions are too much too soon, and others might see these questions as an intriguing catalyst for deeper connection.

Here's how it works: there are three sets of questions—every set goes a little deeper.

- Ask each other the first set of questions for fifteen minutes. Each person should answer each question, but alternate who asks each question ("I'll ask the first one, you ask the second one . . .").
- Then, after fifteen minutes, even if you haven't completed all the questions, move on to set two.
- After fifteen minutes, begin set three, the last set of questions.

SET I

1. Given the choice of anyone in the world, whom would you want as a dinner guest?
2. Would you like to be famous? In what way?
3. Before making a telephone call, do you ever rehearse what you are going to say? Why?
4. What would constitute a "perfect" day for you?
5. When did you last sing to yourself? To someone else?
6. If you were able to live to the age of ninety and retain either the mind or body of a thirty-year-old for the last sixty years of your life, which would you want?
7. Do you have a secret hunch about how you will die?
8. Name three things you and your partner appear to have in common.
9. For what in your life do you feel most grateful?
10. If you could change anything about the way you were raised, what would it be?
11. Take four minutes and tell your partner your life story in as much detail as possible.
12. If you could wake up tomorrow having gained any one quality or ability, what would it be?

SET II

13. If a crystal ball could tell you the truth about yourself, your life, the future, or anything else, what would you want to know?
14. Is there something that you've dreamed of doing for a long time? Why haven't you done it?
15. What is the greatest accomplishment of your life?
16. What do you value most in a friendship?

17. What is your most treasured memory?
18. What is your most terrible memory?
19. If you knew that in one year you would die suddenly, would you change anything about the way you are now living? Why?
20. What does friendship mean to you?
21. What roles do love and affection play in your life?
22. Alternate sharing something you consider a positive characteristic of your partner. Share a total of five items.
23. How close and warm is your family? Do you feel your childhood was happier than most other people's?
24. How do you feel about your relationship with your mother?

Set III

25. Make three true "we" statements each. For instance, "We are both in this room feeling . . ."
26. Complete this sentence: "I wish I had someone with whom I could share . . ."
27. If you were going to become a close friend with your partner, please share what would be important for him or her to know.
28. Tell your partner what you like about them; be very honest this time, saying things that you might not say to someone you've just met.
29. Share with your partner an embarrassing moment in your life.
30. When did you last cry in front of another person? By yourself?

31. Tell your partner something that you like about them already.

32. What, if anything, is too serious to be joked about?

33. If you were to die this evening with no opportunity to communicate with anyone, what would you most regret not having told someone? Why haven't you told them yet?

34. Your house, containing everything you own, catches fire. After saving your loved ones and pets, you have time to safely make a final dash to save any one item. What would it be? Why?

35. Of all the people in your family, whose death would you find most disturbing? Why?

36. Share a personal problem and ask your partner's advice on how he or she might handle it. Also, ask your partner to reflect back to you how you seem to be feeling about the problem you have chosen.

What Helps Love Go the Distance?

Once you have built some trust and history together, a relationship can get stronger or it might get somewhat fixed. You might know couples who have stayed together forever, and some were probably happier than others. What goes into a successful long-term relationship? In an interesting experiment, people in their fifties and sixties who said they were still madly in love were compared with younger couples, aged eighteen to twenty-six, who had just fallen in love.[9] In brain scans, the same love-related regions in the brain lit up for both, but for the newly in love, the areas of anxiety also showed more activity.[10] (Probably they were thinking things like: "Did I say the right thing, do I look fat, is he/she the one?")

By comparison, the older couples had more activity in the area of the brain associated with calm and pain suppression, linked with "positive illusions." Hmmm—does that mean that for a relationship to last, we need to live with illusions and not see the reality? Actually, it's not about deceiving yourself; rather it has more to do with a shift in perspective. What the experiment showed is that the older couples were able to overlook qualities in their partners they didn't like and put their attention on the ones they did. They were able to look for the good aspects and basically turn lemons into lemonade. For example, "He/she talks so slowly and takes their sweet time with everything—it drives me crazy! But on the other hand, I love and appreciate that we have really deep, fascinating, unrushed conversations that are off the charts." When you focus on the positive and make a conscious decision to bring that front and center, you are grateful for the good stuff and help it grow. More joy, more adventure, more appreciation, contentment, patience, humor. That makes you happier, raises your vibration, influences those around you, and makes everyone feel good.

What Is Your Language of Love?

For a long-term relationship to flourish, whether it is between lovers or friends, family or coworkers, communication is key. Depending on how we are wired, we all have different ways that we communicate and receive love from others. Some respond to words of appreciation and kindness, some feel more connected through touch, others prefer a little token of affection for no reason at all. Gary Chapman, in his book *The 5 Love Languages*, describes how it works.[11]

There are five languages:

- Words of affirmation
- Quality time
- Physical touch
- Receiving gifts
- Acts of service

Each person on the planet prioritizes these in their own order. Some people might prefer acts of service, then quality time, followed by physical touch. Their partners might choose physical touch, then words of affirmation, followed by quality time. It's different for all of us. A kind word may mean the world to one person, but another may say talk is cheap and prefer action. ("I'm exhausted; if you could help me with this errand I'll love you forever.") Some may enjoy tokens of affection, while for others nothing replaces physical affection itself and a warm embrace means the world. ("Flowers are okay, but they just die; all I need is to be held.") For others, the experience of having adventures together makes them feel loved and connected.

It's easy to see that if we don't know another person's love language, even with all the best intentions of showing our love, we are speaking a foreign language, and everything we do just doesn't translate. Many people have used the Five Love Languages quiz for better personal relationships or to create a work culture where everyone feels appreciated.[12] It's all about letting people you care about know, in a language that they understand.

JOURNAL CHALLENGE

After you take the Five Love Languages quiz, write down in your **journal** your top three languages. What are some ways you can share this with those around you?

Friendship

In a time of extreme busyness, FOMO (fear of missing out), and competing priorities, you are lucky to have a few true friends who know your heart and want the best for you no matter what.

You want the best for them, too. Aristotle equated it to "shared goodwill," not only because the friendship is useful and enjoyable, but because you consider your friend to be a good person. You see the best in them as they see the best in you. There is mutual respect.

The great thing about real friendships is that there is a trust that has built up over time, which allows you to let down your guard and be more vulnerable than you would be with others. Think of a real friendship as a bubble of love. According to Barbara Fredrickson, social psychologist and author of *Love 2.0*, "Love unfolds and reverberates between and among people—*within* interpersonal transactions—and thereby belongs to all parties involved . . . It resides within connections."[13] And it can create a loop. Kindness begets kindness; smiles bring on more of the same. It is in this connected and safe space that you can laugh or cry, feel accepted, share your challenges, and know your friend will have your back. While fair-weather friends are there during the good times, real friends maintain the connection and show kindness even when times are tough.

Friends also know that mistakes do happen and we're always learning. They also have the desire to look beneath the words to how you really are doing. . . . Friends can forgive each other because they care to understand the cause of the conflict. Most of the time, it's not personal. When times are good, they will also be there to celebrate your victories. Instead of being threatened or jealous, they are genuinely happy for your success.

Have you ever noticed that you may have different kinds of friends for different activities you enjoy? One friend loves to go to movies, another one is perfect for outdoor adventures, another delights in philosophical discussions that go late into the night. The thing is you have many sides, so don't expect one person to be the always-on, all-purpose friend. As you begin to identify what you want, and all your areas of interest, new friends will come in to share that aspect with you.

When you have a love of people and enjoy being with them, they will sense it and want to be around you, too. When you are genuinely interested in them, they feel it. Even in situations when you don't yet know the person, if your energy is welcoming, as if it is saying, "Hi, old friend, it's so good to see you again," you will interact in a much more connected way. Everyone wants to be seen as a friend, and people crave being around those who give them feelings of acceptance, friendship, and love.

Here's a thought—what if the person you consider to be your adversary was actually a friend in disguise? What if someone you consider an obstacle was actually there to help you grow? Think of your relationship as an obstacle course that made you faster, stronger, more understanding, and certainly more discerning. Is there anyone in your past who played that role for you?

Loving-Kindness Meditation

Have you ever noticed that when you think in your mind that someone is a good-hearted person, the next time you see them there is a beautiful warm connection? The opposite is true, too— if you are dreading getting together with someone you view as just a nasty human being, when you run into them, it feels like there is a wall between you.

Loving-kindness means tenderness and consideration toward others. This meditation, easily available online, is a deceptively simple way to develop feelings of kindness, warmheartedness, and connection with others, while making yourself feel better in the process.

Research has shown that loving-kindness meditation[14] will make you feel more content in your own skin and more connected to others.[15] It also increases positive emotion, emotional intelligence, and the length of your telomeres (slows down aging), while it reduces self-criticism, chronic pain, migraines, and depressive symptoms.[16]

My friend Chade-Meng Tan, formerly Google's "Jolly Good Fellow," now *New York Times* bestselling author of *Joy on Demand*,[17] likes to talk about loving-kindness. He sometimes introduces his audiences to a curious experiment. For the next day, every hour for eight hours, he challenges them to choose two random people walking past their desk, office, or wherever they are, and simply send these thoughts to them: "I wish for this person to be happy, and I wish for this other person to be happy, too." They are to think this for ten seconds; that's it. No need to talk to the people or even make eye contact; simply send them that silent message.

The following day, after a talk, Meng received an email from one of the people there. She explained, "I hate my job. I hate coming to work every single day. But I attended your talk on Monday, did the homework on Tuesday, and Tuesday was my happiest day in seven years." The happiest day in seven years came from a total of eighty seconds (ten seconds each hour for eight hours) of loving-kindness, without one word being spoken. Sending good wishes to someone else is a secret strategy, undetectable to anyone else, that can elevate *your* happiness and feelings of connection in unforeseen ways. Thoughts are powerful.

Love for People

Is there anyone in your life who really cares about people and about making this world a better place? There are people in the news who change the world in business, science, and tech, among many other disciplines. Some get Nobel Prizes, but most do not. There are famous change-makers like Gandhi or Martin Luther King Jr. who grab the public's attention. But most people never are known—they make an impact, but much more quietly.

Actually, many of these people are probably right in front of your nose. Look at the teacher who is showing kids their potential, the musician who brightens the lives of people through his instrument, the tech leader who is raising the human bar by giving generous paternity leaves as well as maternity paid time off. There's the social entrepreneur who fights for sustainable resources, and the yoga teacher teaching a classroom of kids or seniors, the artist who is bringing beauty into the world. When a natural disaster strikes, people from all walks of life rally to save those who are stuck in the wreckage. A firefighter returns to the scene of the fire to save those who were left behind. Someone starts a crowdsourcing campaign to help a colleague pay for a necessary medical operation. A kid stops the bully and befriends the one who has been singled out.

Unsung heroes come in all shapes and sizes. They are all around us, among us, and within us. Recognize the people in your community as the leaders they are, and recognize that quality in you as well. It doesn't matter how big the gesture—it matters that you make it. Everyone has the capacity to be that person for someone else.

At the core, people are good. They want the best for themselves, their families, and even for people they do not know. The question of our age is how we can work together to create a world where everyone can thrive. It starts with small actions, and everyone can join the party. Everyone, no matter what age, stage, or stature can be a force for good.

Love for Something Greater

I can remember a time when I was about seven years old. It was near the summer solstice and the days were long. It was a balmy night, barely a breeze. I was sitting with my family in the yard, and we were gazing at the heavens. The sky was a dome filled with countless stars, and we were looking for the North Star, the Milky Way, and any constellation my parents could think of. It was magical, it was holy—I felt like a tiny element in a vast mysterious cosmos yet so connected to it all. It was as if my heart stopped and time stood still in this indelible moment of awe.

How could such majesty, such unspeakable beauty come into being? That was the instant I knew that we are part of something greater. Some find this feeling in church, temple, mosque, or a spiritual group. Some find it in climbing mountains, skiing down cliffs, being immersed in the ocean, or jumping from a plane. It could be discovered at the Grand Canyon, looking at the sequoias, or even the shoot of a flower emerging from its winter slumber. Maybe it is in the witnessing of a baby being born, or when a soul passes from this realm to the next. Call it God, the divine, source, spirit, *ruach*, or prana, there is a life force that energizes each of us and gives us life. Befriend the mystery, know you are part of it, and that you are much more vast than you can even imagine.

Love, no matter what its form, opens the doors to our true nature and to us showing up as our best selves in the world. It is what brings us together, helps up connect deeply, and fuels positive change. When we love, it cracks us open to experience the fullness of life. It reminds us of why we are here and allows us to see that life is calling us forth. Love is who you are; let it shine, and you will send a ripple farther than you know. You have the seeds of greatness already. Water them often—you will see through your own experience that everything you need is inside of you.

Conclusion

THERE IS AN ENERGY in each and every one of us that knows what it is to feel centered, strong, and connected to who we really are. Call it your true nature, inner compass, or higher self; it is what we return to in the quiet moments, or in nature, or when we are in flow. I, for one, would love to live there. For me, it is where time stands still. The good thing about our emotions is that though they may seem to guide us *away* from this calm state, especially when we're in the midst of an episode, they are actually the *vehicle* for us to break through the old patterns and reconnect with our essential self.

Emotions are the clarion calls to help us understand what may be off track in our lives, or what may be so wonderful that just taking it in helps us resonate with who we truly are. As we learn to navigate, work with, and learn from our emotions, we remember that we have choices, and the world can open up in response.

Emotions are fleeting. They come and go, unless we choose to ruminate on them and thereby give them more energy. When we're savoring the good stuff, like a lovely conversation, a great meal, or the beauty around us, our emotions are making us feel better. When situations are more challenging, our emotions let us know and, with a little reflection, point us to other ways of handling what is before us.

Awareness

When we think of emotional episodes, the ones that seem to come from nowhere and take over our minds, it is good to know that we can have some awareness. When feelings start to escalate, you can check in with yourself and understand what the conditions are that are helping that emotion take on a life of its own. If you feel anger brewing, are you hangry? Or have the little irritations been building up all day? That could be an instigating factor. If you feel sad and you didn't get a good night's sleep, your emotions may be more raw. If anxiety is taking over, are you already worried about work, money, taking your dog for an operation? What is lurking in the recesses of your mind? We call this the pregame. Just like athletes go through drills and visualizations to get ready for a game, what kind of thoughts are you practicing to get ready for your day? Are they thoughts that pull you down, or thoughts that move you to what you enjoy and want in your life?

Then come the mental triggers. Is there an incident (an exam, a wedding, a trip) that is either giving you joy and anticipation, or a feeling so heavy you don't know what to do with it? Maybe you remember when you last saw an old friend and you can't wait to pick up where you left off, or you may still have guilt over a nasty breakup that colors every new person you date. Past attitudes can linger and trigger you unless you disarm them with your awareness. For example, "I know I'm walking into a room with all my ex's old friends. What can I do to get through the evening and even have some fun?" For happy emotions, this is a nonissue, but for challenging ones, you can prep with a game plan.

Don't forget about your body. We hold our energy in our body, and it is amazing at giving us clues, if we choose to pay attention! If you have a tight feeling in your gut, the message may be that something is not right. If your heart is pulsing, then anticipation is building. If you have butterflies in your stomach, you are harnessing your courage for what you're about to do. Some people suggest we have three brains: head, heart, and gut. Don't discount the messages from the heart and the gut. The body has a wisdom that senses the emotions that your mind may deny. There are ways to loosen the tensions that get lodged in the body. Acupuncture, massage, deep tissue, and cranial sacral therapy are modalities that have been used by many to release emotional blockages. We can't separate the body from the brain. Both give us important messages about our emotions and increase our awareness.

Choice

In complex times, when it feels like the world is in chaos, it's good to remember that we still have some choices. A greater awareness of our emotions and their triggers allows us entry to the next level of taking agency for the life we want to create by making choices. Imagine yourself an athlete. You are about to run the race, play the game, or kayak down the rapids. It's getting intense and you know it. This is the time that you make some choices. Are you just going to let the momentum take you along (a potentially destructive path), or will you choose to be the navigator of whatever comes your way (a constructive path)? What is your game plan? How do you want to feel in that situation? An athlete might say: "If a runner comes in front of me, I'll pace myself and move toward the inside lane. If someone is blocking my throw, I'll pass the ball left. If there's a quick drop in the water level, I'll do plan B. . . ." By considering your choices, you are ready in that moment to **guide your energy toward the outcome you intentionally want**. In doing that, you effectively deselect the other option, which is to passively not make any choice at all and default to old patterns that did not let you move forward. When we realize we have choices, we get to hear the message of our emotions, choose how we want to steer them, and so use the power of our emotions to transform our life for good.

Integration

After the emotion has erupted and subsided, and even after we have successfully used our emotions to guide us to a better outcome, we might be tempted to just exhale, go on with our day, and walk away from the playing field. That would be passing up a huge opportunity. Rather, take a moment and ask yourself: What did I notice, what worked well, and what would I do differently next time? The best coaches recap the game with their athletes and review the plays in their minds to plan strategies for the next event. This is how we grow, both in skills and in wisdom. Then there are much fewer injuries, greater success, and a whole lot more fun.

Our emotions are poised to help us. We see this when guilt moves us back to our values, when anger helps us set boundaries, and when fear helps us be more aware. If we are open to gaining *perspective* on our emotions, instead of having them take us on a ride, we can discover their messages, their guidance, and their gifts. We all have that opportunity.

What if it's hard to change? We are often attached to familiar patterns even if they keep us stuck. As always, there is personal choice. Granted, it can be unsettling to move out of our comfort zones, but to feel fully alive there is a dance between familiar territory and new situations, landscape unknown. If you are called to stretch and your intuition whispers ideas in the night, then don't shut them down. A part of you is ready to expand. Some fears of change have to do with black-and-white thinking. But it's not a question of sticking to old ways or abandoning everything. Rather, the question is how we can integrate who we are now with who we can be.

The good news is that we can learn how to stabilize our emotions and also allow for curiosity, change, and growth. If you are naturally cautious, then venture out of your comfort zone and try a new approach. If you are all about chasing novelty, let it be grounded in some of the practices you resonate with and keep at them. You will notice the change.

There are so many choices in this book that you will instinctively be drawn to some in each chapter. Let that be your guide.

The Gifts of Your Emotions

Happiness introduces you to retraining your brain by taking on the seven happiness habits: mindfulness, gratitude, self-care, generosity, authenticity, social connection, and aligning with your purpose. See which one(s) calls out to you—it's a perfect place to jump in.

Sadness is to be honored instead of pushed down. It is not the same as depression, but a provider of a safe harbor when we need it most. It can wash away the illusions with its tears and provide clarity and resolve for next steps. It prioritizes meaningful connections above all.

Desire is a force. It moves mountains, gives you the fuel to reach your goals, and allows your passion to ignite. When you desire what aligns with your core values, you are unstoppable.

Fear sharpens your senses and keeps you aware. It is an instinctive physical reaction. Mental fear can either be your protector or your jailer. If you have old patterns that no longer serve you, don't suppress them—set them free. Fear is not who you are. It's a reminder to reconnect with your core self and what truly matters.

Anxiety has much to do with the culture we live in and all the hidden pressures we face. We can decide how much of that even makes sense. Some anxiety is healthy. Other types have proven pathways to get to the other side. This emotion invites us to course correct and architect a life of our design.

Confidence invites us to connect to the clear energy we want to exude, which comes from choosing our mind-set, acknowledging our gifts, and self-acceptance—just knowing that as human beings we are more than enough.

Anger arises when boundaries have been disrespected. It can be a force that destroys everything in its wake, or it can be used skillfully, as did Gandhi and Martin Luther King Jr. In that sense, anger provides the fire to right a wrong and draw a line in the sand where there was none.

Tolerance is the path to being aware of the core needs every human has: to be respected, to belong, to be safe, and to be loved. No one was born a bigot. At some level, we are all connected. If we could recognize that our enemies are actually our teachers and that through them we are reclaiming disowned parts of ourselves, we'd all be better off.

Guilt lets us know in a heightened way that we have veered from our inner values. It provides the opportunity for us to make things right. Shame cuts deeper, because we perceive not that we made a mistake, but that we are the mistake. Both open the door to positive change, if we address the causes with compassion.

Love is the primal force of the universe and has many faces. Though it is designed to be addictive in the first stages of romantic love, it also elevates us to our higher natures and can spark a feeling of transcendence. Love holds enormous power, as do we when we tap into it, because it is the core essence of who we are.

Getting Back to Your True Nature

In this journey of demystifying our emotions, we have learned that there is a reason for every emotion to exist. Each plays a role in guiding us back to our true nature. The world preaches separation, lack, competition, and conflict. We are born in wholeness, innate peace, and full awareness. We can choose to believe we are not enough, or we can cut through the illusion to connect to the fullness of who we truly are. Each person has that capacity—no exceptions.

We have to take off the blinders to remind ourselves that we are not resonating with separation, but ready to make the choices that will keep us in alignment with our core values, higher nature, and inner resources. Emotions are our friends and guides on this journey, pointing us to what is working and what is not, what we want and what we don't and what is the quality of energy that we are boomeranging out into our world. **We are responsible for our own energy, and when we learn how to navigate it, we take charge of our lives.**

In these complex times, we need to remember that each of us is the architect of our own life. We can't control what we encounter, but we can influence our own reaction. We can decide how we want to feel about an issue right now. That alone gives us a sense of agency—we are not at the whim of the winds. We are grounded in our own values, preferences, and the ability to steer our energy. That vibrant energy ripples out way beyond us and touches others in our lives and our world. So embrace your potential, reclaim your flow, your creativity, and your love. Your emotions are tools to get you there. And when the ego tries to keep you stuck—and it will—remember you are so much bigger than that. The best is yet to come—and I am cheering you on. Come alive to all you have inside of you, and let your emotions reveal the power of you.

Acknowledgments

I have to start with my parents, who gave me the exact upbringing I needed to propel me in the directions of my passions. To my mom, whose empathy is unsurpassed, and to my late father, who had a joie de vivre right up to his last days.

My brother and sisters, I am grateful for each of you. Alana, words cannot describe my appreciation for your steady and deeply felt encouragement along every step of this journey.

Some people are lucky enough to have a teacher who sees in them what they cannot see in themselves. Mrs. Bardo, who took me into her ninth-grade class at lunchtime, playing Mozart in the background and encouraging me to write, you touched my life beyond measure.

Thank you to Heidi Berger, Donna Bernstein, Dana Cappiello, Mimi Cukier, Hector Estrada, Melissa Hollatz, Minerva Jeminez, Diane Leeder, Vivian Lehmann, Patricia Schermerhorn, David Waldman, and Joe Webber—you are dear and special people in my life. Karen Joiner, your insights, wisdom, and consistent support have been a beacon through the years.

To Joseph Carbone and Grace Loo, you are guiding forces in my life—my love and gratitude go deep—you are family.

My wonderful friends from the Dalai Lama Foundation, I appreciate you so much, especially Marsha Clark, who saw the glimmer of an idea and opened the door for this adventure to begin. Jim Doty, Tony Hoeber, Darlene Markovich, Tom Nazario, Jim Schuyler, Tenzin Tethong—I am so proud of the ripples that we started.

I am grateful to George Lucas, who made time for a class of teenagers with profound questions. Richie Davidson, you are such an inspiration, and Richard Gere, it was clear to see your dedication to the path of the heart. I will forever be moved by the generosity and kindness of the Dalai Lama—you have imprinted my heart with your compassion.

My talented team, past and present, at Project Happiness— putting our energies together has given birth to a dream. Special thanks to Maria Lineger, cowriter of the *Project Happiness Handbook*, and Isabella Anderson, Julie Arnheim, Kavita Avtar, Holly DeYoung, Brook Dorff, Samantha Feinberg, Ellie Ford, Stefie Gan, Seema Handu, Emmanuel Ivorgba, Abby Konopasky, Jill Pettegrew, Brian Rusch, Rolando Sandor, Sarah Tambling, our dear advisor Carole Pertofsky, and friend Shankar Hemmady.

Thanks to the whole team at Folio, to Scott Hoffman, who I met first and who told me, "I have the exact person for you." You were so right. To my literary agent, Jeff Silberman, you believed in this book and in me from the start, and your diligence and tenacity throughout this whole process, not to mention your innate kindness, has made this experience a joy.

To Daniela Rapp, senior editor at St. Martin's Press, I so appreciate your insights, openness, and nuanced perspective. You had a vision for the book from the outset and gave me the freedom to dig deeper than I had thought possible. I feel so lucky that our paths have crossed. To the team at SMP, your talent and care is front and center.

David, my love, my partner, my dearest friend—I know our deep connection goes beyond this lifetime. Thank you always for your presence, passion, and insight. Alex, Benjy, and Zoe, my beloveds, my teachers: each one of you is wise beyond your years and a gift to all who know you—I am so proud of who you are and what you stand for. I can't forget our dog Happy, the best writing companion in the universe.

Finally, a special thank-you to friends past, present, and future. We are all so connected—I hope this book creates a vehicle for us to meet and recognize that we are all one.

Notes

Introduction

1. Antonio D'Amasio, "How Our Brains Feel Emotion," Big Think, June 14, 2011, www.youtube.com/watch?v=KsSvlKzdiWU.
2. "The Ekmans' Atlas of Emotions," http://atlasofemotions.org.
3. Yasmin Anwar, "How Many Different Human Emotions Are There?" *Greater Good Magazine*, September 8, 2017, https://greatergood.berkeley .edu/article/item/how_many_different_human_emotions_are_there.
4. Brené Brown, "List of Core Emotions," https://brenebrown.com /downloads.
5. "The Ekmans' Atlas of Emotions," http://atlasofemotions.org/#triggers.
6. Paul Ekman, "Basic Emotions," in *Handbook of Cognition and Emotion*, eds. Tim Dalgleish and Mick J. Power (New York: John Wiley & Sons Ltd., 1999).

Happiness

1. "Positive Psychology 2.0: Towards a Balanced Interactive Model." Dr. Paul Wong. May 1, 2011. http://www.drpaulwong.com/positive -psychology-2-0-towards-a-balanced-interactive-model-of-the-good-life/.
2. Susan David, *Emotional Agility: Get Unstuck, Embrace Change, and Thrive in Work and Life* (New York: Avery, 2018).
3. Jordi Quoidbach, June Gruber, Moira Mikolajczak, Alexsandr Kogan, Ilios Kotsou, and Michael I. Norton, "Emodiversity and the Emotional Ecosystem," *Journal of Experimental Psychology: General* 143, no. 6 (December 2014): 2057–66, www.hbs.edu/faculty/Pages/item.aspx?num=47718.
4. James Baraz, "Are Your Happiness Goals Too High?" *Greater Good Magazine*, January 17, 2017, https://greatergood.berkeley.edu/article /item/are_your_happiness_goals_too_high/success

5. "Dalai Lama Quote." A-Z Quotes. https://www.azquotes.com/quote /849367.

6. Martin E. P. Seligman, *Flourish: A Visionary New Understanding of Happiness and Well-being* (New York: Free Press, 2013).

7. Mihaly Csikszentmihalyi, *Flow and the Foundations of Positive Psychology: The Collected Works of Mihaly Csikszentmihalyi* (New York: Springer, 2014).

8. Rick Hanson and Forrest Hanson, *Resilient: How to Grow an Unshakable Core of Calm, Strength, and Happiness* (New York: Harmony Books, 2018).

9. Hanson, Rick. "The Importance of Learning." Dr. Rick Hanson. March 26, 2018. https://www.rickhanson.net/the-importance-of-learning/.

10. Lyubomirsky, Sonya, Kennon Sheldon, and David Schkade. "Pursuing Happiness: The Architecture of Sustainable Change." http:// sonjalyubomirsky.com/wp-content/themes/sonjalyubomirsky/papers /LSS2005.pdf.

11. Fiona MacDonald, "Mindfulness Meditation Linked to the Reduction of a Key Inflammation Marker," *ScienceAlert*, February 10, 2016, www .sciencealert.com/a-key-inflammation-marker-is-lower-in-people-who -meditate-research-finds.

12. "Mindfulness Can Improve Heart Health," Harvard Health Publishing, February 2018, www.health.harvard.edu/heart-health/mindfulness-can -improve-heart-health.

13. Robert A. Emmons, *Thanks! How the New Science of Gratitude Can Make You Happier* (Boston: Houghton Mifflin Company, 2007).

14. Robert Emmons, "Pay It Forward," *Greater Good Magazine*, June 1, 2007, https://greatergood.berkeley.edu/article/item/pay_it_forward.

15. "Health and Happiness." Obesity Prevention Source. https://www.hsph .harvard.edu/health-happiness/.

16. Nadine Burke Harris, *The Deepest Well: Healing the Long-term Effects of Childhood Adversity* (Boston: Houghton Mifflin Harcourt, 2018).

17. Christopher Willard, *Raising Resilience: The Wisdom and Science of Happy Families and Thriving Children* (Boulder, CO: Sounds True, 2017).

18. Delia Fuhrmann, "Being Kind Makes Kids Happy," *Greater Good Magazine*, August 1, 2012, https://greatergood.berkeley.edu/article/item/being _kind_makes_kids_happy.

19. Fred Luskin, *Forgive for Good: A Proven Prescription for Health and Happiness* (San Francisco: HarperSanFrancisco, 2003).

20. "The Hug That Helped Change Medicine," CNN, February 22, 2013, www.youtube.com/watch?v=0YwT_Gx49os.

21. Bruce K. Alexander, "Addiction: The View from Rat Park," 2010, www .brucekalexander.com/articles-speeches/rat-park/148-addiction-the -view-from-rat-park.

22. Dhruv Khullar, "How Social Isolation Is Killing Us," *The New York Times*, December 22, 2016, www.nytimes.com/2016/12/22/upshot/how -social-isolation-is-killing-us.html.

23. "Geordie Shore's Vicky Pattison Visits a Japanese Cuddle Cafe | World of Weird," Channel 4, October 18, 2016, www.youtube.com/watch?v =8PvaUAYowvM.

24. Cuddle Up to Me, http://cuddleuptome.com.

25. Nicholas A. Christakis and James H. Fowler, "Dynamic Spread of Happiness in a Large Social Network: Longitudinal Analysis over 20 Years in the Framingham Heart Study," Digital Access to Scholarship at Harvard, *British Medical Journal* 337, no. a2338 (2008), www.bmj .com/content/337/bmj.a2338.

26. Randy Taran, "The Alphabet of Happiness: 'P,'" *The Huffington Post*, December 6, 2017, www.huffingtonpost.com/randy-taran/the-alphabet -of-happiness_4_b_5684891.html.

27. Sarah Green, "Post-traumatic Growth and Building Resilience," *Harvard Business Review*, March 30, 2015, https://hbr.org/2011/03/post -traumatic-growth-and-buil.

28. Lorna Collier, "Growth After Trauma," *Monitor on Psychology* 47 no. 10, American Psychological Association, November 2016, www.apa.org /monitor/2016/11/growth-trauma.aspx.

29. Ginny Graves, "Is There an Upside to Tragedy?" Oprah.com, July 2015, www.oprah.com/inspiration/post-traumatic-growth/all.

Sadness

1. Allan V. Horwitz and Jerome C. Wakefield, *The Loss of Sadness: How Psychiatry Transformed Normal Sorrow into Depressive Disorder* (Oxford: Oxford University Press, 2012).

2. Bruce Y. Lee, "Antidepressants Found in the Great Lakes and Fish," *Forbes*, September 4, 2017, www.forbes.com/sites/brucelee/2017/09/04 /antidepressants-found-in-the-great-lakes-and-fish/#46cc617b87db.

3. Jean M. Twenge, Thomas E. Joiner, Megan L. Rogers, and Gabrielle N. Martin, "Increases in Depressive Symptoms, Suicide-related Outcomes, and Suicide Rates Among U.S. Adolescents After 2010 and Links to Increased New Media Screen Time," *Clinical Psychological Science* 6, no. 1 (2017): 3–17, https://doi.org/10.1177/2167702617723376., http://journals.sagepub.com/eprint/qeIxKSaE5auQCM8Pfb4Z/full

4. Rangan Chatterjee, *How to Make Disease Disappear* (New York: Harper-One, 2018).

5. "Reverse Disease and Reclaim Your Health with Dr. Rangan Chatterjee," interview by Lewis Howes, *The School of Greatness*, podcast,

April 30, 2018, https://lewishowes.com/podcast/reverse-disease-and
-reclaim-your-health-dr-rangan-chatterjee.

6. Ellen Vora, "The Real Cause of Depression Is About Way More
Than Just Serotonin," Mindbodygreen, August 30, 2018, www
.mindbodygreen.com/articles/real-cause-of-depression-serotonin.

7. Joseph P. Forgas, "Four Ways Sadness May Be Good for You," *Greater
Good Magazine*, June 4, 2014, https://greatergood.berkeley.edu/article
/item/four_ways_sadness_may_be_good_for_you.

8. Todd Kashdan and Robert Biswas-Diener, *The Upside of Your Dark Side:
Why Being Your Whole Self—Not Just Your "Good" Self—Drives Success and
Fulfillment* (New York: Hudson Street Press, 2014).

9. Victoria A. Visser, Daan van Knippenberg, Gerben A. van Kleef,
and Barbara Wisse, "How Leader Displays of Happiness and Sadness Influence Follower Performance: Emotional Contagion and
Creative versus Analytical Performance," *The Leadership Quarterly* 24
no. 1 (February 2013), www.sciencedirect.com/science/article/pii
/S1048984312000896.

10. Tim Lomas, *The Positive Power of Negative Emotions: How Harnessing Your
Darker Feelings Can Help You See a Brighter Dawn* (London: Piatkus, 2016).

11. Tuomas Eerola, "Why Do Some People Love Sad Music?" *Greater Good
Magazine*, September 29, 2016, https://greatergood.berkeley.edu/article
/item/why_do_some_people_love_sad_music.

12. Maraboli, Steve. *Unapologetically You: Reflections on Life and the Human
Experience*. Port Washington, NY: Better Today, 2013.

13. Sandberg, Sheryl, and Adam M. Grant. *Option B: Facing Adversity, Building Resilience, and Finding Joy* (New York: Knopf, 2017).

14. Lomas, *The Positive Power of Negative Emotions*.

15. Zygmunt Bauman, *Liquid Love: On the Frailty of Human Bonds* (Malden,
MA: Polity Press, 2003).

16. Bronnie Ware, *The Top Five Regrets of the Dying: A Life Transformed by the
Dearly Departing* (Carlsbad, CA: Hay House, 2003).

Desire

1. "Desire | Definition of Desire in English by Oxford Dictionaries." Ox-
ford Dictionaries | English. https://en.oxforddictionaries.com/definition
/desire.

2. *Merriam-Webster*, s.v. "desire (v.)," www.merriam-webster.com
/dictionary/desire.

3. Liz Day, Katie Hanson, John Maltby, Carmel Proctor, and Alex
Wood, "Hope Uniquely Predicts Objective Academic Achievement
Above Intelligence, Personality, and Previous Academic Achievement,"

Journal of Research in Personality 44, no. 4 (August 2010): 550–553, www
.sciencedirect.com/science/article/pii/S009265661000067X.

4.   Shane J. Lopez, "C. R. (Rick) Snyder (1944–2006)," obituary, American
     Psychologist 61, no. 7 (Octoer 2006): 719, http://dx.doi.org/10.1037/0003
     -066X.61.7.719.

5.   Shane J. Lopez, *Making Hope Happen: Create the Future You Want for Yourself
     and Others* (New York: Atria Paperback, 2014).

6.   Neel Burton, "The Relationship Between Desires and Feelings," *Psy-
     chology Today*, October 31, 2015, www.psychologytoday.com/us/blog
     /hide-and-seek/201510/the-relationship-between-desires-and-feelings.

7.   Alan Richardson, "Mental Practice: A Review and Discussion Part
     I," *Research Quarterly*, American Association for Health, Physical Educa-
     tion and Recreation 38 no. 1: 95–107, https://doi.org/10.1080/10671188
     .1967.10614808.

8.   Emma Seppälä, "How Desire Fools Us: The Benefits and Dangers of
     the Chase," *Psychology Today*, August 13, 2013, www.psychologytoday
     .com/us/blog/feeling-it/201308/how-desire-fools-us-the-benefits-and
     -dangers-the-chase.

9.   Randy Taran and Maria Lineger, *Project Happiness Handbook* (Palo Alto,
     CA: Project Happiness, 2009).

10. Lynn Grabhorn, *Excuse Me, Your Life Is Waiting: The Astonishing Power of
     Feelings* (Charlottesville, VA: Hampton Roads, 2015).

11. Robert J. Vallerand, *The Psychology of Passion: A Dualistic Model* (Oxford:
     Oxford University Press, 2015).

12. Emilie Wapnick, "Why Some of Us Don't Have One True Calling,"
     TEDxBend Talk, October, 2015, www.ted.com/talks/emilie_wapnick_
     why_some_of_us_don_t_have_one_true_calling.

13. Smith, Jeremy Adam. "How to Find Your Purpose in Life." Greater
     Good Science Center. January 10, 2018. https://greatergood.berkeley
     .edu/article/item/how_to_find_your_purpose_in_life.

Fear

1.   Sam Duncan and Josh Hanrahan, "The Seven Signs Mount Agung
     WILL Erupt," *Daily Mail Online*, September 23, 2017, www.dailymail
     .co.uk/news/article-4914086/Bali-volcano-Animals-flee-mountain-sign
     -eruption.html.

2.   "What Happens in the Brain When We Feel Fear." Smithsonian.com.
     October 27, 2017. http://www.smithsonianmag.com/science-nature/what
     -happens-brain-feel-fear-180966992/

3.   "Prof. Bruce Lipton Teaches Life-changing Truths About Fear,"
     interview by Billy Atwell, *Fear Not*, podcast, August 9, 2017, www

.livingbeyondyourfears.com/prof-bruce-lipton-teaches-life-changing -truths-fear.

4. Dailymail.com, Cheyenne Macdonald For. "University of Salzburg Study Says 70% of People Feel like a Fraud in the Office." Daily Mail Online. November 21, 2016. https://www.dailymail.co.uk/sciencetech /article-3958742/Do-feel-like-fraud-office-Researchers-say-70-people -think-impostor-harms-work.html.

5. Sam Parnia and Josh Young, *Erasing Death: The Science That Is Rewriting the Boundaries Between Life and Death* (New York: HarperOne, 2014).

6. *Megyn Kelly Today*, "Doctor Describes the Science Behind a Near-death Experience," interview with Sam Parnia, August 17, 2018, www .today.com/video/doctor-describes-the-science-behind-a-near-death -experience-1301059139948?v=raila.

7. Nissan Dovid Dubov, "The Soul and the Afterlife," February 27, 2006, www.chabad.org/library/article_cdo/aid/361897/jewish/The-Soul-and -the-Afterlife.htm.

8. "Emotions Expressed by the Dying Are Unexpectedly Positive." Association for Psychological Science. https://www.psychologicalscience.org /news/releases/emotions-dying-positive.html..

9. Karla McLaren, *The Language of Emotions: What Your Feelings Are Trying to Tell You* (Boulder, CO: Sounds True, 2010).

10. Ibid.

11. Sandra L. Brown, "Is It Fear or Anxiety?" *Psychology Today*, November 15, 2012, www.psychologytoday.com/blog/pathological -relationships/201211/is-it-fear-or-anxiety.

12. Bruce H. Lipton, *The Biology of Belief* (Carlsbad, CA: Hay House, 2016).

13. Candace B. Pert, *Molecules of Emotion: Why You Feel the Way You Feel*. Touchstone, 1999.

14. Thomas Curran and Andrew P. Hill, "Perfectionism Is Increasing over Time: A Meta-analysis of Birth Cohort Differences from 1989 to 2016," *Psychological Bulletin* (December 28, 2017), http://dx.doi.org/10.1037 /bul0000138.

15. Brené Brown, *The Gifts of Imperfection: Let Go of Who You Think You're Supposed to Be and Embrace Who You Are* (Center City, MN: Hazelden, 2010).

16. Kristin D. Neff, "Self-compassion, Self-esteem, and Well-being," *Social and Personality Psychology Compass* 5, no. 1 (January 2011): 1–12, http://self -compassion.org/wp-content/uploads/2015/12/SC.SE_.Well-being.pdf.

17. Christian Mickelsen, *Abundance Unleashed: Open Yourself to More Money, Love, Health, and Happiness Now* (Carlsbad, CA: Hay House, 2017).

18. "Overcoming a Fear," Greater Good in Action, https://ggia.berkeley.edu /practice/overcoming_a_fear#.

19. Mel Robbins, *The 5 Second Rule: Transform Your Life, Work, and Confidence with Everyday Courage* (Savio Republic, 2017).

Anxiety

1. Brené Brown, *Daring Greatly: How the Courage to Be Vulnerable Transforms the Way We Live, Love, Parent, and Lead* (New York: Avery, 2015).
2. "Facts & Statistics," Anxiety and Depression Association of America, https://adaa.org/about-adaa/press-room/facts-statistics.
3. Helen Odessky, *Stop Anxiety from Stopping You: The Breakthrough Program for Conquering Panic and Social Anxiety* (Coral Gables, FL: Mango Publishing, 2017).
4. *Diagnostic and Statistical Manual of Mental Disorders, Fifth Edition: DSM-5* (Washington: American Psychiatric Publishing, 2013).
5. Guy Winch, "10 Crucial Differences Between Worry and Anxiety," *Psychology Today*, March 14, 2016, www.psychologytoday.com/blog/the -squeaky-wheel/201603/10-crucial-differences-between-worry-and -anxiety.
6. Harris, *The Deepest Well*.
7. "Got Your ACE Score?" ACEs Too High, July 10, 2018, https:// acestoohigh.com/got-your-ace-score.
8. Laura Starecheski, "Take the ACE Quiz—and Learn What It Does and Doesn't Mean," NPR, March 2, 2015, www.npr.org/sections/health -shots/2015/03/02/387007941/take-the-ace-quiz-and-learn-what-it-does -and-doesnt-mean.
9. "Beyond Worry: How Psychologists Help with Anxiety Disorders," American Psychological Association, October 2016, www.apa.org /helpcenter/anxiety.aspx.
10. Jill Suttie, "Can Meditation Lead to Lasting Change?" *Greater Good Magazine*, September 15, 2017, https://greatergood.berkeley.edu/article /item/can_meditation_lead_to_lasting_change#gsc.tab=0
11. "5 Things to Know About Relaxation Techniques for Stress," NIH National Center for Complementary and Integrative Health, September 24, 2015, https://nccih.nih.gov/health/tips/stress.
12. Dawson Church, *Psychological Trauma: Healing Its Roots in Brain, Body, and Memory* (Fulton, CA: Energy Psychology Press, 2016).
13. "The Science of HeartMath," www.heartmath.com/science.
14. Olivia Remes, Nick Wainwright, Paul Surtees, Louise Lafortune, Kay-Tee Khaw, Carol Brayne, "Sex Differences in the Association Between Area Deprivation and Generalised Anxiety Disorder: British Population Study," *BMJ Open* (May 4, 2017), http://dx.doi.org/10.1136/bmjopen -2016-013590.

15. "Video: Dr. Weil's Breathing Exercises: 4-7-8 Breath," September 20, 2017, www.drweil.com/videos-features/videos/breathing-exercises-4-7 -8-breath.
16. Odessky, *Stop Anxiety from Stopping You.*

Confidence
1. Margo Wickersham, "How to Stop Limiting Beliefs from Crippling Our Happiness." *Money Inc.* February 09, 2018. https://moneyinc.com /how-to-stop-limiting-beliefs-from-crippling-our-happiness/.
2. Carol S. Dweck, *Mindset: Changing the Way You Think to Fulfill Your Potential* (New York: Ballantine Books, 2016).
3. "Mindset Works Programs Case Studies: Fiske Elementary School," Mindset Works, www.mindsetworks.com/science/Case-Studies.
4. Carol S. Dweck and Ellen L. Leggett, "A Social-cognitive Approach to Motivation and Personality," *Psychological Review* 95 no. 2 (April 1988): 256–273, http://dx.doi.org/10.1037/0033-295X.95.2.256
5. Amy Morin, "How Do You Measure Your Self-worth?" *Psychology Today*, July 11, 2017, www.psychologytoday.com/us/blog/what -mentally-strong-people-dont-do/201707/how-do-you-measure-your -self-worth.
6. Ibid.
7. Kristen Neff, "Why Self-Compassion Trumps Self-Esteem." Greater Good Science Center. May 27, 2011. https://greatergood.berkeley.edu /article/item/try_selfcompassion.
8. Kristin Neff, *Self-compassion: The Proven Power of Being Kind to Yourself* (New York: William Morrow, 2015).
9. Lin Bian, Sarah-Jane Leslie, and Andrei Cimpian, "Gender Stereotypes About Intellectual Ability Emerge Early and Influence Children's Interests," *Science* 355, no. 6323 (January 27, 2017): 389–91, http:// science.sciencemag.org/content/355/6323/389.
10. James Gallagher, "Girls Lose Faith in Their Own Talents by the Age of Six," BBC News, January 27, 2017, www.bbc.com/news/health -38717926.
11. "Total Undergraduate Fall Enrollment in Degree-granting Postsecondary Institutions, by Attendance Status, Sex of Student, and Control and Level of Institution: Selected Years, 1970 through 2026," Digest of Education Statistics, National Center for Education Statistics, https:// nces.ed.gov/programs/digest/d16/tables/dt16_303.70.asp.
12. Christine Lagarde, "Daring the Difference: The 3 L's of Women's Empowerment," International Monetary Fund, May 19, 2014, www.imf .org/en/News/Articles/2015/09/28/04/53/sp051914.

13. Lola Akinmade Åkerström,"10 Things That Make Sweden Family-friendly," Sweden.se, January 10, 2018, https://sweden.se/society/10-things-that-make-sweden-family-friendly.

14. Susan Nolen-Hoeksema and Benita Jackson, "Mediators of the Gender Difference in Rumination," *Psychology of Women Quarterly* 25 no. 1 (March 1, 2001): 37–47, https://doi.org/10.1111/1471-6402.00005.

15. Tara Sophia Mohr, "Why Women Don't Apply for Jobs Unless They're 100% Qualified," *Harvard Business Review*, August 25, 2014, https://hbr.org/2014/08/why-women-dont-apply-for-jobs-unless-theyre-100-qualified.

16. "Men's Honest Overconfidence May Lead to Male Domination in the C-suite," press release, Columbia Business School, November 28, 2011, www8.gsb.columbia.edu/newsroom/newsn/1879/men8217s-honest-overconfidence-may-lead-to-male-domination-in-the-c8211suite.

17. "Women in the Workplace 2016," McKinsey & Company, September 2016, www.mckinsey.com/business-functions/organization/our-insights/women-in-the-workplace-2016.

18. Code, The Confidence. "Journalists Claire Shipman and Katty Kay Talk about The Confidence Code." YouTube. April 11, 2014. https://www.youtube.com/watch?v=NSPshvn56sk.

19. "The VIA Survey," VIA Institute of Character, www.viacharacter.org/www/Character-Strengths-Survey.

20. Brendon Burchard, *High Performance Habits: How Extraordinary People Become That Way* (Carlsbad, CA: Hay House, 2017).

Anger

1. Paul Ekman, *Emotions Revealed: Recognizing Faces and Feelings to Improve Communication and Emotional Life* (New York: Henry Holt, 2007).

2. Honor Whiteman, "Angry Outbursts May Raise the Risk of Heart Attack." Medical News Today. February 24, 2015. https://www.medicalnewstoday.com/articles/289864.php.

3. McLaren, *The Language of Emotions.*

4. Krista Tippett, "On Being with Krista Tippett: John Lewis—Love in Action." On Being. May 07, 2017. https://www.youtube.com/watch?v=YIqzCYf10LY.

5. "Dan Siegel: Name It to Tame It," Dalai Lama Center for Peace and Education, December 8, 2014, www.youtube.com/watch?v=ZcDLzppD4Jc.

6. Todd Kashdan and Robert Biswas-Diener, "The Right Way to Get Angry," *Greater Good Magazine*, October 20, 2014, https://greatergood.berkeley.edu/article/item/the_right_way_to_get_angry.

7. Jessica Stillman, "5 Tips to Productively Channel Your Anger," Inc., October 28, 2014, www.inc.com/jessica-stillman/5-tips-to-productively-channel-your-anger.html.

8. Michael Levittan, "Anger and Anger Management: What Are Some of the Triggers for Anger?" YouTube. December 04, 2011. https://www.youtube.com/watch?v=kXQmcA3VQMg.

9. "Channel-cleaning breath," *Yoga Journal*, August 28, 2007, www.yogajournal.com/poses/channel-cleaning-breath.

10. "The Power of Forgiveness," *CBS News*, June 7, 2011, www.youtube.com/watch?v=o2BITY-3Mp4.

11. "Mary Johnson and Oshea Israel." The Forgiveness Project. https://www.theforgivenessproject.com/mary-johnson-and-oshea-israel.

12. Fred Luskin, "Forgive For Good—Greater Good Magazine." Greater Good Science Center. https://greatergood.berkeley.edu/images/uploads/Forgiveness_-_Fred_Luskin.pdf.

Tolerance, Acceptance, and Empathy

1. "Sally Kohn and Erick Erickson—Relationship Across Rupture." The On Being Project. October 11, 2018. https://onbeing.org/programs/sally-kohn-and-erick-erickson-relationship-across-rupture-oct18/.

2. *Merriam-Webster*, s.v. "tolerance (*n.*)," www.merriam-webster.com/dictionary/tolerance.

3. Gay Hendricks and Kathlyn Hendricks, *Conscious Loving: The Journey to Co-commitment* (New York: Bantam Books, 1992).

4. Gay Hendricks and Kathlyn Hendricks, "A Big Clue You Don't Love Yourself." HuffPost. February 24, 2016. https://www.huffpost.com/entry/a-surprising-reason-youre_b_9298854.

5. Miguel Ruiz, *The Four Agreement*. (San Rafael, CA: Amber-Allen Pub., 1997).

6. Daniel J. Siegel and Tina Payne Bryson, *The Yes Brain Child: Help Your Child Be More Resilient, Independent and Creative* (London: Simon & Schuster, 2018).

7. Ekman, *Emotions Revealed*.

8. Chris Voss and Tahl Raz, *Never Split the Difference: Negotiating As If Your Life Depended on It* (London: Random House Business Books, 2017).

9. "How to Talk Politics Without Starting Fights and Ruining Relationships." Oprah.com. April 2018. http://www.oprah.com/inspiration/how-to-talk-with-people-you-disagree-with-politically.

10. Siegel, Dan, and Tina Payne Bryson Bryson. "How to Raise a Child Who Cares." Ideas.ted.com. May 16, 2018. https://ideas.ted.com/how-to-raise-a-child-who-cares/.

Guilt and Shame

1. "The Twelve Steps of Alcoholics Anonymous," Alcoholics Anonymous Great Britain, www.alcoholics-anonymous.org.uk/about-aa/the-12 -steps-of-aa.
2. "Lawrence Kohlberg: Stage Based Moral Development," Domain Based Moral Education Lab, www.moraledk12.org/lawrence-kohlberg.
3. Lomas, *The Positive Power of Negative Emotions*.
4. "Lawrence Kohlberg: Stage Based Moral Development," Domain Based Moral Education Lab, www.moraledk12.org/lawrence -kohlberg.
5. "Post-traumatic Stress Disorder," NIH National Institutes of Mental Health, www.nimh.nih.gov/health/publications/post-traumatic-stress -disorder-ptsd/index.shtml
6. "Sandy Hook Promise." Sandy Hook Promise. https://www .sandyhookpromise.org/.
7. Janey Davies, "What Is a Guilt Trip and How to Recognize If Some- one Is Using It on You," Learning Mind, June 3, 2017, www.learning -mind.com/guilt-trip.
8. Holloway, J. Daw. "Guilt Can Do Good." Monitor on Psychology. https://www.apa.org/monitor/nov05/guilt.
9. Andrea Estrada, "You Should Be Ashamed—or Maybe Not," *The Current*, UC Santa Barbara, March 7, 2014, www.news.ucsb.edu/2014 /014006/you-should-be-ashamed-%E2%80%94-or-maybe-not.
10. Guy Winch, *Emotional First Aid: Healing Rejection, Guilt, Failure, and Other Everyday Hurts* (New York: Penguin, 2014): 123–28.
11. Jon Kabat Zinn, "The Science of Mindfulness," *Greater Good Magazine*, May 2010, https://greatergood.berkeley.edu/video/item/the_science_of _mindfulness.
12. Byron Katie, "Do the Work." The Work. http://thework.com/en/do-work.
13. David Sack, "5 Ways to Silence Shame." *Psychology Today*. https://www .psychologytoday.com/us/blog/where-science-meets-the-steps/201501/5 -ways-silence-shame.
14. Jeffrey M. Schwartz and Rebecca Gladding, *You Are Not Your Brain: The 4-step Solution for Changing Bad Habits, Ending Unhealthy Thinking, and Taking Control of Your Life* (New York: Penguin Group, 2012).

Love

1. Randy Taran, "Alphabet of Happiness: 'L,'" *The Huffington Post*, Janu- ary 23, 2014, www.huffingtonpost.com/randy-taran/happiness-tips_b _4216428.html.
2. Ibid.

3. "The Quick Coherence Technique for Adults," HeartMath Institute, www.heartmath.org/resources/heartmath-tools/quick-coherence -technique-for-adults.

4. James R. Doty, *Into the Magic Shop: A Neurosurgeon's Quest to Discover the Mysteries of the Brain and the Secrets of the Heart* (New York: Avery, 2017).

5. "What Is Romantic Love?" The Anatomy of Love, https:// theanatomyoflove.com/what-is-love/what-is-love.

6. "The 3 Stages of Love and Hormones," MyVita Wellness Institute, www.myvitawellness.com/3-stages-love-hormones.

7. "Helen Fisher: What We Want," The Anatomy of Love, https:// theanatomyoflove.com/what-is-love/helen-fisher-want.

8. Arthur Aron, Edward Melinat, Elaine N. Aron, Robert Darrin Vallone, and Renee J. Bator, "The Experimental Generation of Interpersonal Closeness: A Procedure and Some Preliminary Findings," *Personality and Social Psychology Bulletin* 23, no. 4 (1997): 363–77, http://journals .sagepub.com/doi/pdf/10.1177/0146167297234003.

9. "Helen Fisher: What We Want."

10. "Love Forever." The Anatomy of Love. https://theanatomyoflove.com /blog/videos/love-forever/.

11. Gary D. Chapman and Jocelyn Green, *The 5 Love Languages: The Secret to Love That Lasts* (Chicago: Northfield Publishing, 2017).

12. Gary Chapman, "Discover Your Love Language," The 5 Love Languages, www.5lovelanguages.com/profile.

13. Barbara L. Fredrickson, *Love 2.0: How Our Supreme Emotion Affects Everything We Feel, Think, Do, and Become* (New York: Hudson Street Press, 2013).

14. Emma Seppälä, "Loving-Kindness Meditation," Greater Good in Action, https://ggia.berkeley.edu/practice/loving_kindness _meditation#data-tab-how.

15. "Loving-Kindness Meditation (Greater Good in Action)." Practice | Greater Good in Action. https://ggia.berkeley.edu/practice/loving _kindness_meditation#data-tab-why.

16. Emma Seppälä, "18 Science-based Reasons to Try Loving-kindness Meditation," *Mindful*, October 1, 2018, www.mindful.org/18-science -based-reasons-to-try-loving-kindness-meditation.

17. Chade-Meng Tan, *Joy on Demand: The Art of Discovering the Happiness Within* (New York: HarperOne, 2017).

Selected Bibliography

My research for this book was extensive, but these are the resources that stood out. Each offers a wealth of information that can elevate your journey.

Ben-Shahar, Tal. *Happier: Learn the Secrets to Daily Joy and Lasting Fulfillment*. New York: McGraw Hill, 2007.

Brown, Brené. *Daring Greatly: How the Courage to Be Vulnerable Transforms the Way We Live, Love, Parent, and Lead*. New York: Avery, 2015.

Burchard, Brendon. *High Performance Habits: How Extraordinary People Become That Way*. Carlsbad, CA: Hay House, 2017.

Chapman, Gary D., and Jocelyn Green. *The 5 Love Languages: The Secret to Love That Lasts*. Chicago: Northfield Publishing, 2017.

Chatterjee, Rangan. *How to Make Disease Disappear*. New York: HarperOne, 2018.

Csikszentmihalyi, Mihaly. *Flow and the Foundations of Positive Psychology: The Collected Works of Mihaly Csikszentmihalyi*. New York: Springer, 2014.

David, Susan. *Emotional Agility: Get Unstuck, Embrace Change, and Thrive in Work and Life*. New York: Avery, 2018.

Doty, James R. *Into the Magic Shop: A Neurosurgeon's Quest to Discover the Mysteries of the Brain and the Secrets of the Heart*. New York: Avery, 2017.

Ekman, Paul. *Emotions Revealed: Recognizing Faces and Feelings to Improve Communication and Emotional Life*. New York: Henry Holt, 2007.

Emmons, Robert A. *Thanks! How the New Science of Gratitude Can Make You Happier*. Boston: Houghton Mifflin Company, 2007.

Feldman, David B., and Lee Daniel Kravetz. *Supersurvivors: The Surprising Link Between Suffering and Success*. New York: HarperWave, 2014.

Fredrickson, Barbara L. *Love 2.0: How Our Supreme Emotion Affects Everything We Feel, Think, Do, and Become*. New York: Hudson Street Press, 2013.

Grabhorn, Lynn. *Excuse Me, Your Life Is Waiting: The Astonishing Power of Feelings*. Charlottesville, VA: Hampton Roads, 2015.

Hanson, Rick. *Hardwiring Happiness: The New Brain Science of Contentment, Calm, and Confidence*. New York: Harmony Books, 2013.

Hanson, Rick, and Forrest Hanson. *Resilient: How to Grow an Unshakable Core of Calm, Strength, and Happiness*. New York: Harmony Books, 2018.

Harris, Nadine Burke. *The Deepest Well: Healing the Long-term Effects of Childhood Adversity*. Boston: Houghton Mifflin Harcourt, 2018.

Horwitz, Allan V., and Jerome C. Wakefield. *The Loss of Sadness: How Psychiatry Transformed Normal Sorrow into Depressive Disorder*. Oxford: Oxford University Press, 2014.

Kashdan, Todd, and Robert Biswas-Diener. *The Upside of Your Dark Side: Why Being Your Whole Self—Not Just Your "Good" Self—Drives Success and Fulfillment*. New York: Hudson Street Press, 2014.

Katie, Byron, and Stephen Mitchell. *A Mind at Home with Itself: How Asking Four Questions Can Free Your Mind, Open Your Heart, and Turn Your World Around*. New York: HarperOne, 2017.

Kay, Katty, and Claire Shipman. *The Confidence Code: The Science and Art of Self-assurance—What Women Should Know*. New York, NY: HarperBusiness, 2018.

Lomas, Tim. *The Positive Power of Negative Emotions: How Harnessing Your Darker Feelings Can Help You See a Brighter Dawn*. London: Piatkus, 2016.

Lopez, Shane J. *Making Hope Happen: Create the Future You Want for Yourself and Others*. New York: Atria Paperback, 2014.

Luskin, Fred. *Forgive for Good: A Proven Prescription for Health and Happiness*. San Francisco: HarperSanFrancisco, 2003.

McLaren, Karla. *The Language of Emotions: What Your Feelings Are Trying to Tell You*. Boulder, CO: Sounds True, 2010.

Mohr, Tara. *Playing Big: Find Your Voice, Your Mission, Your Message*. New York: Avery, 2015.

Neff, Kristin. *Self-compassion*. London: Hodder & Stoughton, 2013.

Odessky, Helen, and John Duffy. *Stop Anxiety from Stopping You: The Breakthrough Program for Conquering Panic and Social Anxiety*, Coral Gables, FL: Mango Publishing, 2017.

Parnia, Sam, and Josh Young. *Erasing Death: The Science That Is Rewriting the Boundaries Between Life and Death*. New York: HarperOne, 2014.

Pert, Candace B. *Molecules of Emotion: Why You Feel the Way You Feel*. New York: Scribner, 2003.

Robbins, Mel. *The 5 Second Rule: Transform Your Life, Work, and Confidence with Everyday Courage*. Savio Republic, 2017.

Sandberg, Sheryl, and Adam M. Grant. *Option B: Facing Adversity, Building Resilience, and Finding Joy*. New York: Knopf, 2017.

Schwartz, Jeffrey, and Rebecca Gladding. *You Are Not Your Brain: The 4-step Solution for Changing Bad Habits, Ending Unhealthy Thinking, and Taking Control of Your Life*. New York: Penguin Group, 2012.

Seligman, Martin E. P. *Flourish: A Visionary New Understanding of Happiness and Well-being*. New York: Free Press, 2013.

Seppälä, Emma. *The Happiness Track: How to Apply the Science of Happiness to Accelerate Your Success*. New York, NY: HarperOne, an Imprint of HarperCollins Publishers, 2016.

Siegel, Daniel J., and Tina Payne Bryson. *The Yes Brain Child: Help Your Child Be More Resilient, Independent and Creative*. London: Simon & Schuster, 2018.

Tan, Chade-Meng. *Joy on Demand: The Art of Discovering the Happiness Within*. New York: Harper One, 2017.

Taran, Randy, and Maria Lineger. *Project Happiness Handbook*. Palo Alto, CA: Project Happiness, 2009.

Vallerand, Robert J. *The Psychology of Passion: A Dualistic Model*. Oxford: Oxford University Press, 2015.

Voss, Chris, and Tahl Raz. *Never Split the Difference: Negotiating As If Your Life Depended on It*. London: Random House Business Books, 2017.

Ware, Bronnie. *The Top Five Regrets of the Dying: A Life Transformed by the Dearly Departing*. Carlsbad, CA: Hay House, 2003.

Willard, Christopher. *Raising Resilience: The Wisdom and Science of Happy Families and Thriving Children*. Boulder, CO: Sounds True, 2017.

Winch, Guy. *Emotional First Aid: Healing Rejection, Guilt, Failure, and Other Everyday Hurts*. New York: Penguin, 2014.

Additional Resources

These are books, apps, websites, and organizations mentioned throughout the book, and others that may be of interest.

Disclaimer: Websites and apps can sometimes disappear, and some of these links may become outdated in time. So if any of these don't appear as described, this is an opportunity to reflect on impermanence, take a mindful breath, and maybe look them up a different way.

Happiness

The Atlas of Emotions: to identify and describe how you are feeling and why. http://atlasofemotions.org

Greater Good Science Center: excellent source of science-based insights for a meaningful life. https://greatergood.berkeley.edu

Tal Ben-Shahar: www.happier.tv, www.talbenshahar.com

Positive Psychology Center, University of Pennsylvania: https://ppc.sas.upenn.edu

Penn Resilience Program/PERMA Workshops: https://ppc.sas.upenn.edu/services/penn-resilience-training

Rick Hanson resources: www.rickhanson.net/key-offerings

The Center for Compassion and Altruism Research and Education (CCARE), Stanford University: www.ccare.stanford.edu

Center for Mindfulness, UMass Medical School: www.umassmed.edu/cfm

The Seven Happiness Habits: www.facebook.com/projecthappiness, www.instagram.com/projecthappiness_org

Kris Carr: https://kriscarr.com

Forgiveness: https://learningtoforgive.com

Volunteering: www.volunteermatch.org, www.idealist.org

Sadness

Jean Twenge: www.jeantwenge.com

World Health Organization: www.who.int/news-room/fact-sheets/detail
/depression

Functional nutrition: https://drhyman.com

Managing depression online class with holistic psychiatrist Dr. Ellen Vora:
www.mindbodygreen.com/classes/managing-depression-mind-body
-spirit-approach

Option B course on LinkedIn with Sheryl Sandberg and Adam Grant: www
.linkedin.com/learning/sheryl-sandberg-and-adam-grant-on-option-b
-building-resilience/the-importance-of-resilience

Resources for resilience: https://optionb.org/build-resilience

Resources for grief: https://optionb.org/category/grief-and-loss/resources

Living without regret: https://bronnieware.com/6-free-lessons

Desire

Robert Emmons: www.takingcharge.csh.umn.edu/making-gratitude-part
-everyday-life-tips-dr-robert-emmons

Emmons, Robert A. *Thanks! How the New Science of Gratitude Can Make You Happier.* New York: Houghton Mifflin, 2007.

Wapnick, Emilie. *How to Be Everything: A Guide for Those Who (Still) Don't Know What They Want to Be When They Grow Up.* New York: HarperOne, 2018.

Are you a multipotentialite? www.ted.com/speakers/emilie_wapnick

Vallerand, Robert J. *Psychology of Passion: A Dualistic Model.* Oxford: Oxford University Press, 2015.

"Bob Vallerand on the Psychology of Passion," *Making Positive Psychology Work* podcast interview: www.michellemcquaid.com/podcast/mppw05-bob
-vallerand-psychology-passion

Fear

"Overcoming a Fear," Greater Good in Action: https://ggia.berkeley.edu
/practice/overcoming_a_fear#.

Robbins, Mel. *The 5 Second Rule: Transform Your Life, Work, and Confidence with Everyday Courage.* Savio Republic, 2017

Center for Mindful Self-compassion: https://centerformsc.org

Mental Health Foundation resources: www.mentalhealth.org.uk/our-work

Anxiety

Find a therapist (United States): www.psychologytoday.com/us/therapists

American Psychological Association: www.apa.org/helpcenter/anxiety.aspx

Anxiety resources: https://adaa.org/living-with-anxiety/ask-and-learn
/resources

National Suicide Prevention Lifeline: https://suicidepreventionlifeline.org,
1-800-273-8255

Crisis Text Line: text HOME to 741741, www.crisistextline.org

"Got Your ACE Score?" https://acestoohigh.com/got-your-ace-score

"Video: Dr. Weil's Breathing Exercises: 4-7-8 Breath": www.drweil.com
/videos-features/videos/breathing-exercises-4-7-8-breath

Confidence

Dweck, Carol S. *Mindset: Changing the Way You Think to Fulfill Your Potential.*
New York: Robinson, 2017.

Character Strengths Survey, www.viacharacter.org/www/Character
-Strengths-Survey

"Mel Robbins: The Skill of Confidence and How to Take Control of Your
Mind!": www.youtube.com/watch?v=TVAcs5AHhF4

Amy Morin, "How Do You Measure Your Self-worth?" *Psychology Today,*
July 11, 2017, www.psychologytoday.com/us/blog/what-mentally-strong
-people-dont-do/201707/how-do-you-measure-your-self-worth

Anger

Todd Kashdan and Robert Biswas-Diener, "The Right Way to Get Angry,"
Greater Good Magazine, October 20, 2014, https://greatergood.berkeley
.edu/article/item/the_right_way_to_get_angry.

Dealing with anger: www.apa.org/helpcenter/controlling-anger.aspx

Managing anger: www.mayoclinic.org/healthy-lifestyle/adult-health/in-depth
/anger-management/art-20045434

McCarthy, Jenna. "What's Your Anger Style?" *Real Simple* magazine. www
.realsimple.com/health/mind-mood/best-manage-your-anger.

Tolerance, Acceptance, and Empathy

Relationships: Hendricks, Gay, and Kathlyn Hendricks. *Conscious Loving: The
Journey to Co-commitment.* New York: Bantam Books, 1992.

Parenting: Tsabary, Shefali. *The Conscious Parent: Transforming Ourselves, Empowering Our Children.* London: Yellow Kite, 2014.

Accepting all emotions: MacLellan, Lila. "Accepting Your Darkest Emotions Is the Key to Psychological Health." Quartz. July 23, 2017.
https://qz.com/1034450/accepting-your-darkest-emotions-is-the-key-to
-psychological-health.

Guilt and Shame

"Shame Versus Guilt - Brené Brown." Jan Fleury. September 21, 2015. www
.youtube.com/watch?v=DqGFrId-IQg.

Davies, Janey. "What Is a Guilt Trip and How to Recognize If Someone Is
Using It on You." Learning Mind. June 3, 2017. www.learning-mind
.com/guilt-trip.

Holloway, J. Daw. "Guilt Can Do Good." *Monitor on Psychology* 36, no. 10
(November 2005). www.apa.org/monitor/nov05/guilt.aspx.

Love

Anatomy of Love Quiz: https://theanatomyoflove.com/relationship-quizzes
/helen-fishers-personality-test.

Quick Coherence Technique for Adults: www.heartmath.org/resources
/heartmath-tools/quick-coherence-technique-for-adults.

Love Languages Quiz: www.5lovelanguages.com/profile.

Loving-kindness meditation: http://marc.ucla.edu/mindful-meditations

Molly McLaughlin

As founder and CEO of Project Happiness, RANDY TARAN has created a nonprofit organization that has amassed a following of 2.5 million people globally. She has produced an award-winning documentary, also titled *Project Happiness,* and has written the *Project Happiness Handbook.* She has worked with first ladies, ministers of education, and major thought leaders; been covered in multiple publications; and served as a board member for the Dalai Lama Foundation and the International Day of Happiness.